# Angel Kisses
# And
# My Beating Heart

*With fond memories of The Larrabees and times we shared!*
*Jack Ramsay*

## By Jack C. Ramsay, Jr.

My Life And Near-Death Experiences

Library of Congress Control Number: 2004104697

© 2004 Jack C. Ramsay, Jr.

All Rights Reserved

No part of this book may be reproduced in any form or
By any means without permission in writing from
Historical Resources Press

Printed in the United States of America

ISBN 0-9642511-2-4

November 27, 2004
First Edition

All inquiries for volume purchases of this book should be addressed to Historical Resources Press, 2104 Post Oak Court, Corinth/Denton, Texas 76210-1900. Telephone inquiries may be made by calling 940.321.1066.

## About This Book

"I enjoyed *Angel Kisses And My Beating Heart,* especially the year-to-year account of a pastor."
— Marj Carpenter, 1995 Moderator of the 207$^{th}$ General Assembly of The Presbyterian Church (U.S.A.)

•

"Don't miss this wonderful story of how Jack and Karin Ramsay ministered to thousands of people for over 50 years. Their delight in serving God through leadership of congregations is documented on every page of this remarkable book."
— C. Ellis Nelson, President Emeritus, Louisville Presbyterian Seminary and presently Research Professor, Austin Presbyterian Seminary

•

"Interesting interplay between Jack and Karin in many settings of ministry through the second half of the 20$^{th}$ century, the golden era of mainline church history."
— David R. Sawyer, Director of Graduate Studies and Lifelong Learning, Louisville Presbyterian Theological Seminary

•

"I thought you had asked me to proof read your manuscript, but I had difficulty in looking for any mistakes because I was so caught up in the stories."
— Leila McGeath, Director of Christian Education, Local, Presbytery, Synod and General Assembly levels, Presbyterian Church (U.S.A.)

## My Book

This *book* did not begin as *a book:* it began as a manuscript written especially for my children and grandchildren after my hospital and *near death experiences*. It began in response to conversations I had with my son while awaiting my surgery. He mentioned he had "passed through" places that had been significant in my life story. He had "passed through" Sweetwater which appeared to have only one grocery store. He had "passed through" Spur with a lonely hilltop ice cream drive-in; Brownwood, which to him did not seem to have a thriving economy; and Crane, which was off the main highway. I had planned to make two manuscript copies for Christmas gifts 2004, one copy for my daughter and one for my son. Early chapters carry information some say, "Does not directly relate to the main thread of the story." Since my near death experiences, I have become aware my children and friends, in order to understand my story, need also to hear how I was influenced as a small child by my father who organized twenty-seven churches in Virginia; how Karin's father started a business in the early years of *The Great Depression* and the impact that had on Karin; how my mother and aunt influenced my faith and my life; how Sweetwater brought Karin's and my lives together. This *book,* the story of my life, starts slowly, "once upon a time", like a child waiting for Christmas and accelerates as quickly as that same child eagerly unwraps a special gift. What I then began as two copies of a manuscript for Christmas presents I now finish as *a book* written for my children and grandchildren, and, perhaps, for my church family, classmates, friends in communities in which I have lived and a vast host of readers who have never met us, readers who will remember with me who was where and what was happening yesterday that made today what it is and tomorrow what it will be.

- Jack Ramsay, August 2004

## *Dedication*

This book is dedicated to the memory of
Billy (William Allen) Baine,
My best friend in High School,
My first year Seminary roommate, and my lifelong friend.

Billy was the first to suggest that I turn my biographical efforts into autobiography. Without Billy, this book would never have been written.

William Allen Baine,
Billy, entered into the Eternal Presence without pain or struggle on June 20, 2004.
He and his wife, Margaret, were watching television, relaxing after a busy day.
When he failed to respond to her comments, she believed he had drifted off to sleep.
I regret he was never able to read
what he encouraged me to write.
I miss you, Billy.

## Table of Contents

| | | |
|---|---|---:|
| Preface | | ix |
| One | A Plane Falling From the Sky | 1 |
| Two | The Victorious Journey | 5 |
| Three | A Loud Hurrah for Silas and Seth As Though Thousands Backed Them | 11 |
| Four | The Streets of Laredo | 23 |
| Five | Decisions, Decisions And Approaching War | 33 |
| Six | The First Glimpse | 41 |
| Seven | The Scottish Adventure | 51 |
| Eight | Sunlight On The Heather | 59 |
| Nine | The Final Year | 67 |
| Ten | The Course of True Love | 73 |
| Eleven | An Accident And A Honeymoon | 81 |
| Twelve | Laughter At A Phantom Siren | 89 |
| Thirteen | An Unsettling Revelation | 99 |
| Fourteen | "You And Jack Just Murdered A Man" | 109 |
| Fifteen | Five Percent of A Chance | 119 |
| Sixteen | "Nobody Is Home" | 131 |
| Seventeen | A Cross Hanging On A G String | 141 |
| Eighteen | He Lay Limp On The Floor | 149 |
| Nineteen | Sparkling Rays Across The Water | 157 |
| Twenty | God's Spell At Covenant | 165 |
| Twenty-One | We Cried, We Laughed, We Prayed | 175 |
| Twenty-Two | A Bit of Urban Witchery | 183 |
| Twenty-Three | A Decorum Broken By Applause | 193 |
| Twenty-Four | Spouse Trailers | 203 |
| Twenty-Five | Eastward To The Sea | 211 |
| Twenty-Six | The Great Adventure | 223 |
| Twenty-Seven | At One P.M., The Snow Began To Fall | 235 |
| Twenty-Eight | The Last Bicycle Ride | 249 |
| Twenty-Nine | Kissed By An Angel | 255 |
| Thirty | Two Bicycles on A Garage Floor | 265 |
| Thirty-One | A Bundle of Joy | 271 |
| Thirty-Two | When Nightmares Become Pleasant Dreams | 279 |
| Index | | 287 |
| To Order | Other Books By Jack Ramsay | 296 |

## *A Preface*

Since I had written several biographies, friends suggested that I write my own story. I had chronicled the lives of beleaguered politicians, the deeds of one considered a ruthless pirate, a Civil War photographer, and a female who had chosen to live among the fiercest of the South Plains Comanches. I did not fit in any of those categories about which I had written, but I knew my efforts had been widely accepted as authentic accounts. Yet recording my own history was quite another matter.

In researching, writing and publishing my first books, I had always taken my eyesight for granted. I now have one serious impediment: I am legally blind. I can no longer read that which I write. I hesitated to write my story as my friends suggested, to continue writing any book now. Yet, why should becoming legally blind be a problem? One of the greatest of the English epic poets, John Milton, authored his finest work after he lost his eyesight. Mathew Brady, the best known of America's photographers had lost most of his ability to see when he trained others to do his work. The famed Scottish hymn writer George Matheson produced his greatest hymn after he became blind. Perhaps those with failing eyesight have some measure of inner consciousness that others do not have. I am hopeful such will be the case in my continuing efforts as an author.

The words that follow are an account of a relationship between two persons, a relationship that is both physical and spiritual. This is a true account, one that is true in the telling and also one in which the persons involved are true to each other. What began as a friendship, in time, evolved into what others recognize as true love. Without love, my life would have ended years ago.

Most important, this is my life story including my near death experiences.

x

*One*

# A Plane Falling From The Sky

*1922*

My life did not really begin until a beautiful young lady named Karin married me. Perhaps that is the point in time at which this account should begin. Yet, since there were many events in my life that preceded my first glimpse of Karin, I will start at the beginning.

One of my earliest memories was that of an airplane falling from the sky. A plane crashed into a larger aircraft and then spiraled downward into the deep waters of a nearby bay. My mother, Lilian Cook Ramsay, was painting the eaves of our home in Larchmont, a suburb of Norfolk, Virginia. I was four years old. I was watching.

My father, John Cummins Ramsay, was at work organizing new Presbyterian churches along the eastern coast of Virginia. His official title was superintendent of Home Missions for the Presbytery of Norfolk. Before I came on the scene, November 27, 1922, 11:20 A.M., Mt. Sinai Hospital, Norfolk, Virginia, Lilian had helped her new husband in his work. Together they visited towns near Norfolk that had come into being during World War I. She led singing while my father played a portable organ and then preached to any of the defense workers or navy yard employees who would gather around. Sometimes this took place out of doors beneath a large shade tree. Once enough interested persons had agreed to sign a new church charter, my father would find a student minister or unemployed pastor to lead the fledgling church. He would then move to another location and start all over again.

When my mother saw the falling plane, she cried out in horror. An even more frightening sight appeared. We watched a larger aircraft heading toward us, one, which came so close we could see the aviators in open cockpits. We later learned the larger plane was a U.S. Navy bomber that had collided with the smaller aircraft. The crippled plane was piloted to a nearby field where it crash-landed.

When my father came home in the family car, a Model T Ford, he took me to see the crash site. The Navy pilots had guided their craft beyond the residential area without further loss of life. Only the pilot of the small plane would be listed as a casualty of the accident. There were less frightening memories of the home in Larchmont, the earliest residence I can recall. It was a two story, white stucco building in a residential area which could have been seriously damaged had not the Navy pilots skillfully guided their aircraft to a landing immediately beyond the last home in the subdivision.

I can remember walks with my mother in a stand of trees she called "the woods". When we walked in the opposite direction we could reach the shore of the deep-sea entry into the Bay. There we could watch the great ships come into port, count the number of funnels on each, guess their size, cargo and land of origin. There were often trips to nearby beaches, one quite close called Ocean View. Virginia Beach was another place for swimming and enjoying the rolling white caps that came directly from the Atlantic.

Just after my fourth birthday, a baby sister came to live with us. At about the same time, an aunt, Elizabeth Lavinia Cook, joined the household. I knew her as Aunt Bessie. It was her given name, Elizabeth, which would be bestowed upon my little sister.

I remember one other traumatic event: the wreck of our Model T. Ford that happened near the Larchmont house. I saw the car with front wheels askew. This called for the purchase of another motor vehicle, an Essex. This was a car with a powerful motor and a beautifully upholstered interior complete with delicately shaped flower vases on each side of the spacious back seat. It was also one with a history. It had been used by bootleggers, had been confiscated by the government, and was purchased at a fraction of its original cost. My father took pride in owning such a car and often showed the small hole in the back seat that he believed had been made by a drop of acid that somehow had been left there by the former owners. The pride of ownership was heightened by the fact the car could now be used for both legal and religious purposes.

Soon after my fifth birthday, my father decided he was through with vagabond preaching. In the nine years he was employed by Norfolk Presbytery, he had organized twenty-seven churches. By this time there were no longer new communities completely devoid of religious services. He wanted a congregation of his own in a settled community. I remember a Christmas when my father had announced that all he wanted was a church. My mother found a picture of a tall steepled building that she framed and wrapped as a Christmas present. This she presented her husband when the family opened gifts. He thanked her for her efforts but he made it plain this was not what he had in mind.

Soon after this, an offer came that fulfilled his highest expectations: the position of minister of the First Presbyterian Church of Alexandria, Louisiana. This was a congregation that boasted of a membership in excess of six hundred, a large church for the time. The former pastor had died after supervising the construction of a handsome new building that included an attractive sanctuary with dramatic stained glass windows and a large basement for informal activities. In addition, the structure included three levels of well-equipped classrooms.

My father was elated with the prospect of his new position. Soon my parents, John and Lilian, along with Elizabeth, Aunt Bessie, the Essex and I were en route to Louisiana.

*My sister, Elizabeth, my Mother, and I on our way to Alexandria.*
A picture made in the Richmond, Virginia studio of my famous grandfather, George L. Cook, and great grandfather, George S. Cook, who had parted company with the Civil War photographer, Mathew Brady, to become famous on his own. My great grandfather had studios in New York City, Charleston and Richmond.

## Two

## The Victorious Journey

*1928*

I clearly remember the celebration of my sixth birthday on the spacious enclosed front porch of the Ramsay's Alexandria home, a manse provided for the new pastor and his family. It was a large building directly across the street from the high steps on the front of the sanctuary. A huge room served as the entrance to the home but had yet another purpose: a parlor for formal church social events. Each Christmas Eve, the Sunday School party took place in the church basement. Immediately afterwards the fully decorated tree was taken across the street to the manse parlor for the Ramsays to share Christmas with parishioners who might drop by during the festive season.

    The front room was separated from the dining area by double doors with beveled glass. I remember the consternation that existed when I was responsible for breaking one of the panes. This was an item that had to be properly replaced before one of the deacons noticed the damage.

The dining room was serviced from a kitchen presided over by a capable black maid, Bea, who came with the house. She prepared Sunday dinners to which the pastor was expected to invite any visitors who had attended morning worship.

My father had a large first floor room for his "Study". In those days churches did not have "offices". All serious pastors were expected to maintain an area either in the church building or his residence where he could spend endless hours in careful sermon preparation. This room contained my father's extensive library, his roll top desk, and his Underwood typewriter. He could leave his Study and go directly across the street to the church building.

The family living quarters were upstairs. Father and mother and baby sister slept in the master bedroom; my room was next, followed by an ample guest room. Aunt Bessie's room was at the end of the hall. An open area at the top of the staircase served as an informal family room. Canned food was kept there in case the Red River levee, six short blocks away, should break.

Central Elementary School was directly across the street, just south of the new church building. I began my education there. My Kindergarten was a crowded basement room. The only activity I could remember was that of tossing large wooden blocks back and forth with my fellow kindergartners. One of my return tosses must have been poorly aimed. The lone supervisor, who had more five-year-olds than she could possibly handle, severely admonished me for my participation in the action.

I began the first grade in another dark, gray, basement room. Toward the end of the year, the teacher insisted that her students begin to memorize the multiplication table. When I was called upon to give the sum of three times five, I froze. I was told to write out the entire table one hundred times before the next morning. Aunt Bessie who had been a teacher herself felt this demand was unreasonable, but since my teacher had made this an assignment, it must be done. She enlisted the entire family in the project showing how two pencils could be held for writing at the same time, one above the other, and the result would be two lines of multiplication table written instead of the usual one line. By bedtime, the multi-page task was complete. I went to class the next day to find I was the only one who had missed a sum who could take credit for completing the full chore. Aunt Bessie had a conference with the teacher who was extremely nice to me for the few remaining weeks of the school year.

Another educational crisis developed shortly before I was to enter the fourth grade. The school principal was concerned with the fact a single teacher would have at least forty pupils. A possible solution would be that of allowing certain students to skip a grade. When Aunt Bessie learned this double promotion would include me, she objected. The principal proposed another solution: twenty-eight students would be selected from the elementary school overage and remain with an able teacher, a Miss Sinclair, for two full school years.

Under Miss Sinclair's tutorship, I found the learning process both challenging and exciting. There were trips to museums and parks. On occasion, we attended concerts. When we journeyed to a well-treed area of the town, the teacher introduced the class to poetry. She read Joyce Kilmer's *Trees*. Seven decades later, I can still remember lines from Kilmer's work:

"I think that I shall never see
   A poem lovely as a tree.
A tree that may in Summer wear
   A nest of robins in her hair.
A tree that looks at God all day,
   And lifts her leafy arms to pray.
Poems are made by fools like me,
   But only God can make a tree."

I had friends both at school and in the neighborhood. Two Italian boys, a bit older than I, lived immediately behind the manse. My closest friend was a Cajun boy, Leroy, who lived on the opposite side of the block. Together we fished for Crawdads in Louisiana storm sewers. Leroy was my age but physically larger and more muscular. His ambition was that of becoming a riverboat captain. Such vessels still sailed the Red River and the not too distant Mississippi. Leroy told me that if anyone ever tried to give me a hard time, let him know and he would take care of anyone who threatened me. No one did as long as I lived in Alexandria.

Aunt Bessie did much more to aid my educational development than occasionally objecting to administrative mistakes made by the officials of the school across the street. She spent hour upon hour reading to me. Although I remembered some stories about a gingham dog and a calico cat, I can also recall much more advanced themes. There were stories of distant lands, of a pirate ship painted blood red that had to be hunted down by dauntless seamen. She read tales of the sea, of undiscovered islands, of exploration and adventure, *Swiss Family Robinson* and Verne's *Twenty Thousand Leagues Under the Sea*. These followed the account of *Robinson Crusoe*. There were books about the Old South, the bayou country, of gentlemen of honor and of those who were without any vestige of respectability.

One that burned its way into my memory was that of a woman disgracefully treated by a male who was no gentleman. Aunt Bessie read the story as it was written. She then answered my questions about the facts of life in her uniquely genteel style.

She was a student and a teacher. Throughout her life she had been an avid reader. She read current literature, the classics and the scriptures of the Old and New Testaments. Soon after she came to Alexandria, she was invited to teach an adult Bible class in the church. She was the *Bible Teacher*, teaching in the auditorium while others taught in classrooms as long as she was physically able to do so.

Her favorite work was Bunyan's *Pilgrim's Progress*. She read this in the classic edition to me and read it to me later in a modernized version. A deeply spiritual person, she was truly one who was on the journey beyond the Shining River to the Eternal Presence.

Aunt Bessie encouraged me in learning the Westminster Catechism. Once she told the story of a Black youth from the slums of Richmond who had been charged with shoplifting.

"Honest to God, I did not steal anything," he kept repeating to the magistrate.

The judge looked at him and said: "Young man, you are using the name of God very freely. What do you know about God?"

Without hesitation the Black youth replied. "God is a Spirit, infinite, eternal and unchangeable in His being, wisdom, power, holiness, justice, goodness and truth."

The judge had no choice. He dismissed the case. I knew I had better not freeze if I ever needed my catechism. Although I never found need for such a recitation in a court of law, this knowledge did grant me the right to become a communicant member of the church at an early age. When I did, Miss Sinclair was there to congratulate me on what she called my "special red letter day."

There came a time when Aunt Bessie spent most of her daylight hours in the great bed in which she had been born. My mother told me not to bother her when she might not be feeling well, yet whenever I entered the room, she would speak gently and make an effort to resume reading to me. One morning my mother insisted I go outside and play. I sat on the front steps most of the day. Suddenly a car pulled up in front of the house. The family doctor got out and went quickly inside ignoring the child near the door.

When he came out, I asked if Aunt Bessie was feeling better.

The doctor paused and replied, "Your Aunt Bessie is feeling far better now than she has for a very long time."

Somehow I understood what I was being told. I went into the house crying. My mother took me in her arms as she shared my tears. We both knew the Pilgrim had crossed over the Shining River.

For my Aunt Bessie, the victorious journey was complete. For me, the months, which followed, were times of extreme loneliness.

*Angel Kisses And My Beating Heart*

## Three

# A Loud Hurrah For Silas and Seth As Though Thousands Backed Them
### 1930

Hundreds of miles west of Alexandria, deep in the heart of Texas, an event took place that would have a profound impact on my life. Although I knew nothing of this at the time, this event would eventually bring an end to my loneliness.

A child was born to Kirby Luther Kinsey and Ina Wood Kinsey in Brownwood, Texas August 10, 1930. The proud father gave her a name that would perpetuate his own initials: Karin Lucille Kinsey and spent hours designing a linoleum block and printing a three-color tri-fold birth announcement.

Kirby met Ina in Sweetwater on a Sunday night when Ina was singing in the Methodist Church choir where he and his family were active. The fact that he had a friend arrange a blind date with her after he saw her in the choir is a family joke since even Ina admits she couldn't carry a tune in a bucket. She was teaching biology and chemistry in Sweetwater High School and Kirby working as a printer for Watson-Focht newspapers. The friend, John R. Cox a local jeweler, served as best man when Kirby married Ina Rebecca Wood August 25, 1929 in her parents Zephyr home. As a honeymoon, Kirby and Ina traveled on the train to Jefferson City, Missouri where Kirby enrolled as a student in the School of Journalism of the University of Missouri. His father worked for the Santa Fe Railroad, enabling Kirby to go any place trains traveled. His major trip before the honeymoon was a trip to New York City for a World Series game and to see the Statue of Liberty.

During his second year in the University of Missouri, a professor told Kirby that there really was not much more they could teach him that experience would not provide and he might consider leaving before graduation to find a job. He was a natural artist of the printing profession. Yet 1930 was no time to begin a business career, for the Great Depression held the entire nation in its grip and the two lovers, especially Ina with a college education and certified as a high school science teacher, really did not want to abandon their idea of Kirby's college degree and certainly not the end of what they had hoped would be a *four-year honeymoon* on the campus of the University of Missouri. They reluctantly accepted the guidance of the University and returned to Zephyr, Texas where they awaited the birth of Karin and while Kirby searched for a job. Karin celebrated her first and second birthdays while Kirby, Ina and Karin were living with Ina's parents in Zephyr and while Kirby was seeking employment as a printer, or actually any job.

Famed newspaperman Houston Hart of San Angelo was notified of the young printer's potential and agreed with the University professors. In the middle of *The Great Depression* Houston Hart suggested he assist Kirby in financing and setting up a printing shop of his own in Sweetwater, Texas. In 1932 Ina, Kirby and two-year-old Karin moved to an apartment above the garage of the Trammel home and later to a duplex on Broadway in the town of Sweetwater where Kirby had been raised. The business opened under the simplest possible trade name: *Kirby*

# A Loud Hurrah For Silas and Seth As Though Thousands Backed Them

*Kinsey, Printer.* This logo appeared in the window of a building directly across the street from the town's only post office. In later years, when Kirby was able to purchase his own building, the trade name became a familiar lighted sign in the town's business district.

Kirby became one of Sweetwater's leading citizens, active in city events and in the local Lions Club. He served on the School Board, an office he gained with an expenditure of only five dollars. This was the cost of his single political advertisement that read:

"Kirby Kinsey for School Board.
*Qualified and willing to serve."*

He was known throughout the area as one of West Texas' most able printers. Decades after his death, his name would be remembered. His successors would rely on his reputation by using his business name well into the twenty-first century.

Ina and Kirby, after two years at the University of Missouri School of Journalism and two more years living with Ina's parents while Kirby searched for employment, found themselves in the midst of a most uncertain economy. When Kirby had received Houston Hart's endorsement and offer of help, Ina, had agreed to return with Kirby to his home town of Sweetwater, willing to assist in the printing shop. Married and now a parent, she would not return to her teaching profession but would, ahead of her time, become a working mon. As the business grew she became the bookkeeper, financial officer, fed presses, ran the perforator, assembled and stapled or tabbed books, answered the phone, swept the floor ......

Not only did she possess a keen economic acumen, but also she developed a unique system for printing season football tickets. Football was the major sport for the area. Sweetwater was proud that Bulldog Turner of the Chicago Bears and Slinging Sammy Baugh of the Redskins both played on the same Sweetwater High School Team. Presbyterians usually added that Sammy Baugh married their preacher's daughter. Every West Texas town cherished it's own sports tradition and needed attractively printed tickets for the intense fall competitions. Sweetwater had built what was one of the first true football *bowls* (a stadium surrounded with dirt so that seating was below ground entry level) and needed tickets for the new bowl. Ina planned and she and Kirby perfected, a process in which each ticket was perfectly printed and no two of the tens of thousands produced were identical (each game date a different color ticket; each ticket a different section, different row, different seat number). When a football fan from an opponent of Sweetwater attended a game he was fascinated with the Sweetwater ticket and took his stub to a printing firm known for printing tickets in the Dallas area to ask them to reproduce similar tickets for his school district. He was told that they had already been alerted to tickets made in Sweetwater by *Kirby Kinsey, Printer* and experts with their company, so famous for printing tickets that they thought they held a monopoly, were at a complete loss in determining "how that West Texas printer is doing it".

    The Sweetwater printing shop was a family operation. Karin often brags that she was "raised in the printing shop" where she loved the perfume of printer's ink and the musical rhythm of the printing presses. Sleeping soundly as an infant in a large box for shipping envelopes as long as presses were running, she would awaken only when presses stopped and it was time to go home. Her mother often told how, at age two, Karin was identifying Coca Cola trucks and other vehicles and buildings by the *cuts* used in the printing shop to print advertising circulars, images that should have confused her because they were backward mirror images. When she was taught to read, she did not seem to be confused and easily read type that was backward and upside down as easily as she read her schoolbook texts. Karin, the "printer's daughter", always amazed me by easily reading upside down what I was writing or reading from across the table. As an elementary school student, she spent her after school hours in the shop. At the age of ten, Kirby lovingly taught her and watched as she was allowed to run a full size printing press, printing *tags* for the cotton oil mill in town. Whenever cotton was

## A Loud Hurrah For Silas and Seth As Though Thousands Backed Them

picked and the cotton gin began to process seed for the mill, Karin could smell the wonderful aroma of the cotton oil mill that drifted across Sweetwater and would start begging for the job of running *oil mill tags*.

Receipt books were necessary for duplicate copies before there were copy machines and assembling books in triplicate was another job of Karin who was paid a penny for every book assembled. Karin was extremely fast and assembled with her own method in which she crossed over her hands with speed which was such fun to see that Kirby often brought in printers who knew the usual system to watch her. Karin's sisters both had the options of learning the printing trade, but to the best of Karin's knowledge neither particularly liked to work in the printing shop.

Nelda, four years younger than Karin, has said, "I don't know why you got so many printing genes and I ended up with so few."

Karin often tells friends that she has printers' ink in her veins rather than blood. Her first paying job was that of a proofreader, Copy editor and summer Society Editor for the town's daily newspaper, *The Sweetwater Reporter*. As a high school student she was editor of the school newspaper, a position her father created when he wrote and printed the first *Pony Express* on Watson-Focht presses. His high school classmate, Laura Sheridan, became Karin's journalism teacher and she was more than a little disturbed when Karin, prompted by Kirby, showed her teacher the *cut* (image) and offered to print her high school picture in a 1946-47 issue of the paper. Kirby enjoyed good jokes and that one did not seem funny to Laura Sheridan.

Though Karin's feeling is that neither of her sisters particularly enjoyed press work in the printing office, both Nelda and Marilyn followed in their father's steps with *The Pony Express*: when they were High School Seniors Nelda was Editor and, Marilyn was Business Manager.

As well as being editor and winning awards for the Sweetwater High School *Pony Express,* Karin was elected and served for several years as editor of the Synod of Texas statewide newspaper for the Presbyterian Church, *The Tex-Syn News*, and as editor of the summer conference youth daily news, *The Howl of the Hills*. Karin was unique as editor for the *The Tex-Syn News* in that she not only edited but also printed and mailed the paper which was published several times each year. In later years she would round out her career in the media by working as Continuity Editor in charge of writing commercials for the local radio station KXOX.

Karin's mother, Ina, was not only an able partner of her husband but also the mother of three daughters. Karin was the first-born, Nelda next and Marilyn the youngest. Like Kirby, Ina was a leading citizen of the town. She held membership and was an officer (often president) in several women's organizations including local literary study clubs and the Daughters of the American Revolution. As President of the historical society in Sweetwater, she is credited with being responsible for placing a historical marker on and almost singly handedly saving the Municipal Auditorium from demolition, an auditorium where numerous nationally and internationally known performers had appeared. (i.e.: Scotland's Sir Harry Lauder, touring vaudevillians such as Bob Hope, George Burns and Gracie Allen, ... most of the famous violinists and pianists touring in the 30s and 40s and ... vaudeville provided by the company of Harley Sadler who made his home in Sweetwater.)

Ina's ancestry was not only traceable to Colonial America; she also was a descendant of pioneers who had survived the Fort Parker massacre. Her ancestors had entered Texas in 1833 in a train of covered wagons. Some had settled in East Texas but an adventurous few had dared go beyond what was then the ultimate frontier. There they built homes and planted crops.

On a balmy April morning, a renegade band of natives of the plains attacked the settlement, raped the women and scalped the men who were present in the fort. Five hostages were taken, one of who was the famed Cynthia Ann Parker. In maturity she would become the principal wife of Peta Nocona, the most

# A Loud Hurrah For Silas and Seth As Though Thousands Backed Them

dreaded of the South Plains War Chiefs. On at least three occasions, Cynthia Ann had a chance to return to white settlement. Each time she had such an opportunity, she resolutely refused to do so. When a band of well-armed Texas Rangers forced her back to Anglo civilization, she made repeated efforts to return to the home she considered her own on the South Plains.

The raid on the Parker settlement would have resulted in the taking of more hostages had it not been for two brothers, Silas and Seth Bates. They were among the men tending crops a mile from the makeshift frontier fort. Once they realized their home was under siege, Silas and Seth ran toward the massacre site. They had no weapon, only the hoes they had been using in the field. According to Rachel Plummer's eyewitness account, Silas waved his hoe in the air and shouted "a loud hurrah as though he had thousands to back him". Only his brother accompanied him. This was a courageous act that prevented additional ravaging of the colony.

Though I heard the story from those who believed Ina was a direct descendent of Silas Bates, recent research indicates her ancestor was Seth Bates. It was he and he alone who backed up Silas in the daring charge toward the Fort. Seth later married one of the females who had been saved from becoming a Comanche captive. Ina Wood Kinsey was a direct descendant of that union. Karin would be a seventh generation heir of one of the most traumatic events in the history of the Texas frontier. I feel I should give a loud hurrah for Seth!

Karin was born in Brownwood and, as has been mentioned before, lived with her parents in her grandparents home in Zephyr, Texas, a small community near Brownwood, until she was two and moved to Sweetwater where her other Grandmother, widowed while Kirby and Ina were in Missouri, lived.

Karin and her sister Nelda spent many of their summers in the home of their grandparents in Zephyr. Three churches in the village, Presbyterian, Methodist, and Disciples of Christ, shared a circuit-rider plan, sending a pastor from their denomination to preach one Sunday each month. Each church had a building on one of the four corners of the intersection of two roads and members would gather in their own church for Sunday School. Karin went to the Presbyterian Church where her Grandfather was Sunday School Superintendent and her Grandmother taught her pre-school class in the choir loft. On the fourth corner was a *brush arbor* where on every fourth Sunday the church members shared *dinner on the ground.* Though too young to remember exact details of the schedule, Karin knows that on at least Fifth Sundays and, she remembers more often than that, they had *all day singing* and members of the original Stamps Quartet always were there.

When back home in Sweetwater she became a regular attendee of the Sunday School of the town's First Presbyterian Church. At the age of nine she made a decision to profess her faith and unite with the church. Her greatest joy was the surprise on the Sunday she was to join to suddenly realize her parents, Kirby and Ina, were standing beside her, having decided to join with her as all three became Presbyterians. Wise parents they were, for Karin never realized until adulthood that this action deeply hurt her Sweetwater Grandmother (Kirby's mother) who had been and remained until her death a very prominent and active member of the Methodist Church in Sweetwater.

Kirby, who surprised Ina when he was the first to start down the isle to stand with Karin and join the Presbyterian Church with Karin, served as both a Deacon and a Ruling Elder of the Presbyterian congregation. For a time he held the very important position of Church Treasurer. For years he used his professional skills to print the Sunday morning worship bulletins without cost to the Church. It was a day when few churches had bulletins of any sort, much less professionally printed bulletins. This he often had to do late Saturday night or early Sunday morning when the appropriate information had not been given him during working hours.

Kirby was a leader in the local Men of the Church organization. Ina was active in the congregation's Women's program, usually the Circle Bible Teacher and later President of the Women of the Church. Karin's leadership ability was also recognized. She was chosen to serve on Presbytery's Youth Council before she was 14 and later the statewide Synod Youth Council, attending Presbytery camps, Synod Conferences and national General Assembly youth gatherings in Montreat, North Carolina.

Karin received her entire preparatory education in the efficient Sweetwater school system. She painfully recalls one dismal event during her elementary school years. Her school allowed a music teacher to audition students for a school choir. More than anything at that time in her life, Karin wanted to be accepted into the choir. She was the first to volunteer to *try out*. The teacher asked Karin to sing the scales. At this point Karin had no tutorship in music and, not knowing what the *scales* were, she simply began to sing, causing snickers, giggles and laughter from the other students. Elementary student Karin was declared totally devoid of musical talent and was the *only* student who was rejected. Each day thereafter, for that school year, she was required to sit in the classroom with one other student, a boy who did not want to be in a singing group. The two sat downstairs without a teacher in their classroom doing homework, which their teacher would later check. Sounds of music for the coming event made by all other members of their class upstairs floated downstairs to the homework room. Karin accepted the inept instructor's verdict of her lack of musical ability, a verdict that she has carried into adulthood. Yet I occasionally hear her singing in a lovely, clear soprano voice when she thinks no one is listening. I often wondered what beautiful music might have come forth from Karin if a certain instructor had been even marginally able to instruct.

Karin excelled in mathematics in an age when only male students were supposed to be good at sums. She proved herself capable of working the most complicated math problems, usually attributing that talent to the fact that she was challenged to try to solve a problem when a Junior High Teacher offered to pay ten cents to anyone who solved a certain problem that day. She solved the problem and she and two boys collected ten cents each from the pocket of their teacher, Mr. Overton. That teacher inspired Karin to carry his picture in her billfold throughout high school and college and to remain resolute in the face of any challenge, mathematical, or otherwise. Perhaps ten cents paid by a teacher resulted in Karin being named valedictorian at her High School graduation.

The level prairie land on the outskirts of the town provided an ideal site for training pilots of military aircraft. Karin remembers the city airport where her second grade class in 1937 went to watch Amelia Earhart land during one of her last cross-country flights before her tragic disappearance.

Sweetwater's Avenger Field housed three unique groups who underwent training during World War II: the U. S. Army Air Corp trainees (one with his new bride rented the Kinsey's guest bedroom, sharing the upstairs bathroom and limited kitchen privileges with the Kinseys), elite British Royal Air Force cadets who were sent by Britain to complete their pilot training away from the terror of Hitler's bombing, and a group of women trainees who would be known as America's first female military aviators called WASP (Women's Air Service Pilots known for flying practice targets for the Airmen). Each member of WASP had to be wealthy, for each had to be already a licensed pilot before entering as WASP. Most of them were debutantes, a concept new to Sweetwater citizens. Many were golfers, some famous, and especially enjoyed the golf course on Lake Sweetwater.

The Kinsey family took special interest in the young men and women who underwent training at the nearby field. Holidays at the Kinsey's always included guests from Avenger Field. Kirby would go out the morning of the holiday to find any willing guests while Ina prepared the holiday meal. Often while they were preparing to accept his invitation he would rush to the print shop and print a box of stationary with the name of each guest as an added gift. Young British cadet pilots who were far from their homes in a strange, new land were invited into the Kinsey home, often in groups of three or four. The family's meager gasoline allotment was used to take some favorite guests on trips into the

# A Loud Hurrah For Silas and Seth As Though Thousands Backed Them

nearby countryside and even included for trips the Kinseys found necessary to make when Ina's mother was critically ill in Zephyr. Geoffrey became a favorite. When he learned that Karin was near the same age as his younger sister, Pearl, he helped set up a penpal correspondence between the two. This was a relationship that would last a lifetime.

Sources of history for The Women Air Service Pilots state, "Fifinella, the Official mascot, was designed by Walt Disney for a proposed film. During WWII, the WASP asked for permission to use her as the official mascot and the Disney Company generously agreed. Official Fifinella 'went to war' and was worn in the form of patches. Some were leather, some were cloth...worn on WASP flight jackets."

Somewhere a WASP or someone who appreciates WASP history should own a framed letter that tells another story about the mascot for WASP (no "s" added to denote plural since the "P" stands for more than one pilot, "*Pilots*"):

When female pilots known as WASP became frequent customers for personalized stationery, Kirby Kinsey wrote Walt Disney and told him that the WASP members were doing a brave job and he felt they needed an identity of their own. He asked if it would be possible for Walt Disney to design something for him to use on stationery the women stationed at Avenger Field were buying. Walt Disney immediately responded with the drawing of Fifinella and a letter allowing Kirby to print stationery with the famous Fifinella mascot. When the letter from Walt Disney arrived, Kirby asked the officials at Avenger Field if they also wanted to use it. Karin was too young to know whom he asked, but it could even have been Jacqueline Cochran who created the WASP unit since Kirby and most of the businessmen in Sweetwater knew her. They were always invited to special events at Avenger Field. Karin remembers her family attending a WASP graduation where Jacqueline Cochran spoke. Karin heard most of the speech and then fainted in the heat and was taken to an "off-limit" section of Avenger Field, the Infirmary! Fifinella appeared first on stationery printed for members of WASP by Kirby

Kinsey then began to appear on their clothing and on airplanes they were flying. The original black and white drawing and brief letter from Walt Disney was framed and hung above the front desk of *Kirby Kinsey, Printer* for years. One day, many years later, Karin met a former WASP and introduced her to Ina who was so excited to again meet a WASP that she, to Karin's amazement, immediately took the framed letter off the wall and gave it to the former WASP. Karin quietly cried on the inside. She had hoped to inherit that letter and drawing from Walt Disney. Actually, that letter really belongs in a WASP Museum!

The Sweetwater printer produced so many boxes of the special stationery at $2.00 per box that his shop made an unexpected profit. It was this money that made it possible for the Kinseys in 1940 to build a beautiful new Cape Cod two-story home on Twelfth Street and pay the $6,000 price for it in two years.

It was in the back yard of that Cape Cod home where I first met Karin. She was serving ice cream to the Men of Church meeting her father was hosting. She was fifteen.

*Four*

## The Streets of Laredo

*1932*

Soon after the death of Aunt Bessie the one person to whom I had always been able to talk about anything, a strange feeling of uncertainty seemed present in the Ramsay household in Alexandria, Louisiana. One night in late summer I was outside in front of the manse talking with neighborhood friends. One said there would be a meeting at the church at which my father would be fired. I asked Leroy about this. Leroy, who was a Roman Catholic, said that could not happen in his church. No one could fire the priest, but he did not know about Presbyterians.

The next Sunday a strange minister preached. After the worship service, my mother took me home. I would not be allowed to attend a meeting of the congregation in spite of the fact I was a full member of the church. There were no Sunday guests at the manse that day.

A few days later, a moving van took some of our furniture

away for storage. This included Aunt Bessie's bed. A painter came to repaint her room and the guest room. He would soon return to complete the refurbishing of the large house. Before he returned, most of Lilian Cook Ramsay's prized possessions were moved to the Louisiana storage facility. There they remained for several years during which time the river overflowed its banks wreaking havoc on my mother's treasured possessions. Only one item was salvaged from the inundation: the bed in which my aunt had been born and died.

My mother especially treasured the bed. Aunt Bessie (Elizabeth Lavinia Cook) was the daughter of famed pre-Civil War photographer George S. Cook, ex-associate of Mathew Brady, and she was my mother's aunt, my great aunt. The spool bed, beautifully finished inside and on all four sides, is marked on the inside of one side rail, "made in Charleston, S.C. 1860 for George S. Cook". It was made for the house at 28 S. Battery, built by George S. Cook in 1861 and completed shortly before the Civil War. During the many moves the Ramsays made, mother carefully used quilts to protect the bed, which she entered in antique shows and bragged when it won first place. The fact that it was a winner is amazing because it survived the flooded storage and as well as what I caused to be done to the bed only a few months before Aunt Bessie died in it.

When Karin and I were living in San Antonio, Mother gave the bed to us. Mother cautioned Karin that she hesitated to give it to us because she was afraid our children might get their head caught, as I did, between the carved spools, which rotate enticingly. Though Karin thought she was merely a cautious grandmother, we kept the treasured bed covered until our children were safely in college. After that time, we hung a picture of 28 S. Battery on our master bedroom wall, centered the bed below the picture and have been sleeping in it as *our bed*. Only while writing this book did I confess to Karin why two of the spools do not turn. Together we examined the footboard and discovered where the top section had been skillfully sawed in two and even more skillfully repaired. I remember how Aunt Bessie was more concerned on that day for my head than she was for the bed and how a whole crew was brought into the bedroom while I was caught between the spools. I also showed Karin the place, still evident by a slight indention above my temple, where I had been caught. At times I touch my temple and still remember the pain and panic of that day. Karin, now that she knows my story, marvels even more that Mother was able to enter the bed into antique fairs and that the bed would be declared a winner in spite of repairs I caused!

About six months before we knew we would be forced to move, the grand old Essex had been traded in on a brand new Chevrolet. Although the old car brought a substantial trade in, a considerable amount of cash was necessary to complete the purchase. This was only possible at the depth of the Depression because my mother provided the funds from savings she had accumulated during her eight-year teaching career, a career she had to abandon when she married.

As the new car took the Ramsays over the Alexandria Red River Bridge, I remembered my mother saying something about shaking the dust off our feet and going on. When I heard her say that, I knew that persons who were not wanted in a town had no choice but to go elsewhere.

The dismal journey took us eastward to Richmond where my father had enrolled in a graduate school of Theology, Union Seminary. He had already earned three degrees including a Master of Arts at the University of Texas. Our new home was quite different from the spacious manse in which we had lived for nearly five years. We would dwell in a Seminary owned apartment, one of several created from a pre-Civil War home. Since the decision by my father to go back to school was finalized after the beginning of the semester, we had to take the only lodging still available, one with two rooms below ground level with a single bedroom upstairs. Only my mother's ingenuity made the quarters livable: she strung wires across the sleeping room upon which she hung sheets that provided a reasonable amount of privacy for the four of us.

The centuries old building in which we lived had once been the mansion of one of Robert E. Lee's trusted subordinates. The famed Confederate Commander's ghost was said to have roamed the multi-story house since the General had often spent nights there during the effort to defend the southern capital. My father took me to a site a mile or two beyond the area. There he pointed out several mounds of dirt that he believed had once been a site for Confederate cannon aimed northward. We never met Lee's phantom spirit, but he would have had no reason to enter our below ground living area. Obviously our apartment had been servant's quarters that had been inhabited by black slaves before the year 1865.

My school was six long blocks away in what was then a well to do neighborhood of aristocratic Virginians, Ginter Park. Since I had missed the first several weeks of the school term, I had some catching up to do. A very different style of penmanship was taught, one which required a unique type of capital letters. Although the teacher was encouraging, she was no Miss Sinclair.

On my way home from school, several older boys took delight in jumping out of the bushes and chasing me the rest of the way to the basement apartment. I finally confessed to my mother why I was so out of breath upon my arrival at home. She suggested that my father might walk me home the next day. I refused the proposed escort service and made her promise not to embarrass me in such a fashion.

The following day, on reaching the ambush site, once more my tormentors appeared. This time I started to run but did not. My father suddenly emerged from a larger row of bushes. He grabbed the oldest of my antagonists and got the name of the leader of the gang who turned out to be the son of the president of the graduate school in which my father was enrolled. The next day a conference took place between the two fathers. The gang of bullies ceased to exist.

I later attended the same seminary where the President who was there when my father attended was still serving. To my amazement, the president's wife once teased me by saying she remembered me as a small boy, one her son had "given some trouble". I still felt embarrassed, so I did not respond, though I was and always have been curious to know her version of the story.

Richmond was a very different place than Alexandria. The winter was colder and several times snow fell. Often ice covered the steps that led up to level ground from the door of the basement apartment. In March the family arose well before daylight and drove to Washington for the first inauguration of Franklin D. Roosevelt. There were trips to Williamsburg, Jamestown and Yorktown. When spring came I found friends nearby. The large trees around the old building put forth green leaves carefully covering their bareness. A field of grain took on a shimmering hue. For the first time, the state in which I had been born appeared to be a land of beauty.

In late spring, the news came of the death of my grandfather, Foster M. Ramsay. My father was named executor of the estate. As soon as the residence requirements for the Master's degree in Theology were completed, we moved once more. This time we would go to Laredo, the Texas town on the Rio Grande where Grandfather Ramsay had lived most of his life.

The family moved into the large brick home where my grandfather had lived near downtown Laredo. There were friends aplenty in the immediate neighborhood. I can still remember several: Ed Mann, Wendell Pogell, Arthur Schuemaker, and later Pat Stanford and Monroe Chapman. I was delighted Texas had no gang of bullies to chase me about the streets of Laredo.

At the end of the summer, the family took a trip to Mexico. This was my first time to cross an international border. The Chevrolet carried us over high mountains to Monterrey. From there we went to Saltillo. This required a river crossing where there was no bridge. Water got into the car's engine causing it to stall out. A Mexican national stopped to help. He spent over an hour helping my father dry out the motor. At last the car was running well and when money was offered for the help rendered, the Mexican refused. My father had spoken to him in the Spanish he had learned in Laredo and they were "*compadres*", more than friends, comrades on the road. He would not take pay for aiding a fellow traveler.

After an overnight stay in Saltillo, the return trip began among towering mountains that cast dramatic shadows across the land. As we headed north toward the border, a cloud of Monarch butterflies enveloped us. Although some of the magnificent creatures died on the automobile's radiator, most survived to continue the southward journey deep into a land of amazing beauty.

For a year, we lived in the downtown brick house. The family moved to the Heights, a newer area east of the older part of the city. The new home had two tall palm trees in front and sixteen citrus fruit trees in the spacious back yard. My father enlarged the house by adding an additional bedroom and a sunroom, one similar to the enclosed porch of the Alexandria Manse. We lived there for the next several years. During this time, I completed Junior High School and the eighth and ninth grades, attending both the old High School perched on the edge of the Rio Grande and the newer Martin High on the city's north side.

In the Texas Centennial Year, the family decided to see the western United States as a prelude to a visit to the Texas Exposition in Dallas. The Chevrolet was traded in on a new Dodge and the journey began. On the first morning in the new car we were on a road that was being repaired when we ran over a large stone on the road that cut a hole in the crankcase. The car was hauled to the nearest town, Langtry, a village with only three businesses: a small motel, the restored Judge Roy Bean Saloon, and a filling station. The stranded travelers had no choice other than to take up lodging in the Spartan accommodation then called a *Tourist Court*. The filling station operators sought help from the nearest car repair facility in Alpine, a process that could take as much as a week. We had barely settled into our temporary home when a ranch welder arrived and made the necessary repair. The journey could continue.

Each evening the search for clean lodging began well before five o'clock. When an adequate tourist court was sighted, my father would stop and ask to see an available cabin. If the interior was neat, white towels were on the bathroom rack and the price was no more than two dollars, payment was made and we spent the night. Only once the two-dollar limit was exceeded: a California national park charged four dollars for a tent. My father never forgot that over charge.

The Ramsays spent several days in the Grand Canyon area, a full week in Los Angeles, visited Sequoia, Yosemite, San Francisco, Portland, the Canadian Rockies, Glazier National Park, Pikes Peak, Estes Park and finally arrived in Dallas for the Centennial celebration. Years later Karin and I discovered we had both been at the Exposition at about the same time. Yet I had failed to get a glimpse of the most fascinating person I would ever be able to meet.

The year after the grand western tour, my father decided to return to full time religious work. He became pastor of the First Presbyterian Church of Taft, Texas. This required another move, one that took the family away from the home in Laredo's heights to a two-story manse next door to the church building. This was a long established congregation in a flourishing community. Yet from the beginning I had an uneasy feeling about my father's position as minister. On one occasion I overheard a bitterly argumentative discussion between my father and a leading member of the church.

I became the sports editor of the Taft High newspaper. I carefully recorded each play by the football team and provided a typed copy for the towns paper and carbons for the school coach. I did this each week on my father's Underwood typewriter. This gave me ample keyboard practice time. I soon became a fast typist. I won the local speed-typing contest and went on to place high enough in county and regional interscholastic league events to qualify for a try at the state championship at the University of Texas in Austin. Although I failed to win first place, my typing teacher assured me I would have won had I not drawn an inferior machine, one, which was prone to mechanical errors. I wondered if I had been able to use an Underwood, perhaps I could have won the championship.

John Ramsay's pastoral position at the Taft church did not last long. In the summer of 1939, the family moved to the West Texas town of Spur. This would be my father's longest and most successful pastorate. His forthright and energetic style was appreciated among the hearty ranchers of the broken lands just beneath the Caprock where the vast south plains began.

The area around Spur was an interesting portion of Texas. Just north of the town, a dramatic mesa known as *Soldiers' Mound* rose high above the surrounding prairie. The flat-topped hill had taken its name from the fact that cavalry units had often camped there in the on-going wars against the natives of the plains. Only a single trail led to the top of the high mesa, one which could easily be defended against Comanche attacks led by war chiefs like Peta Nocona and his son, Quanah Parker.

I completed my state-mandated education in Spur High School, a small institution with a limited curriculum. One teacher, a dedicated educator I knew as Miss Cavness, voluntarily took on the task of aiding several of us who were college bound by providing tutorship in mathematics. Each day she would assign an algebra problem just beyond our ability. One of the students kept asking, "Miss C., do we really have to do that one?" Her reply was always, "In this life, you do not have to do anything but die." I knew she meant even the most difficult task was an absolute must.

It was during this time I began to struggle with the question of my future. I had wondered if I might be able to become a minister. My father never mentioned this possibility to me, probably realizing the heartbreak and pain his own pastorates had brought to his family. By this time I had attended eight different schools and we had lived in seven homes.

The immediate decision before me after high school graduation in Spur, Texas May of 1940 was which college I should attend. My college bound fellow classmates all planned to attend Texas Tech University in Lubbock. Just before graduation I had won the preliminary round of an extemporaneous speech contest held at Tech and one of my judges was a professor there. When, on the final round I came in second, he called me aside and told me why I had not won in the finals. I had used a trite illustration regarding the flag outside the window. He did not want me to be discouraged. He assured me that I had all the "earmarks of a forceful platform speaker". This was an ability I should continue to develop. He, an outsider gave me encouragement I needed. Still, though I was impressed with Tech and especially that professor, I did not want to go there. It was too close to home.

My mother was in favor of Tech. She wanted me to have the option of coming home for weekends. My father hoped I would attend Austin College in Sherman, his own alma mater.

## Angel Kisses And My Beating Heart

*Five*

# Decisions, Decisions And Approaching War

*1940*

After graduation, I attended what had become a highlight of my summers, ten days at Westminster Encampment in Kerrville, Texas. That was one of the high points each year. The conference drew an attendance of several hundred high school and college age youths. The gathering always concluded with an act of dedication. The entire conference would go on a *mystery ramble*. This was an event that involved several miles of walking to a final worship service in some spot in the nearby hills. After an inspirational message by one of the ministers on the staff, a fire was lighted below the cross. We would then sing a hymn of dedication. With the flames still burning we would then march into the hill country night with a new resolve within our hearts.

Since I was now a high school graduate and a veteran conference attendee, I was asked to serve on the crew that was responsible for erecting the cross, preparing the sand and gasoline mix, and finally setting it aflame at the precise moment that would have the greatest emotional impact. This cross ceremony was abandoned a few years later, fearing that any form of emotionalism was to be questioned. Yet, for me, I believe this ceremony had a profound impact, one that contributed to my decision to make a try at becoming a minister.

I spent the month of July that summer in Laredo. My father was still engaged in settling Grandfather Ramsay's estate. He believed I needed a bit of help in understanding financial reality. The estate included about thirty-five rental properties that required monthly collections. My father did not go to Laredo with me. He simply arranged with the collection agency for me to do the job for one month and for me to room with the son of Cousin Maude in their Laredo home.

My high school graduation gift was a factory reconditioned Underwood typewriter. My father had written a Master's thesis at the University of Texas about the huge images on Easter Island in the Pacific Ocean. He hoped to have this published and needed a carefully revised copy plus two legible carbons. This was a tedious task but he drilled me in the fine points of entering footnotes correctly. This would be a skill that would be highly usable in college, and later in preparing a thesis of my own.

I am not sure when I decided to go to Davidson. I remember considerable correspondence during my senior year in high school with the college. At some point I signed an application form. There was no SAT test in those days, but Davidson's requirements were stricter than those of most other institutions of higher learning. In any case, by the beginning of the summer, I knew I was going to a college as far away from home as possible.

My father wanted me to attend a Presbyterian College. Although I think he would have preferred that I go to Austin College in Sherman, Texas, his alma mater, he was willing to send his son to Davidson College in Davidson, North Carolina. I think I chose the far distant school knowing only that the college had an excellent reputation. I had been told Davidson was considered the Harvard of the South. I later learned this was not

## Decisions, Decisions And Approaching War

necessarily so: Harvard was the Davidson of the North.

That fall the family took a trip east, visited New England, Canada, New York including several days at the World Fair. The journey took me to North Carolina in time to enroll at Davidson. One of the major hurdles necessary for acceptance into the college's student body was that of successfully passing a rigid math exam. I was able to pass on the first try, thanks to the diligence of Miss Cavness.

I spent long hours walking the beautiful North Carolina countryside making my next decisions, deciding a major and seeking an answer to the question of what career I should pursue. I found my first year Physics class an exciting one particularly the rapidly developing science of Meteorology. Many other Davidson students were planning to go on to Medical School. I took courses that led to a Bachelor of Science degree rather than one in Arts. Once or twice I tried predicting North Carolina weather. I soon ruled that out as a career. One year of inorganic chemistry cooled my interest in becoming a physician.

It was late in my freshman year at Davidson, just before the summer of 1941, that I decided to ask my presbytery to received me as a candidate for the ministry. This they did. I met with the committee in Cisco, Texas in the summer of 1941. One member of the committee, a Dr. McCall, a retired minister living in Weatherford, Texas, corresponded with me throughout my pre-ordination years.

I hoped that if the Candidates Committee believed in me, I might be able to make it in spite of the doubts I had about my own ability which were probably based on my father's difficulties as a pastor.

I returned to Davidson as a sophomore. On the morning of December 7, 1941, we awoke to the reality of war. I was spending the weekend with a Charlotte friend, Linus Banker. We had gone to a war movie the night before, *Sergeant York*.

My mother insisted that I come home for the Christmas holidays that December when Pearl Harbor had been attacked. This was the only year during my college years that I was home for Christmas. I took my ROTC uniform with me and wore it in downtown Spur. No one was sure who would be called up or how any of us would be involved in the approaching war.

On one occasion soon after Pearl Harbor I visited the local chairman of the draft board who was also a Davidson College official and asked if I should volunteer for military service. I was told to stay in school if I wanted to be of real service to my country. He was confident that the War would be a long one, fought not only on the world's battlefields but also in the realms of the mind and spirit.

I attended the University of Texas the summer of 1942, taking courses in Texas History and Sociology. I was back at Davidson the next fall. The following summer, 1943, I returned to Texas University in Austin where I was able to complete enough work in English Literature to be able to claim a valid major.

Billy Baine, a good friend I had made while my father was pastor in Taft, came to Austin for a visit midway through the summer of 1943. Together we went to see the acting president of the Austin Seminary. Dr. Thomas Currie, long time president of the institution had died early that spring. We both decided to go to Union Seminary in Richmond, Virginia since there appeared to be some doubt about the future of Austin Seminary as to what seminarians entering that fall could expect.

We were roommates for our first year at Union Seminary in Richmond, Virginia. Billy married Margaret in the summer of 1944 and I spent my summer going back to Davidson in spite of the fact I now had enough hours to graduate. Davidson had a requirement that no degree would be granted unless a student took his final credit hours at Davidson. These hours in Davidson were at the sacrifice of time I wanted to have at the Seminary. An important part of our Seminary training was that of working in a church where members of the teaching staff could later evaluate us. Since I still had to complete the work at Davidson, I was only able to spend two months of this time in what was then called "Practical Theology", a situation that would not be allowed today, but in times of advancing war exceptions are allowed.

I enrolled in the last term of summer classes at Davidson so I could graduate and instead of working in Richmond near Seminary Staff who could evaluate me, I was invited to spend the first part of the summer of 1944 in Anson, Texas as a student pastor. This was a small town twenty miles west of Abilene. A retired rancher met me at the bus stop.

He immediately commented that he hoped I "would not be like their last pastor".

When I inquired about my predecessor, I was told he had failed to speak to everyone he passed on the street. Since I had come directly from a Virginia seminary, the same institution the former minister had attended, my greeter feared I would not fit in.

Once more I wondered if I could make it as a pastor. I slept but little my first several nights in Anson. I soon learned to greet every person I met with true West Texas enthusiasm. In addition I visited every family in the congregation as soon as possible. I must have passed muster, for it was my original greeter who vigorously urged me, even offering me a full time salary if I would consider switching to a Texas seminary so I could return as student pastor and eventually become full time minister of the Anson church.

With summer classes back in North Carolina and Davidson diploma granted, I returned in the fall of 1944 to Richmond for my middle year of Seminary and was fortunate enough to find a new roommate, Roy Sherrod, once Billy had traded me off for Margaret. Friendship with both Billy and Roy would last a lifetime.

During the following summer, 1945, I worked in West Virginia. I was responsible for conducting Vacation Bible Schools in a rural community near Fayetville and in two coalmining towns, a mile a part. During this time, I lived in Summerlee and walked the mile over a high mountain pass to Scarboro. In addition to working with a staff of teenage teachers, I was expected to preach each Sunday as many as four times. I had an early service in the only church in the coalmining camp of Summerlee. I set out immediately after the service for the mile trip to the site of the small church on the other side of the mountain. I was never late since the organist was not supposed to begin until I arrived. After I completed my second service, I was expected to preach in the county home where I preached the same sermon to the elderly residents who lived there as I had preached earlier. I then walked back to Summerlee for the evening service. It was there that a *love offering* was always taken. This offering consisted of coins and a few dollar bills, which were presented to me, wrapped in a miner's large red bandana. Since I had all of my meals free at the Company Boarding house, I ended the summer with plenty of cash, mostly coins and one-dollar bills.

A few weeks before receiving my degree from Union Seminary, my father proposed that I consider going abroad for further advance study. He believed he could finance a year of academic work in Europe. I consulted with my theology professor, John Newton Thomas. He urged that I apply for admission to the University of Edinburgh in Scotland. He assured me I would be accepted since the Virginia seminary was known for its high standards in language studies.

While I was uncertain that I would be accepted for further study after Seminary, the War was an even greater uncertainty in my mind. Billy Baine, and I visited the Sea Bee base in Williamsburg where Navy chaplains received their final training before joining a ship's company in the Pacific. At the time I believed this was the direction I should go, one possibly inspired by the tales of the sea Aunt Bessie had read to me as a child. The war ended before my final year at Union Seminary and there was no longer a need for sea going preachers.

My love of adventure in far away places led me to volunteer for missionary service in Africa, taking preliminary exams and deciding that I would fulfill the requirement of a year's experience in a local church. I am not sure what happened, yet in time I realized that I could use what talent I possessed at home. During my final Seminary year, I had preached on a regular ba-

# *Decisions, Decisions And Approaching War*

sis in two towns in southern Virginia, Kenbridge and Victoria. They wanted me there. Since I had worked in West Virginia my last seminary summer I was invited by the Presbytery Executive to visit the mountain state and consider a call there. None of these possibilities seemed quite right.

One morning I was called out of class to receive a long distance call. Clifford Williams, pastor of the Presbyterian Church in Sweetwater, Texas, asked me if I would consider coming back to Texas and work in a three point preaching situation. I immediately said yes. Somehow I knew this was right. I had yet to understand how right it was.

# Angel Kisses And My Beating Heart

## Six

## The First Glimpse

### 1946

I arrived in the West Texas town of Roscoe only a few days after graduation from Union Seminary. The five-room manse next to the white wooden church building was rented in part to a young couple that had been lifelong residents of the town. Since I had agreed to only one year as resident pastor, I would live in the front room and share the house's lone bathroom with the renters.

On my arrival in town, I made the mistake others may have made. I asked for the residence of Mr. William Gordon.

After a moment of hesitation, I heard this response: "Do you mean Uncle Bill?"

I responded with an affirmative nod. I learned, "he was known as Uncle Bill throughout Nolan County". His wife was called "Aunt Bessie" and was equally well known. I was immediately directed to a small home about a half block from the bus stop. It was there I spent my first night in Roscoe. Aunt Bessie would not let me go to the room that would be my headquarters until everything was properly prepared.

Uncle Bill was the local magistrate. He had long served as Justice of the Peace. He had a style that was unique. He had the ability to assess a fine without making the charged person angry. He was also a Presbyterian elder. He was known throughout Mid-Texas Presbytery and never missed a meeting of that governing body. There were only two elders in the church. The other was a man named Nemir who was seriously disabled. He made efforts to attend church on occasion, but could not sit through morning worship.

Since one elder able-to-attend and one yet-to-be-ordained pastor do not make a quorum, thereby making no possibility of holding regular meetings of the Session, I organized Church Council. This included Uncle Bill, Aunt Bessie as Superintendent of the Sunday School, a representative of the women, two younger men who were elected as deacons and the president of the youth group of the church.

Aunt Bessie was the heart and soul of the congregation. She visited everyone in the community of eleven hundred people who needed any kind of help. She saw to it that all needs were adequately met. When the church building had to be moved six blocks across town because of highway construction and Sunday morning arrived, she found the building in the middle of the road halfway to the new site. She helped others climb into the building, then on rollers. There she conducted Sunday School as usual since she was the life long Sunday School Superintendent.

Another stalwart member of the church was a woman I knew as "Mrs. Clausell". She had raised a family by operating the only washateria in the town. She rendered whatever cleaning service one needed which included ironing white shirts, washing and ironing sheets or pressing Sunday attire. She had two daughters. One lived in Abilene and was a leader in a Presbyterian Church there. The other was a young woman about my age who was a student in the General Assembly's Training School across the street from the Seminary I attended in Richmond, Virginia. Lena Clausell was a graduate of Austin College, a school she was able to attend on her mother's Washateria earnings. When I received my invitation to go to Roscoe, I consulted her. She urged me to accept the call believing I would be a good choice for her home church. Lena would later have a long and highly successful career as a Church Educator.

I made use of my day off to spend at least the morning hours learning Latin. Each Monday morning I completed a chapter of my Latin textbook and mailed my work to Austin. By the time I applied for admission to Edinburgh University, I could claim college level credit in one additional language. Although I never had reason to make use of my year of personal study in Latin, this may have helped me in being accepted as a student in a European university.

Not only was Scotland the ancient home of Presbyterianism, it was the place for Presbyterians to study with Edinburgh's New College faculty which included such names as Dr. James Stuart, an internationally known New Testament scholar, and Dr. John Baillie, a world renown theologian. Both had published books that were widely read throughout the English-speaking world.

I had been advised that I would be accepted as a serious student if I passed my Presbytery's examination for ordination and had at least one year of experience as a full-time pastor. The Church of Scotland would accept my ordination and consider me a candidate for income-producing work in the Scottish Kirk (church), income that I would need if I were accepted in The University of Edinburgh and stayed for the two years necessary for the degree I sought.

Since my freshman year at Davidson, spring of 1941, I had been what Presbyterians call "under the care of my home Presbytery", Mid-Texas. Soon after moving to Roscoe, I met in Cisco, Texas with the Examination Committee of my home Presbytery, a committee chaired by Tom Currie, Jr. I was approved in a routine meeting of Presbytery for ordination as a minister of the Gospel. Ordination as a Presbyterian minister was an action confirmed by full presbytery at a stated meeting held in July 1946 in Anson, Texas. The ordination rite was administered in my behalf in the sanctuary of the Roscoe church in late July, probably the only time the Roscoe Presbyterian Church ever hosted an ordination of a Presbyterian Minister.

For the next twelve months my duties would include three different tasks: serving as pastor of the small Roscoe church which had a membership of 72; preaching on Sunday afternoons in a Methodist church for Presbyterian ranching families who lived on the Divide, the high mesa south of Sweetwater; and on the Sunday afternoons when I was not scheduled to go to the Divide, preaching and leading worship at Westminster Chapel in Sweetwater, a flourishing new project which had been instigated by the youth group of Clifford William's Sweetwater church.

Westminster Chapel in Sweetwater, described before as a *project of the youth group*, is a special memory for me because it was in this place I had my first two baptisms: September of 1946, Frances Bartlett, age 13, and her 12 year old sister, Helen Bartlett the Sunday afternoon before Christmas of that year.

The Roscoe congregation received me with warmth. No one questioned my ability to fit in. Aunt Bessie gave me a standing invitation to her home for Sunday dinner unless someone asked me to eat elsewhere. Not only was I well fed during my stay; I also felt genuinely appreciated from the beginning. Although I began my work with considerable uncertainty, the loving concern shown by the entire congregation soon quenched my fears.

One essential for serving such a widespread parish was a suitable means of transportation. At the time I had no car. About two weeks after my arrival in Roscoe, I was offered a chance to buy a Hudson-Terraplane. The total cost would be three hundred dollars. I purchased the vehicle and drove it several thousand miles in the year I was in Roscoe. I then traded it back to the previous owners, a father and son repair shop that specialized in maintaining automobiles made by the venerable Hudson

## The First Glimpse 45

Company. The trade back a year later was for the exact amount I paid in June of 1946. The car had only one drawback: it was painted a bilious yellow. I could not imagine myself following a hearse in a dignified funeral procession in a car that had been repainted such a color.

I purchased a large can of jet-black enamel. I also bought a spray gun, which at that time was usually called a "Flit-gun" and was used to jettison mosquito-destroying mist (Flit and Flit-guns were sold before spray paint in cans was invented.). I began on the large right front fender. By the time I finished, my arm was completely exhausted. I attempted to do the opposite side in a similar fashion. By then half the day was gone. It was a Saturday and I had to finish before sundown. I managed to do so by resorting to using a brush to complete the job. Although some of the paint beaded, few noticed since the town was on a level area of West Texas that was always muddy. The mud usually adequately covered my painting mistakes.

I soon felt affirmed by the ranch families who lived on the divide between the Brazos and Colorado watersheds, mostly red sandy loam. *The Divide* was not an organized community: it was a group of ranchers who settled on a mesa, a high and flat table land, a dozen miles long and seven or eight miles wide, an area quite visible and dramatic as you approach Sweetwater when coming from the east. Actually, the Divide includes most of Nolan County. The prominence, south of Sweetwater and north of the city of San Angelo, truly has the flavor of the real west. One of my three assigned duties was to preach on a regular basis in the Methodist Church to families who lived there. On the Saturday before the Sunday I was scheduled to preach, I would travel to the area in my Terraplane. Once on the mesa, I visited five different ranches. I was always asked to stay for a meal if I reach any of the homes near mealtime. One rancher kept asking me to take a few hours off of my pastoral rounds to saddle up and ride with him over his range. On one of my trips to the Divide I did so. For most of the day, I was in the saddle. I rode over a part of West Texas that few people ever see. It was a unique section of rugged lands with occasional watering places where both riders and horses can rest in shady green dells before mounting and riding on. Although I thoroughly enjoyed the day, it took this inexperienced horseman several days to regain my ability to sit comfortably behind a study desk.

On one very warm summer evening, I was invited to a Sweetwater Presbyterian Men of The Church meeting in the backyard of the Kirby Kinsey's home. It was there I had my first glimpse of Karin. She served ice cream to her father's guests. A few days later she was a volunteer worker in a Vacation Church School at Westminster Chapel. The Chapel had been a project of the Sweetwater Church, mostly a project of the Church Youth group to low-income families living in a small tourist court area of Sweetwater. Someone told me that Karin had been the driving force behind a campaign to raise funds to build the small but attractive building.

I had an opportunity to learn more about Karin when I attended a church youth meeting. Someone suggested we go on a snipe hunt. Karin was assigned the task of holding the sack into which the mythical creatures would be herded on the assumption she was as naïve as she was beautiful.

The group then took her in a car to an isolated bit of terrain surrounded by deep gullies behind the high school property and left her holding a bag. After thirty minutes or so, the youth group returned and could not find Karin. The adult sponsors including Jack became frantic fearing she may have fallen into an abyss. An extensive search began, ranging over several acres of broken, deeply furrowed land. There were no signs of Karin or her empty snipe sack.

It was time to call in the authorities. Clifford Williams decided it was his duty as pastor to go to the Kinsey home to notify Karin's father and mother. When he went to his car, he discovered Karin in the car, hiding between the front and back seat. The youth meeting was quickly dismissed and Clifford drove Karin home and explained to her parents what had happened. After Clifford left, when she told her father the details of the night,

Kirby chided her for not coming home instead of going back to the meeting. He would have enjoyed waiting for Clifford to come tell him his daughter was missing because the group took her snipe hunting. Kirby and Karin would have had fun chuckling over the joke she had played on the group who thought she would believe there was such a thing as snipe. I realized I had found a truly amazing person. It suddenly dawned on me that this might have been the reason for my certainty that the answer to Clifford's invitation to return to Texas had been right.

Clifford Williams had been my counselor at Westminster Encampment in Kerrville while I was in high school. Once you know Clifford, he is always interested in you. After I came to Sweetwater to work on projects he dreamed, my experiences as a minister took on special meaning. Especially meaningful was the fact that he and his Mary Agnes trusted me with my first Infant Baptism: the baptism of their two-month-old son, John Rowland Williams, January 26, 1947.

The next summer, 1947, I was invited to be the Adult Advisor for the editor of the newspaper at Westminster Encampment at Kerrville, the statewide youth conference. Karin was the editor I was supposed to advise. (When Karin read my manuscript, she asked me if it had ever occurred to me that as a member of the Texas Synod's Youth Council she had input as to who might help her as adult advisor for the daily newspaper.) One afternoon the mimeographed daily paper was completed well ahead of schedule and I asked Karin to go swimming with me.

She replied, "I do not know how to swim."

I had been certified the previous summer as a Red Cross Water Safety Instructor. When we got to the pool I demonstrated my best technique for each proper stroke. Karin pretended to listen attentively. She then proceeded to swim across the pool with amazing ease, showing perfect form with every movement of her graceful body.

Back in Sweetwater, Karin invited me to a swimming party at the lake. She suggested that we swim out to the float where boats were docking. At first I questioned the advisability of such a swim since the lake was full and deep and the distance too great for safety. When she insisted she could make the swim, I threw away all caution. About two thirds of the way, I thought I saw Karin struggling to keep above water. I grabbed her and demonstrated my safest life saving technique. I had been taught to use the hair carry on female swimmers since this was a method that gave the rescuer greater mobility. I was so fearful that I might lose her in deep water. I used the cross-chest carry. When we reached the floating platform, I was exhausted, and Karin was not. This was something about which she proceeded to chide the mighty swimmer. Although she claimed she could make the return swim without difficulty, I took no chances and called for a boat to carry us back to shore. Karin never told me whether or not I really saved her life. Even to this day I can do nothing other than assume she was merely putting me on. There was only one certainty for me: Karin Kinsey was a unique individual.

By this time I had only a few weeks left in my twelve-month agreement. I spent as much of those remaining days as possible in seeing Karin and taking her out on more conventional dates. In September Karin would enter Trinity University in San Antonio on a scholarship she had been awarded for being valedictorian of her high school graduating class. By then, I would be in the middle of the Atlantic Ocean, thousands of miles away. I had received notice the University of Edinburgh accepted me. I had booked passage on the R. M. S. Queen Elizabeth, the largest ship afloat. I would sail from New York harbor on September 18.

I knew I was hopelessly in love with seventeen-year-old Karin. She had all the charm and physical beauty of any of my high school or college friends, yet she had much more. She had the resolute wisdom and deep spirituality of Aunt Bessie.

I had at last found someone with whom I could share anything, yet I had never conveyed to her the depth of my feelings for her. When I left her at the front door of the Kinsey home I had only gained a promise from Karin to answer when I wrote from afar. I could not help but wonder if such a romance could survive for a year or more over a distance of at least five thousand miles. I was well aware of the sensation such a beautiful and vivacious young lady would be as a freshman at Trinity University.

*Jack Ramsay on board the forward deck of the Queen Elizabeth September 18, 1947. Picture taken by Charles McCain, Union Seminary Classmate and Cabinmate on the Queen Elizabeth.*

Post Card mailed from Southampton 24 Sep 1947:

*"Dear Folks,
Here's a picture of the ship that I'll mail when we dock. Thinking of you.*
                                    *Love, Jack"*

Cunard White Star R.M.S "Queen Elizabeth"

Church of Scotland

Richmond, Craigmillar

*Seven*

## The Scottish Adventure

*1947*

One of the first things I did on board the *Queen Elizabeth* was to sit down and write a letter to Karin. The ship's steward furnished me writing paper with the letterhead that read "R.M.S. Queen Elizabeth". I asked how best to mail such an important letter. The Steward assured me that I was on board a Royal Mail Ship, thus the lettering *R.M.S* at the top of the page. The Queen of the Sea, the great Elizabeth herself, would carry my letter back to Karin as quickly as possible.

The voyage was uneventful, for once out on the northern Atlantic there was little to see, but the ship itself was a wonder to behold. The food was excellent, as was the service. The huge vessel carried three thousand passengers and during wartime had transported more than five times that number of troops with each voyage. The ship moved so rapidly that enemy submarines could not threaten the vessel's passage. The ship had been completely reconditioned after the war and returned to its original luxurious condition.

I explored the vastness of the ship. Although I was a passenger in Third Class, then discreetly called *Tourist Class*, I was permitted to pass through most of the two upper levels as long as I did not linger in First Class. I spent much of my time in the large forward cabin where there were small shops, writing desks, movie theaters and exercise equipment. The cabin windows provided a view of the sea when there were no heavy north Atlantic clouds hovering beyond the vessel's prow. Even when dark masses appeared ahead, an occasional sunbeam fell on the rolling waters of the great ocean.

When there was relative calm, I took the ship's elevator up fourteen levels to the upper deck immediately behind the vessel's huge funnels. There the ship's forward motion was much more noticeable than below decks. It was then that I felt truly at sea as I moved across a vast ocean toward an unknown adventure.

The on board swimming pool was available when the rolling Atlantic allowed the vessel to ride on an even keel. I made a reservation for this amenity on two occasions and swam for a time in seawater. I then enjoyed a conventional bath administered by a steward before returning to my cabin.

I disembarked at South Hampton and took the train to London. During WWII a British Cadet stationed by Britain's Royal Air Force at Avenger Field, only eight miles from Sweetwater where choice cadets could safely finish their training during days when Hitler was bombing England, had become a special friend of the Kinsey's and was a frequent guest in their home. He had a sister, Pearl, slightly older than Karin, and the two became special friends, sharing letters and packages/parcels through the years though they had never seen each other in person. Karin had written her World War II pen pal, Pearl Maunder, and alerted her to my arrival. Pearl, nearly 50 years later, confessed to Karin that she did not want to do any thing as improper as entertaining a male guest in her home nor did she want to jeopardize her relationship with the person in whom she was interested, now away and studying in United States, so she enlisted her brother to help her entertain me. Pearl's brother, Geoffrey, the brother who was "a favorite British Cadet" of the Kinsey's, took me on a grand tour of the London area. He explained the intricacies of British currency to me and gave me a crash course in understanding the peculiarities of the language spoken in Great Britain. Pearl and Geoffrey could not do enough to help me. Before they let the wandering student board the train north to Edinburgh, they had done everything possible to make me feel at home in a strange new land.

Once in the northern capital, I enrolled as a Ph. D. candidate and had a conference with the Principal of New College, Dr. Hugh Watt. I explained that I wanted to enter into a full course of study but I was not sure that I had enough money to stay for the entire two years of university-required residence. Principal Watt seemed sympathetic to my confession of economic insecurity.

Scots had experienced financial difficulties since the final days of the Seventeenth Century. All available funds in Scotland had been invested in a failed colonial plan known as the *Darien Scheme*. Darien was the Seventeenth Century name of what is today Panama. The Scottish plan or scheme envisioned establishing a colony on the Atlantic side of the Isthmus of Panama. There ships could be unloaded, natives hired as burden bearers to carry all goods through the fifty miles or so to the Pacific side of the landmass. The very long and dangerous voyage by sea around South America could be avoided. The failure of the *Darien Scheme* left the nation destitute and caused the Scottish people to be forced, because of economic necessity, to give up their Parliament. The Scottish Parliament had given Scotland independence to make laws that benefited Scotland without dependence on English law as determined by the House of Lords in London. Without a Parliament, Scotland would remain merely an integral part of Britain.

Success in the Edinburgh Ph. D. program did not depend

entirely on passing certain prescribed examinations. This degree was granted only when a researcher produced fresh information that would be of value in understanding the totality of the human experience. Only two of the five candidates who had fulfilled all requirements the previous year were awarded degrees.

Dr. Watt suggested that I consider researching the Darien Scheme since this colonial endeavor had taken place in the Americas. He admitted this was a difficult project but it was one that he believed should be done. He gave me as much help as possible. He suggested inexpensive eating-places in order to aid me in stretching my limited finances. Since I was an ordained Presbyterian minister, a paying position in a Scottish church was a possibility.

Dr. Watt saw to it that I was one of the first American students to be offered a paying position in an Edinburgh church. It was soon after the beginning of the academic year that I became an Assistant Minister at Richmond Craigmillar Church. The stipend for this position would pay for all of my room and board. Although I knew nothing about Darien at the time, I accepted the challenge since it came directly from the Principal of the College who was a respected scholar and a published historian.

My University assigned lodging was a small residence hotel, the Wardie. My roommate was a fellow American student, Wade Huie who was pursuing a similar course of study. Huie would later become the respected professor of Homiletics at Columbia Theological Seminary in Atlanta, Georgia.

From our second story window we could look out at Granton Harbor. A stone jetty extended for a mile or more into the waters of the Firth of Forth, several miles wide. This view fascinated us especially in the winter when a lone Scottish worker would venture out the jetty and, not realizing we could see him from our second story window, would disrobe, take a swim in the icy waters of the sea, return to the jetty, robe and go wherever he went for the day. The view to the west included the famed Forth High Bridge under which major ships could pass with ease.

Each morning the two students ate Scottish Kipper, a bony

fish and drank British tea. The very word *Kipper* turns my stomach and I still refuse to eat it today. Eggs were seldom available since few chickens had been kept alive during the war years. The British had eaten them when they could not have beef. Even Britain's Beefeaters could not eat beef because Britain could not secure beef from Peron's Argentina. Rationing of beef, four ounces per week per person, caused the British to eat chicken, thus no eggs. This rare delicacy was on the table only on an occasional Sunday morning.

After breakfast we boarded the tram for the twenty-five-minute ride to New College, the theological branch of the University of Edinburgh. Once there we attended classes in the cold stone buildings. We ate the noon meal in the high vaulted College Refectory. I spent most of my afternoons in one of the libraries of the University.

Winter days in Scotland were short. The sun arose, if it came up at all, at about nine o'clock, the time classes began. By three p.m. daylight was over, earlier if a heavy fog had descended on the city. The Gulf Stream kept Edinburgh from extreme cold. Most mornings were frosty, but never more than a few degrees below freezing. When the sun did come up by noon the temperature could be in the forties or low fifties, yet even that could be a penetrating cold which required heavy underwear and at least two pairs of socks to keep feet accustomed to southern climes from suffering.

The city itself was uniquely interesting. The famed Edinburgh Castle dominated the skyline. Each day at noon a canon would roar from the esplanade immediately below the bonnie blue flag of Scotland. The cobbled stone High Street made its way down hill for a mile to Holyrood, the residence of the Queen when she made an official visit to the northern kingdom.

Midway down the slope were the somber gray stones of New College, the National Library and the General Assembly Hall nearby. The massive form of Old College Quad lies south of the High Street. The gold dome of McEwan Hall, the auditorium where graduating ceremonies were held, presided over other college buildings. Many of the surrounding structures predated the University's four centuries of existence.

I plunged into my research project with enthusiasm seeking every possible source of help. I traveled to Scotland's oldest university, St. Andrews, where the students wore crimson robes whether in class, on the street or bicycling against the north wind, which came in vigorous gusts off the North Sea. I sought the help of the university's professor of history.

This interview resulted in nothing other than total discouragement. The St. Andrew professor assured me there was nothing more to be known about the Darien Scheme. This project was a futile quest that could never produce a degree from any European University.

The only helpful information I received from the dour professor was an answer to my question of why students were required to wear bright red gowns. His reply was that this was a centuries old custom which he believed had come into being for the same reason fire plugs were always painted red: "we can know where they are".

I found my work at Richmond Craigmillar a pleasant relief from my intense efforts at Edinburgh University. I was an assistant to a Scottish minister named Alexander Hutchison. He assigned me the responsibility of working with a large group of youths in their late teens.

On each Saturday night one hundred and fifty young Scots filled the parish hall for social activities, at least half of who returned for the Sunday night program which involved serious discussion on Biblical themes. My work assignment included planning the Sunday night programs, visiting in the community near the church, conducting funerals in the parish, and assisting the minister when called upon to lead worship or preach. I was honored when he had me baptize infant Marion Macgill Hay, age 3 months, only my second infant baptism. He also set me up for a wedding, but the couple never showed. By December I felt accepted by the youth despite the fact that at first I had as much trouble understanding the Scottish youths as they did with my

## The Scottish Adventure

Texanized English.

During the lengthy Christmas holidays, I found relief from the continuing search for Darien materials by attending Edinburgh's theaters. For one or two shillings, ten to twenty cents, I could sit in the third balcony and enjoy shows ranging from comic ballets to serious musical dramas. On New Year's Day I heard the entire four-hour presentation of Handel's Messiah in the city auditorium by a five hundred-voice chorus.

I was asked to join a student delegation that would take part in a convention in London where there would be representatives from universities throughout Great Britain. I rode all night on a small bus with thirty other students. Several of the Scottish girls good-naturedly teased me about my *foreign accent*. One young woman who sat near me insisted I must be from Australia since she had never heard anyone speak exactly like I did. This was the kind of teasing which meant acceptance, an indication I was a part of the group.

Once at the London conference, I found myself involved in serious discussions on the importance of human worth. The event's theme was "Persons in a Modern World". After hearing prominent speakers discuss the importance of understanding person-hood, the conference broke up into small groups where there was vigorous discussion of how to apply the concept of human worth to the political structures of the day.

One of the more out spoken members of my seminar group was a young man who appeared to be slightly older than I. He took me to nearby eating places known only to a native Londoner. On one of our lunch breaks, we stopped by the British Museum. I tried to show off my newly learned knowledge of British history by identifying the pictures of several Sixteenth Century monarchs. My companion gently corrected me a time or two. Later he told me he was a lecturer in English history at Oxford University.

On my return to Edinburgh, I continued to find the ancient city both fascinating and exciting. Only one thing concerned me. Although I had written to Karin on a regular basis, I had heard from her only once or twice. I decided to keep writing and hope for the best.

Each evening the intensely penetrating cold of the North Sea crept in to my room at the Wardie. I had little hope of gaining the academic degree I sought. I was almost certain the Scottish adventure was a futile quest.

*When my first Christmas arrived, I received as a Christmas present the above picture of Karin. Charles McCain teased me:*

*"Just think. When you go back to America, you can go back to the U.S.A., marry her and help her through puberty."*

*Nevertheless, when she asked for a picture of me, I sent her the picture you see here.*

# Eight

## Sunlight on the Heather

*1948*

Soon after the first of the year I believed I had located documents that could assure the success of my academic quest. One of the unsolved riddles of Darien was that of the payment of the Equivalent. After the failure of the scheme to colonize Darien, the British offered to repay Scots an *Equivalent*, a large sum of money equivalent to money Scots had invested, money which had been used to finance the venture. A wagon train of sterling silver was sent to Scotland. Some historians believed the payment had never been made and the disillusion of the Scottish Parliament by the British was an illegal act.

I discovered papers in the archives of the Bank of Scotland that proved the payment had been made. Almost every Scot who had money had invested in the Darien Scheme. After the failure, a vast majority of Scots faced tremendous economic loss and they sold their investment certificates far below face value.

They had believed in the plan so much that they had risked their life savings in the venture. I found other records in the basement of the Tron Church on High Street, which opened up another avenue of understanding Darien: the heavy support and involvement of the Church of Scotland in the colonial adventure. When I presented my discoveries to Dr. Watt, the New College principal assured me that I was well on my way to the successful completion of my project, but I would have to write up my findings in an acceptable form.

An External Examiner, one who was the foremost expert in a particular field, would be assigned by the university to make the final determination as to whether or not a degree would be granted. I had brought my Underwood typewriter with me. This would be a faithful ally in the all-important writing process.

I had one more academic hurdle to overcome: my lack of ability to read and interpret the scholarly languages. I would need to pass a rigid examination in German, a language I had never studied. Most of the American students were enrolled in a class taught by a refugee from Hitler's regime known for working hard at the chore of getting southerners like me to properly pronounce the crisp tones of the Germanic language.

It was the written test I most feared. I spent hours in one of the university libraries going over German tenses, verbs and involved connective phrases. Our tutor assured us he would give us two chances to translate different passages of obscure German documents. If we failed the first, we might be able to succeed on the second. To my surprise, I passed the first test, which was supposed to be the most difficult.

At last I believed I was capable of achieving my academic goal. My stipend from my work in Edinburgh parish solved my economic problems. I wrote home I would stay in Scotland for another full year. My only uncertainty about this decision was that of wondering if Karin might find someone else during my long absence in a far distant land.

In March my roommate, Wade Huie, became the assistant minister at the Cannongate Kirk, the parish church for

Holyrood Palace. The minister was Ronald Selby Wright, known as Chaplain to the Queen and for his weekly radio broadcasts during the war under the name, "The Radio Padre". He was known throughout Britain and had drawn a greater wartime audience than anyone other than Winston Churchill. Wade suggested that I move with him to the four-story manse in which the Padre lived. I agreed, knowing I would have to undergo an interview with The Very Reverend Ronald Selby Wright. This proved an interesting experience, one that involved questions about my university project, my politics, and my religious views. Somehow I passed this test.

Wade and I moved to one of the most fashionable neighborhoods in Edinburgh, one that was within walking distance of New College. When we looked out our window on Regent Terrace, we no longer looked at the cold waters of the Firth, but now, when the Scottish mists were not too heavy, we could overlook the Palace and its well-kept gardens.

Since my roommate was assistant minister of the church down the slope from our residence, he was often called upon to secure the parish hall. Whenever a door had been left open by one of the many groups who used the building, someone from the Manse had to assist the police in searching the area. On occasion I helped with this responsibility. When a call came, I would take the master key from the downstairs rack, cross over the bridge spanning the railroad and walk into the murky darkness below. Once I had followed the officers through the building, I locked up and returned to Regent Terrace as quickly as possible.

Ronald Wright had written a book about ghostly apparitions. This was but one of more than two-dozen publications he had authored most of which had been produced by prestigious Oxford Press. I remember one dinner table discussion with him in which we asked about the Loch Ness monster legend. He responded by noting that the fabled creature often made a convenient appearance at the beginning of the tourist season. When we asked about the validity of the ghost tales about which he had written, his only reply was, "appearances are in their favor". A late night walk through the cobblestone streets of foggy Edinburgh was almost enough to convince anyone of the validity of spirit appearances.

Spring at last came to Scotland. The days were much longer and there were hours of bright sunshine. I had hope for the future since Karin's letters came with greater frequency. My work with the youths of Richmond Craigmillar became even more pleasant. The group took advantage of the Scottish springtime by planning long treks through the countryside. All would take a tram ride to the edge of the city and then walk some eight or ten miles through the Pentland hills. Since the teenagers were the church choir, the group would often sing as they walked, pausing beside a sparkling stream or atop a grassy knoll.

I learned to love the shrill sound of the bagpipes just so long as they were a mile or two away.

Most American students took advantage of the summer, *the between years break* as University students called it. University classes were not held during summer, a period of time lasting from May until the first of October, so both students and professors could see the beautiful Scottish countryside, visit the misty isles or travel on the Continent. On the last day of the spring semester, several students were discussing plans. The college principal happened upon us.

"By this time I thought all of you would be off to the ends of the earth", he said jovially.

"No sir", replied one of my companions. "We believe we are already at the end of the earth."

In early June I spent ten days on the Isle of Iona, a three-mile long stretch of land off the western coast of Scotland. I joined a group of workers who were renovating century old monastic community structures on the island, some dating from 623 A.D. Iona was also a Burial-place of Kings including Kenneth M'Alpine, first King of a United Scotland; and since his burial, over fifty Kings of Scotland, Ireland, and Norway, as well as Duncan and Macbeth. For a few days, I was on the sand loading crew that used the only motor vehicle on the island for loading crystal clear sand. This sand would go into the concrete that would hold stones together for reconstructing an ancient refectory that had long been in disrepair. Another task was that of ditch digging, a far less pleasant chore, but one that was necessary so that a telephone line could be laid to the community center. The cathedral was next to the building being reconstructed. This structure had weathered ten centuries of coastal storms. I participated in worship in the massive stone church using rites as old as the building itself.

Midway through my stay on Iona, the leader of the community, George MacLeod, announced that the bathing water system had broken.

"That should be no problem since we are on an island", he declared. "But to be perfectly frank about the situation, we are now faced with the fact, it is either a case of stink or swim."

The Queen later knighted George MacLeod for his leadership of Iona, for his service to the British nation as a champion of the poor and downtrodden. At least for a brief time, I was a companion of a future knight of the realm.

Sunlight so far to the north in June lasted until nearly ten o'clock after which the glow on the shining sea continued for hours. One of my fellow workers demonstrated the longevity of the Scottish summer light by reading an inscription on a coin at midnight. I witnessed this feat, but found walking across the isle even more exciting when there were brief moments of sunlight on the heather.

In July Wade and I joined two other students, Charles McCain and Jac Ruffin, in a tour of Europe. We crossed the English Channel by boat, rode the train to Paris where we spent nearly a week. Wade's friend, a U. S. Army captain stationed in Europe, joined the four theological students for an evening tour of what he considered to be the more interesting portions of the French scenes.

We began in Pigalle, a noted location for clubs which featured slightly clad dancers. From there we visited two other show clubs where the girls were somewhat better dressed and displayed a measure of talent in their presentations. Our captain friend assured us our education in French culture was not complete until we had seen the Follies. All four of us bought tickets for the highly advertised show.

Wade and I were seated down front on the fourth row. The music and dramatic dances were superb, far superior to the shows we had seen earlier. Even the totally nude scene was handled with such sensitivity that effective lighting displayed only the grace and beauty of the female human form.

At one point, there was a call for a volunteer to join the cast on stage for *An American in Paris* number. Since there were two Americans only a few feet from the foot lights, Wade volunteered Jack who suddenly found himself surrounded by a dozen or more young French women on the stage of the world's best known girlie show. Fortunately, at least for that one scene, all were fully clad in flowing dresses and large hats. I was led around the stage for a few moments before I was allowed to return to my seat. My three fellow travelers refused to promise never to tell that they were in company with the only Southern Presbyterian minister who had actually danced on the stage of the Paris Follies.

From Paris we went south by train to Cannes and Monaco. At the Monte Carlo Casino we had an excellent meal on a balcony overlooking the sea. Each of us ventured several twenty-five franc coins in the institution's slot machines. At the time the franc was worth about one third of a cent in American currency. Our gambling losses were not substantial, yet no one of us could ever deny he had actually gambled at Monte Carlo. In the opinion of some of our more conservative brethren, such an act would have been almost as bad as dancing on a Paris stage.

From the French coast we traveled east to Italy. After visiting Milan, Jac Ruffin insisted we take a side trip into southern Switzerland where we could buy Italian lira legally far below the official exchange value in Italy. This we did and spent a delightful evening in Lugano. The favorable exchange rate made our next two weeks of travel unbelievably inexpensive. For the remainder of the journey, all three trusted Jac Ruffin's advice on financial matters. Only once did his recommendation fail us. A street vendor in Milan offered us an exchange rate even lower than the Swiss price. The vendor insisted each examine the currency involved. When the final exchange took place, we found ourselves holding a huge roll of newspaper covered by a few small lira bills.

Jack's and Wade's host in Scotland, Ronald Selby Wright, had insisted we do two essential acts while in Italy: visit Assisi, the home of St. Francis, and make an effort to gain an audience with the Pope. The journey to Assisi was one of the real high points of the trip for me. This was well off the usual tourist's route, a village that could have changed little since the days of the Saint.

In Rome we immediately went to the American Catholic Club and applied for a papal audience as Ronald Selby Wright had instructed us to do. We were in the Italian capital for a week and on the next to the last day of our stay, a large envelope with the papal seal attached arrived at our hotel inviting us to visit Castel Gondolpho, twenty miles from Rome. This was the Pope's residence during the summer. The envelope was addressed to Jack who was instructed to bring all members of his party to a semi-private audience with Pope Pius XII.

On arrival at the Papal residence, we were greeted graciously by the colorfully dressed guards and ushered into a large hall. We were arranged in language groups since Pius XII was fluent in a dozen different tongues.

The Pope arrived, gave all present a blessing, about eighty people. He then proceeded to speak to each group in turn. Since the Americans were at the head of the line, he came first to me. The Pope asked if I was a student and then inquired where I was studying. He then asked if my parents were alive. When he received an affirmative answer, he pronounced a blessing on both my family and me. The Pope turned to the others in the group. He asked similar questions. Wade had more courage than I and dared interrupt the process by telling His Holiness that all three of us were ordained Presbyterian ministers. The reaction was delightful.

The Pope grinned broadly, threw up his hands as though this was truly a pleasant surprise. He then declared: "a special blessing upon all of you, upon your families and upon your work."

The tour continued to the Isle of Capri, Florence, Venice, over the Alps to Austria, behind the iron curtain to Prague, then Switzerland, across war ravaged Germany to Holland. There we were able to attend the organizing session of the World Council of Churches in Amsterdam. Religious leaders from around the world, including Dr. Karl Barth, the leading theologian of the time, were present. I attended an after session meeting where Barth spoke, declaring his belief that Presbyterian and Reformed churches were the great center of Christendom, the only hope for a united world wide church. He spoke in his native tongue, German, but constantly interrupted the translator by correcting his interpreter in English.

I returned to Scotland where I would need to begin the difficult task of organizing my research and placing it in acceptable form. The greatest academic challenge I had ever faced lies before me.

*Nine*

## The Final Year

*1949*

Once back in Scotland, I went to work at the complex task of organizing my research results. Although I was confident my goal was within reach, I had heard tales of other students who had failed to satisfy the University appointed External Examiner's expectations. Although I had regular conferences with Dr. Watt and Dr. Burleigh, my Internal Examiners, I was never to know the identity of the examiner whose decision was seldom if ever overridden.

    Once I discovered only one living author, George Pratt Insh, had written scholarly works about the Darien Scheme, I made several efforts to contact him. I had met a teacher on a tour of the western highlands who had studied under Insh at Glasgow's teacher's university. She had assured me her mentor was very easy to reach and urged me to continue my effort to make contact with the only person living that knew a great deal about Darien.

By the fall of my final year in Edinburgh, I gave up my effort to reach Dr. Insh. My Underwood would be my only ally in my quest. I also gave up my two shilling visits to the theater. After classes at New College I spent most of my time pounding away on my trusty typewriter.

The University required an original copy of every thesis and two carbons. One additional copy was advised in case the examiners demanded revisions. Since this was long before easy copy devices were available, this meant four sheets of typing paper, and three fresh carbon sheets had to enter the typewriter for producing each new page.

My sturdy typewriter met the challenge. By the end of the year several chapters were beginning to take shape. My intense efforts were broken only by my trips to Richmond Craigmillar Church. My contacts with the Scottish youths proved to be delightful interludes from the hard grind of thesis writing.

On Advent Sundays the group gathered early in the afternoon to rehearse the Christmas drama they would present to the congregation. Then they would go into the streets singing carols. I will never forget the sound of "Gloria in Excelsius Deo" ringing out in the crisp Scottish night, echoing off the stone buildings of the community.

In my final year there was little time for anything that did not contribute to gaining the degree I sought. My only trip outside the city of Edinburgh was one in which I spent several days in Glasgow studying little known documents in the University of Glasgow Library. These were important because the major Darien ships had been built at Clydeside, the area near Glasgow, where the seagoing giants from the *Titanic* to the *R. M. Queen Elizabeth* were later constructed.

Once I had gleaned all of the Darien data possible, I spent an evening in a theater where I saw a British version of *Annie Get Your Gun*. I was able to afford this extravagance by buying a standee ticket where I joined a dozen or more other students leaning against a rail at the back of the large auditorium. All

# The Final Year 69

seemed delighted to have an American in their midst who was willing to take advantage of the *Standing Room Only* section.

As the long dark days of the Scottish winter settled in on Edinburgh, I continued to work feverishly at my project. By early spring, I had a first draft that I carefully began to revise. My Internal Examiners were willing to look over a chapter or two of my work for form and style. Dr. Watt was delighted with my thesis format, but suggested several changes that involved what he called "Americanisms". Everything had to be in proper English and an acceptable style.

The Darien Scheme involved two major expeditions to the Isthmus of Panama, 1698 and 1699. Scotland's effort to become a world power involved establishing a colony on the Atlantic side of the Isthmus that would serve as a base for transporting goods across the narrow piece of land separating the two oceans. Although ships built in Scotland had made England into a major sea power, all profits had remained in the hands of merchants in London. Over two thousand Scots died in the tragedy of the Darien Scheme. Those who survived the mosquito infested jungles, the deterioration of food supplies and Spanish firepower lost their lives in ocean storms. The final Darien disaster was the destruction by a hurricane of a Darien ship attempting to seek shelter and more supplies in the harbor of Charleston, South Carolina.

From the beginning I was fascinated by the subject of my thesis. I was not the only one to be so enthralled. Ronald Selby Wright took special interest in the American student living in his home who was working on a subject that involved the causes of the Anglo Scottish union. He contacted his most important parishioner, the Duke of Hamilton, who was the keeper of Holyrood Palace, which was a part of the Canongate parish. He gained permission for me to go to the extensive Royal Library within the Palace. I found no new Darien data, but gained the interest of the Duke.

The Duke, premier nobleman of Scotland, invited me to dine on venison at Edinburgh's most exclusive gentlemen's club.

There he questioned me about historical facts that might be of interest to Scottish Nationalists who hoped to restore Scotland's Parliament.

At last my three hundred plus page work was ready to go to the book binders shop where the typed pages would become three bound volumes, a process that would take at least ten days. I took this time to tour the midlands and the Oxford Stratford area. I then journeyed north, visited the Highlands, the Hebrides and the western isles before returning to Edinburgh to present the bound copies of my dissertation to the University registrar's office.

A few days after I had turned in my thesis I received a call from Dr. George Pratt Insh who wanted to come by and see me. He apologized for not having answered my calls for help. He spent several hours questioning me about several aspects of my work. He was particularly interested in my opinion about whether or not the *Equivalent* had been paid to individual Scots who had financed the adventurous plan to the Isthmus of Panama. I told him about the papers I had discovered in the basement of the Bank of Scotland, one of which had been an eyewitness account by an individual who watched the unloading of the actual pounds of sterling into the vaults of what would become the premier financial institution of Scotland. He was still seeking answers to the question whether or not individual Scots had received their payment. The challenge in my thesis was to discover if doubts about payment of the *Equivalent* could be proven, and if so how. If true, this would become a basis for claiming the union of Parliaments of England and Scotland was illegal. No matter how long the argument would take, the Scots wanted their independence from England and their Parliament of Scotland.

Our meeting took place in the front room of Ronald Wright's residence. At one point Insh looked up and saw the crucifix that adorned the room. He asked if my host was a protestant pastor? I assured him that he was, but one of rather high-church persuasion. He then asked about the involvement of the Church of Scotland in the Darien Scheme. Since my project had begun as a study of the relationship between Church and State, I told him about extensive documentation in the Church archives in the Tron Church on High Street. These papers had indicated that the Church of Scotland was a primary promoter of the Darien scheme. The Church had sent six chaplains with their families to the colony, one of whom was the best known of the Covenanters, Alexander Shields. Dr. Insh indicated he would like to see the documents I had found. I went to the Tron Church the next morning and found Dr. Insh there ahead of me. Throughout two sessions with him, he seemed pleased with my answers.

I was aware that many theses are written and then stuck away in some place never to be read by anyone other than the student and examiners, yet there were indications that my thesis subject and my thesis eventually would become a major player in the effort to re-establish the ancient Parliament of Scotland. I could not help but wonder why Dr. Insh was so interested in me. Some of his questions implied he had read my thesis although this soon after submission, my work would still smell of binder's glue. I would never know if Dr. Insh was my all-important External Examiner. Nonetheless I had a feeling I had met the man that held my scholastic fate in his hands and that my thesis was important.

Formal graduation ceremonies would not take place until mid July. I could not afford to wait that long, so I packed my trunk and my one remaining copy of my thesis and made arrangement to return home on an American freighter. I traveled by train to Swansea, Wales where I boarded the *S. S. Zoella Lykes* for the voyage home.

Just before I left Edinburgh, I went by the New College office where I saw Miss Leslie, the principal's secretary. She told me I had nothing to worry about. Although the Ph. D. committee had not made the formal decision, she had seen the report of the External Examiner that highly commended my efforts and urged that my thesis on the Darien Scheme be made available for publication.

Miss Leslie was giving me a hint of what actually did happen about a dozen years later. My thesis, *The Darien Scheme and The Church of Scotland*, would be listed as reproduced by the British government, on microfilm, along with other dissertations in a series of works on British history. Microform Limited of London would provide copies for worldwide distribution and I would have correspondence with consulates and people from places as far away as Panama. While Miss Leslie, to assure me that day in 1949, gave only a hint that my thesis would be "made available for publication", she could not have known that people would still be reading my thesis and using it in research over half-a-century later, some still seeking evidence which might be used as partial argument to help regain a Scottish Parliament. Somehow I boarded the *Zoella Lykes* with confidence that I had been successful in my quest.

During my sixteen days at sea on a vessel one twentieth the size of the ship on which I had sailed the Atlantic two years earlier, I now had only one major concern: would Karin still be interested in me after so many months away in distant lands?

# Ten

## The Course of True Love

### 1950

Once on board the four thousand ton Zoella Lykes, I experienced a genuine sea adventure. I was one of four passengers who occupied staterooms just below the ship's bridge. My cabin mate was a young Brit who was immigrating to the United States. A retired British colonel and his wife occupied the other stateroom.

A crew of thirty-three including officers, engineers, and seamen manned the ship. The First Mate reached the dining area ahead of everyone else each day and placed his order with the ship's steward for a six-egg omelet so he could return immediately to duty on the bridge.

The Second mate who was not scheduled to assume control of the vessel until afternoon spent many of his mornings with me. He was an ex-Roman Catholic priest who had given up his ordination to sail the sea. He held a Master's license, as did both the First and Third Mates. This made all three officers qualified to captain a ship of that type.

The captain, an older man, who was a life long seaman, had his meals sent up to his quarters behind the bridge. He came down to the galley at odd hours to fix some special delicacy of his own liking. All the officers and passengers had the same privilege.

The Chief Engineer who occupied a private cabin near the entrance to the engine room welcomed my presence as a fellow crossword addict. He had to be available night and day should there be an emergency. Protocol did not permit him to go below decks unless the First, Second, or Third Engineer asked for assistance. He could escort a visitor on a tour of the efficiently operating machinery, which drove the vessel smoothly across the ocean. He took me on such a tour on several occasions.

Once out of Bristol harbor, the Zoella took a west-southwest course toward the Gulf of Mexico. No one knew the ship's exact destination. The passengers had been promised a landing at a Gulf of Mexico port in the United States. Most of the crew hoped for shore leave in New Orleans. The other three passengers would have preferred Houston.

When the captain received his orders by radio in the mid-Atlantic, I was the only one on board who was completely satisfied. We would land at Port Isabel at the mouth of the Rio Grande, just down river from my home in Laredo.

Only one night of stormy weather marred the near perfect voyage. The captain had plotted a course toward Florida that would take the ship through a passage between island landmasses known to seamen as "the hole in the wall".

The vessel did not have radar. At the time such sophisticated equipment was available only to naval crafts and larger ships. When heavy seas began to pound the Zoella, the captain made a decision to refrain from attempting the dangerous seaway at night. The ship circled in deep water until daybreak.

This delayed the voyage by ten or twelve hours but brought the ship near the shore at Miami shortly before sunset. The passengers and off-duty seamen stood on deck enjoying a calm sea as they watched a magnificent display of golden light behind the towering hotels of the famed beach resort. The ship turned south, rounded the tip of Florida, and headed directly west toward my Texas home.

Once back in Laredo, I could do nothing but wait for an affirmation of my hoped for degree. I knew the unofficial information given me by Miss Leslie before I left Scotland was all the reassurance I really needed. Yet I also knew Edinburgh University did not take the granting of such degrees lightly.

I had paid my diploma fee long before I left Scotland, but I had signed an agreement that the fee would go to the University publisher, James Thin, if the Ph. D. committee should decide against making me a Doctor of Philosophy.

At last the hoped for happened. A large heavy cardboard rolled package was delivered to my parent's home address. Inside was a sheepskin affirmation of my degree written in Latin. In addition a printed copy of the graduation ceremony was included. This was in English. That event had taken place in Edinburgh's McEwan Hall. My name was listed as one of the few who had been granted the University's highest degree.

I began to make known my availability for a paying job. I was asked to serve as a cabin counselor at Mo Ranch, a site the Presbyterian Church hoped to purchase as a replacement for Westminster Encampment. This gave me contact that resulted in possible positions. I was invited to preach in a long established church in Central Texas where I was asked to consider a call to ministerial service. I decided against this since it was too far from Sweetwater.

I next visited a church in near West Texas and continued on to Karin's home. She was just as beautiful as I had remembered her. Much to my amazement she seemed still interested in me. It was during that visit that I first kissed her. I had hoped to give her a kiss on my last date before I sailed for Scotland. My plans to do so had failed. When I parked the borrowed car at her front door, she did not give me time to accomplish my goal for the evening. I was determined to give her the kiss that had been formulating in my mind for a very long time. We were in a secluded portion of the Sweetwater city park. She let me kiss her without objection, a kiss that I had dreamed about for at least two full years.

One other career possibility for me was a recently organized congregation deep in West Texas' oil and ranching country. The church had no building, only a vacant lot purchased by Presbytery for eventual construction of a sanctuary and educational facilities.

This was the kind of challenge I liked. I accepted the call of the congregation and moved to Crane, Texas in early fall soon after Karin began her third year at Trinity University in San Antonio.

I borrowed my father's Ford V8 to transport my personal possessions and books to Crane. On the way through San Antonio I visited Karin again. On the return trip I arranged for my mother, Lilian, who was visiting friends in the city, to meet Karin. From that time, she was an admirer of Karin believing my hope of marrying her was a wise choice.

I threw myself into my work. I preached each Sunday from the judge's bench in the Crane County Courthouse. A plywood pulpit had been built which fitted over the judicial desk, an act that instantly converted the seat of justice to a place for expounding the Scriptures.

I became involved in community activities. I joined the local Lions Club and became a volunteer fireman. Each week I donned my white coveralls with the words *Crane Fire Department* written in large red letters on my back. Thus attired, I took part in the simulated fire drills that were intended to hone a fire fighter's skills.

Each member of the volunteers was expected to be capable of operating all of the department's equipment. When it became my turn to drive the fire truck to the nearby filling station on my own, I climbed into the vehicle's seat and started off in great style. I reached the gasoline pump and had no difficulty in assisting the station attendant in filling the truck's tank. Once properly fueled, I started up the engine and drove forward. I suddenly realized I could not make the sharp turn into the main street without backing up. I could not find the reverse gear. The fire truck was hopelessly stuck in the middle of the town. I turned on the flashing red lights and climbed down from my seat.

By this time several of the village's residents were loudly chuckling about my predicament. One was a retired truck driver who eventually came to my aid and helped me put the gearshift into reverse. I finally got the fire engine back to the firehouse without mishap. Although I had learned to drive the powerful vehicle in reverse, I never again had an opportunity to test my skill as a backward driver.

The congregation was well aware of my activities as a fireman. Since worship services were held in the court room directly across the street from the firehouse, members of the small group often wondered what would happen if the fire siren sounded in the middle of one of my sermons.

One day it did. The call to the volunteers drowned out my final sentences. I managed to complete my concluding words and pronounce a hasty benediction. By the time I reached the site of the fire all was well under control without the help of the recently arrived Presbyterian minister.

I knew that the congregation could survive only if a building could be built soon on the empty lot across the street from the town's high school. I found an Odessa architect who drew up a basic set of blueprints for a structure, which would include a fellowship hall, an office, classrooms, a church kitchen and adequate toilet facilities. This cost the church treasury only one hundred and fifty dollars since the designer would not be available to supervise the construction program. Volunteers would do most of the work.

I answered the fire siren's call on one occasion that took me to a large ranch house west of town. The owner, Gib Cowden an elderly rancher who had become one of the richest men in the area because of oil lease royalties on his extensive land holdings, noted that I was one of the first firefighters to reach the site. A few days later he came by my small house and presented me a check that would pay for the church building's foundation and for construction of all exterior walls. From there the volunteers could take over and in time have a usable structure.

For my first year in Crane, I had to balance my work as pastor with my role as construction boss. The city required that the application for a building permit be issued in the name of a responsible individual. I suddenly found myself a building contractor in spite of the fact that I knew absolutely nothing about the building business. My nine years of higher education had not provided me with even the slightest clue to success in such a role.

I had to borrow an automobile to visit members of my congregation who lived in outlying oil company camps. My only mode of transportation to San Antonio, three hundred and fifty miles from Crane, was by bus.

I had no other means of seeing Karin than that of stopping over on trips to or from Laredo. For a time the romance seemed on track, but there were bumps in the roadway to love. I mentioned my discouragement over my hopes for marrying to my mother who simply quoted the adage: "The course of true love never runs smooth".

I realized a car of my own was an essential to the course of true love. In early spring of 1950, I had saved enough of my salary to make a down payment on a new car, a Ford 6 that I purchased for sixteen hundred and one dollars. This I proudly drove to San Antonio and was able to take Karin out on a date with at least a measure of style.

The road to love continued to be full of pitfalls. In June I was asked to serve on the staff of a youth conference at Mo Ranch, the upscale facility that by this time the Synod of Texas had purchased from the estate of Dan Moran, founder of Continental Oil.

I would serve as dormitory counselor and again be advisor to the editor of the camp newspaper. Karin was the editor I was to advise. I helped her set up her office, but found her extremely cool toward me. Clifford Williams was another member of the staff. He asked me about the obvious lack of my relationship to Karin. I told him I needed all the help I could get to revive what I still believed was the only real romance of my life. He promised to help. He had long been Karin's pastor. Healing the apparent breach between Karin and Jack would be a pastoral responsibility. For most of the remaining days of the conference Clifford and several other minister dropped by the editor's office to counsel with Karin. Some of the outstanding clergymen of the synod assisted, by putting in a good word in my behalf. Although the steady stream of ministerial counselors irritated Karin a bit, on the last night of the event, the intense pastoral effort paid off. She let me give her a kiss and invited me to come to Sweetwater during the summer.

Jack McMichael, the Synod of Texas Minister of Christian Education, commented that my romance with Karin was "like an old refrigerator: sometimes cold, sometimes hot".

I was anxious to warm things up as quickly as possible, but never before having been so much in love, I had no idea of how to win Karin. My mother had another adage in mind from her years of reading English literature. This she passed on to me: "Faint heart never won fair damsel".

I took her advice and continued my quest. At last the magic moment arrived. Karin and I were seated in the Ford 6 parked on a hill overlooking the lake where we once swam. It was a crystal clear night in July. There was no moon in the sky, but the West Texas night was bright with the brilliance of countless stars.

I dared to make the proposal I had long wanted to place before Karin. To my delight, she said, "yes" without hesitation. I wanted to go back to town, wake up her parents and let the whole world know. I had always felt that her father, Kirby, was on my side in my efforts to win Karin. Her mother seemed agreeable to the idea of having a preacher son-in-law in the family, but on more than one occasion she had let me know that Karin was not to be married until she finished her university degree.

Karin wisely stated that awakening her parents at such an

hour might be the improper thing to do. I asked if I could give her an engagement ring on her birthday. She agreed. Since this was less than three weeks away, this would be an adequate proclamation to the entire world that Karin had at last agreed to marry me. I stopped at every possible jewelry store on the way back to Crane: Big Spring, Midland, and Odessa. At last I found just the right ring, purchased it on a ten-month pay out schedule, and proudly presented it to her in the presence of her parents. I could wait one more year in the hope Karin would set a date for a wedding as soon as possible after her graduation.

*The picture I took of Karin on the day I introduced her to my mother.*

*Eleven*

## An Accident and A Honeymoon
*1951*

My life really began after the big event on August 31, 1951. I was dressing in the Bluebonnet Hotel under the supervision of my seminary roommate, Roy Sherrod. I hoped I could appear worthy of the beautiful person I would marry that night.

The phone rang and Roy answered. I heard him say something about an accident. I panicked. I had avoided seeing Karin all day as instructed by my tradition bound best man. I insisted on knowing what had happened. Was Karin all right?

Roy finally told me that the conversation had been about the accidental dropping of the wedding cake. All was well. The cake had been completely repaired by the baker, Jack Spillers, a high school classmate and friend of Karin's, and was now safely at the Kinsey home where the wedding reception would be held.

I remember little about the ceremony itself. All I can recall was the beautiful face of my young bride. Her father had insisted a few days earlier that she get a driver's license since she was twenty-one and soon to be married. Though her father had taught her to drive, the family always had only one car and, especially immediately after WWII, there was a shortage of gasoline and tires. Karin left Sweetwater for college only two weeks after her seventeenth birthday so she had never really had the opportunity or need to have her driver's license.

The Public Safety officer who had not seen her around because she had been away in college thought she was new in town. He looked her over and said, "Young lady, when you get to be sixteen come back and you can take the test".

She had turned twenty-one a few days earlier. Upset at being called a "kid", Karin left and walked back to her father's printing shop. Her father sent her back the next day with instructions to insist on taking the test. Not wanting him to go with her to prove her age, she went. She also passed on the first try and received her driver's license only a few days before her wedding.

On the day of the wedding, Karin, age 21 plus 21 days, for the first time, was told she could "take the car". She drove a few blocks to the home of her Journalism teacher to deliver the wedding guest book over which Laura Sheridan would preside. I was aware of only one fact: I was about to become the mate of a person who would never grow old, a beautiful being I would always love.

After the wedding I was told that I had failed to kiss the bride when the minister paused expectantly. Karin had to kiss me, an act that brought a roar of laughter from the church full of friends and wedding guests. Since Karin had worked all summer at a radio station, the station manager made a professional recording. Actually, the record we have is *almost* the way it happened. In reality, the KXOX manager, Larry Hubbard, also sang for the wedding and when he heard the recording he insisted on singing his solo again and re-recording it. I feel he probably amplified the laughter at the point I was supposed to kiss the angel I married. Nevertheless, when this was played back later, I real-

## An Accident and A Honeymoon

ized the extent of the daze that had possessed me.

I had no fear of the validity of the rites since eight Presbyterian ministers were present: Clifford Williams and Dwight Sharp presided; Best Man Roy Sherrod, Jim McCrary, Lewis Waterstreet, Bob Hawkins, all ministers; and C. D. Birdsong, an elder from Crane who had relatives living in Sweetwater, were male attendants. My father and I were also there to make a total of eight ministers and one ruling elder: almost enough for a meeting of Presbytery!

I clearly remember all else that took place that evening. Kirby, Karin's father, had a grand time. Roy went through the reception line 14 times at Kirby's suggestion, and each time he kissed the bride. While eight Presbyterian ministers helped with the wedding, most of them were in on a plot to delay our departure from the reception. Karin and I were ready to leave, and there was no car.

We were told that the car would be there, "There is just a short delay." It was not until we returned from the honeymoon that we learned what had caused the delay. Though Roy had hidden the car, the groomsmen had found it. They had performed too many weddings. They painted our car with everything they had ever seen painted on a honeymooner's car. Roy, my best man, took Nelda, Karin's maid of honor, and the two of them, dressed for the wedding ceremony, "washed the car" before delivering it to the reception. It wasn't the best wash job you ever saw, but at least you couldn't read what it had said! We had it professionally washed the next day.

There was the usual chase and then the final getaway in a different direction. Fortunately our clever get-away prevented my father from being able to reach us on the phone to tell us we had lost a hubcap! The remaining hubcaps were filled with gravel and rocks that announced our arrival in Abilene at the Wooten Hotel where we would spend our first night together.

Near the end of the journey, I felt a small head upon my shoulder that rested there in trusting repose for at least the final minutes of the trip. My happiness was complete.

Although the well-planned wedding had been slightly flawed by the cake accident and my daze, the honeymoon was flawless. Karin's father, aware we were planning a honeymoon to New Orleans, found the September 1951 Holiday Magazine with an article on *$50 for four days of recreation in New Orleans: see the most interesting sights, eat the best food, visit the top night spots.* He gave it to Karin and we decided we would try to follow their suggestions, spending $10 each day for meals, $50.00 each for five days of New Orleans food.

After a leisurely two-day trip across Texas, we arrived at the Roosevelt Hotel on New Orleans's Canal Street where we had a reservation. In later years this would be known as the Fairmont. "Rates in the best hotels start around $4.50 a day." We splurged: our room at the Roosevelt was $9.00. At the end of five days we gave them $50 to cover the room and parking and received $5.00 in change.

I enjoyed walking through the hotel's plush lobby with my beautiful young bride by my side. Each time we traversed the length of the richly carpeted area, we noticed a flower shop that displayed a wide selection of beautiful flowers. One afternoon, I excused myself and went down to the lobby and purchased a corsage of pink roses. I requested that the flowers be sent up to our fifth story room, Room 553. Karin looked so beautiful wearing her roses that evening that I tried to find similar flowers for her as often as possible throughout the years that followed.

The first evening of our stay in New Orleans, we walked to Arnaud's in the French Quarter where we ordered Oysters Rockefeller. Each morning we had coffee and Beignets at the French Market. We continued to follow the magazine article's suggestions. We took the recommended tours and ate inexpensive noon meals.

On the second night we dined at the Court of Two Sisters and on the third night in the hotel's Blue Room noted for seafood and an excellent, yet proper floorshow. When the waiter asked if we would like our fish to be de-boned, we agreed. Just then the lights went out and the show began. The waiter continued his delicate job in the dark with amazing success. I wondered if I tipped him enough.

Our fourth evening we ate at Antoine's, our most expensive meal where eighty-nine pound Karin out ate Jack. One of the magazine writer's suggestions was that of a trip to Lake Pontchartrain where we rode the roller coaster together and decided one ride was more than enough. We had lunch in a restaurant on a pier in the lake where we both enjoyed a large basket of shrimp. By this time we had proved the Holiday Magazine article was a wonderful bit of advice: great places to see and eat, and we still had enough money to continue the trip.

Only one meal was less than perfect. On one of our tours of the Quarter, we purchased a perfume called *Kus-Kus*, made from several dozen-flower blossoms. That evening the two lovers ate in a courtyard where a horde of mosquitoes descended on Karin, attracted by her beautiful skin and the aroma of a flowery perfume. That night, our second night, I had to go out and find a medication for the multiple insect bites before Karin could sleep. Our final evening in New Orleans was a dinner at world famous Owen Brennan's Creole Restaurant where the head waiter noticed the pink rose corsage and surprised us with a fancy dessert and the entire wait crew gathered around us to sing a special love song.

The trip continued along the gulf coast to Bellingrath Gardens of Alabama. There we saw at a distance the elderly founder of the gardens who had built the extensive display in memory of his wife. I could not help but wonder if the lone figure we saw looking over the beauty his love had created noticed the honeymooners. If he did, he must have sensed our enjoyment of the flowering plants he had arranged.

From the Alabama coast we returned to Louisiana. We then traveled through the Cajun country, spent nights in Galveston and San Antonio. The final portion of the romantic journey took us back to our starting point, Sweetwater where we loaded up some of the wedding gifts, which have become our treasures. From there, the honeymoon continued to Crane.

# An Accident and A Honeymoon

## Twelve

## Laughter at a Phantom Siren

### 1952

I had done all I could to make the Crane Manse as attractive as possible. The house consisted of a very small kitchen, a slightly larger front room and a bedroom with furniture and appliances that had been furnished for their bachelor minister by members of the Crane congregation. There was no bathtub, only a shower. I painted the bare metal around the showerhead. I patched up the rickety kitchen table and painted it twice. I made a valiant effort to get everything in the best possible shape. I had cleaned and re-cleaned, just before I left to go to my wedding.

    This was the type of building once called a *shotgun house*, built so one could shoot a shotgun in the front door and the bullet would exit the back door without damaging the structure of the building. At this point in time it was no longer recognizable as such. It had been turned sideways and a small porch built and a door cut in the center of the middle room as an entrance. An inside door had been hung to provide bedroom privacy. For bachelor's quarters it had been adequate, yet it was a far cry from what would have been considered an appropriate dwelling in Sweetwater.

A few weeks earlier I had tried to build a sidewalk from the street to the front door. Once I had carefully set up the forms, I mixed up two bags of what I thought was cement. After three days the sidewalk still had the texture of Jell-O. A couple of the church members came to my rescue, reset the forms and dug up the substance which turned out to be drilling mud which came in sacks that looked much like cement. The experienced oil field workers quickly replaced it with the proper mix without telling anyone of my goof.

In spite of all of my efforts, I was aware of the contrast between the Crane house and the attractive Kinsey residence. In addition Crane was in a semi-desert land where life was only possible because of the most ardent ranching efforts intermingled with successful oil production. Only days before Karin arrived, something amazing occurred. During my three weeks away from the area, a rare series of rain showers fell upon the land. Never before had there been so many flowering plants. Obviously this was a welcome to the beautiful young bride.

I carried Karin across the threshold of the small house. This was not a difficult task since I weighed nearly twice as much as my bride. The next morning I took her out to see the town. We went first to the Post Office. Walking from the car to the mailbox, I was greeted warmly.

Then Karin heard, "Good Morning, Sister Ramsay."

She was not really accustomed hearing herself addressed as "Mrs. Ramsay". Hearing the greeting "Sister Ramsay" in a community that had seven Baptist Churches and more being organized, one Methodist, one small Disciples of Christ and one newly organized Presbyterian Church was a real shock to her.

When I had left Crane in August, the church building consisted of no more than a foundation and freestanding walls. When I returned as a newly wed pastor three weeks later, the structure was completely under roof. Some of the volunteers were putting the finishing touches to the project that we were told was our wedding present. Never before in all history had two young lovers been presented with such a unique gift: a brand new church roof.

Steel casement windows had been set in place and enough glass panes had been purchased to close in the building. Karin decided that since the roof was half hers, she would need to protect what belonged to her. She suddenly developed a talent for puttying windows and in due time enough of the other ladies joined her that they had all one hundred and forty-four panes neatly in place.

Karin was asked to serve as substitute teacher in the Crane High School. She was assigned to a trigonometry class, an all male class that included most of the school's football team. Many were young men who had attended a Baptist revival and had answered the call to become Baptist preachers. This was a much publicized fact and, years later, we read in a national publication that those members of Crane High School, Class of 1952, had fulfilled their call and were all still serving as Baptist pastors. The class members took one look at their youthful tutor, a *Presbyterian minister's wife*, and decided they could avoid serious work for a time. The group objected to the difficulty of the textbook assignment.

A hand went up. "Teacher," one of them asked, "how do you work that first problem?"

Karin picked up the book, took chalk in hand, and demonstrated her mathematical ability on the blackboard.

The students, all boys, muttered, "She can work it!" and went to work as directed.

When the Superintendent of School heard of this, perhaps from J. B. and Thelma Strickland, members of the church and school teachers who constantly encouraged me, he pled with Karin to stay on the teaching staff for the rest of the year even though she did not have a teaching certificate. He could legitimize her credentials as a math teacher under the emergency clause in the state's educational standards. At the time the Crane school system paid the highest salaries of any in the state. She turned down the lucrative offer believing she had enough to do as minister's wife.

Karin joined the Firemen's Auxiliary. Many took a careful look at her slender figure. Her fellow auxiliary members explained this to Karin: "Just remember that it takes nine months to have a baby, but the first one can come at any time."

Karin was aware that Jack needed to respond to the fire siren's call. One night she awoke from sound sleep and asked if the siren had sounded? I jumped up and pulled my white and red coveralls over my pajamas. I was out the door and on my way to the fire station without another word. At that moment Karin realized she had been dreaming. When I returned she was sitting up in bed laughing. I had no choice but to admit that it was better to answer a phantom call than to miss a real one.

All grocery shopping had to be done at the local store operated by the husband of the church organist. When Karin went from counter to counter selecting items she needed, the proprietor would walk behind her and turn on the light over each as she looked and then turn it off when she moved to another counter.

We found we could buy much more economically at the larger grocery stores in Odessa, thirty-three miles to the north. On Saturdays we would sneak out of town and purchase as many sale items as possible. This usually required explanations to the organist's husband who generally remembered what we had bought and not bought.

There was one item he had in the meat section that beat all Odessa prices: attractive red meat steaks. Months later, after we had left Crane, we learned that a meat salesman who had long serviced the area had been arrested for selling horsemeat as beef. The honeymooners had been among the victims of this scam.

The first visitor to the home of the newly weds was Jack's sister, Elizabeth. Karin was determined to give her an adequate welcome by baking two apple pies. The only cooking device in the house was a gas stove that did not have a working thermostat. Karin had found the stove hopelessly unreliable but she could produce satisfactory results by constantly watching her product. Every few minutes she gently pulled the baking tray out and cautiously inspected the items in the oven.

On this particular occasion, her third pull ended in disaster. Tray and contents came sliding out all over the freshly cleaned kitchen floor. She sent me back to the store for more apples while she cleaned up. I had difficulty in talking the storekeeper into selling me more apples since Karin had bought an adequate supply the day before.

The whole process began all over again and finally Karin had two beautifully baked pies just in time for Elizabeth's arrival. These she put away and greeted her first in-law visitor with the sad story of her pie disaster as she produced the hopelessly scrambled pies. Elizabeth sat down at the kitchen table prepared to accept what had been scraped off the floor while Karin kept telling her, "The floor was very clean!"

As Liz took a spoon in hand, Karin stopped her and then produced the perfectly baked pies that all three of us enjoyed. After the pie tragedy Jack and Karin decided to get a new stove. We found a top of the line electric stove, a Hot Point with a working thermostat for the surprisingly low price of twenty-five dollars, available only because the original owner did not want to use an electric device in oil and gas territory. Although the honeymooners felt a slight tinge of conscience for their decision to go electric, Karin loved her non-gas stove and never again had a cooking disaster.

For six or eight weeks after Karin had completed her task as window glazer, no volunteer work took place. A major problem had developed: the entire building would have to be plumbed for water, gas, and sewer lines before a cement floor could be poured.

The volunteer crew included able plumbers. Most oil field workers were skilled in connecting pipes much larger than that necessary to the project, but the church had no access to heavy digging equipment essential to cutting through the solid rock upon which the building had been built.

Finally I was told this problem had been solved. County owned equipment had been borrowed and the task had been completed on a Sunday afternoon. This was the only time such a tool was available. The volunteers had not told me fearing I might object to breaking the Sabbath.

Another problem surfaced. The ditch diggers did not bother to gain access from me to the blueprints. They had approximated the point at which the sewer and utility lines would enter the building. When measurements were made, the Sunday digging was over nine feet off the plans.

Penciling over the blueprints solved this problem. This resulted in a much more ample kitchen than the original plans had envisioned. There would be less utility space and considerably less room for the pastor's study. This accidental redesign would be a boon to those who would eventually prepare meals there, yet it may have somewhat limited the preparation of spiritual food. Future pastors would have to work in slightly cramped quarters.

As the Christmas season approached, Karin was determined to make the Crane house attractive. Since the whole town was urged to display appropriate decorations, she fashioned a Bethlehem silhouette scene out of cardboard and created a Christmas tree for the front door made of chicken wire. She needed some greenery to fill out the decorations.

I told her I had heard green shrubs grew profusely on the high mesas south of town. We went out to search the area where California bound travelers had once crossed the land. I promised to scale one of the imposing peaks and bring back the greenery Karin needed. I made the steep climb with difficulty but found nothing. When I returned Karin sat in the midst of a bountiful supply of greenery laughing at the exhausted mesa climber. She had gathered up all she needed by searching the low-lying draws. With this she completed her project that won a cash prize from the city.

I soon learned that Karin had a vast host of talents beyond that of winning a prize as holiday decorator. When I came down with a hoarse sore throat just before Christmas Sunday, she agreed to help out by substituting for me in the pulpit. With only a few hours notice, she prepared and delivered a beautiful and dramatic account of the Christmas event. Several members of the congregation commented that the sermon that Sunday was the best they had ever heard. In later years, Karin helped me develop a first hand account of the birth of the Christ child in Bethlehem. This became a standard presentation for later Christmas seasons in other churches. "The Man Who Owned the Stable", the title we gave to the sermon, had to be delivered at least once every Christmas of my preaching ministry. Bill Innes even placed a recording of it in the Farmers Branch Library.

I had looked forward to my first Christmas with Karin. This had always been a lonely time for me. During my nine years of higher education, I had only been able to go home twice during the festive season. We decided to go to Sweetwater for Christmas day. Then we travel to Laredo for a New Year's celebration where Karin was welcomed into the Ramsay family with a border-style reception consisting of raisin-laden tamales and Coca-Cola.

My parents had returned to Laredo where my father's two sisters, Lola Davis and Ellen Phillips lived. My Aunt Ellen was a vibrant and brilliant person who had served as a Presbyterian missionary along side her husband, Harry, during two tumultuous decades in Mexico. Harry had contracted a serious tropical disease while working as headmaster of a mission school deep in the Mexican interior. The Phillips had returned to the United States where Harry eventually regained a measure of his health. All members of the Phillips family were highly talented musicians. Their oldest daughter, Jean, was a Juliard graduate and a star violinist in Phil Spitalny's All-Girl Orchestra that toured the nation and made a Hollywood movie in the late 1930s.

At the first meal together in Laredo, my father asked Karin

"Can you cook?"

I was embarrassed by his overly forthright question. I replied, "Sure, she can cook".

He then asked: "Where did you learn to cook?"

She replied: "I can read". With that answer, Karin proved her ability to parry any challenge that came her way.

In the early spring of 1952, the church floor was laid and work began on the building's interior. A series of non-Sabbath work evenings were established. Congregation members brought meals to the church and ate together on the bare floor picnic style. All then joined in whatever tasks were necessary.

At this point, one more problem materialized. I had been given several boxes of flooring tile. As construction boss, I accepted all donations. The tile was carefully laid out by the volunteer workers and glued to the cement floor. Once the glue dried, the individual tiles began to curl and crack off at the corners. It was finally determined that the donated tile was hopelessly outdated and would have to be removed. This proved to be a much more difficult task than that of laying the tile. At last the resourceful oil field workers brought in blowtorches and cleared the floor of broken pieces of floor covering. Funds were found to have fresh tile professionally installed.

Once the floor tiles had been properly replaced, the Building Committee set a grand opening date for early fall. This would be a time to show off the attractive new church, a building that had been constructed at a fraction of what it would have cost without volunteers.

I had once warned Karin about the severity of the spring sandstorms. She assured me that Sweetwater had such events. Yet the mild winds with which she was familiar were nothing to compare with the prolonged storms that came directly from the high plains. During the late spring, the sand hills west of town could literally move in upon us. One day she placed a freshly washed sweater upon the bed to dry. Shortly later she moved the sweater and discovered the outline of the garment was apparent from the sand that had seeped under doors, around windows, and through the walls into our small home. When Lilliput, the cat, began to paw the buildup of sand on the inside of the front door as though this was another sandbox both of us realized neither of us was prepared for West Texas *sandstorms*.

Serving as solo pastor in a newly organized church was an experience for all. Karin was identified as *minister's wife* or *preacher's wife* in the Baptist Bible Belt. The newly organized congregation was highly educated with oil-related or education-focused careers, most holding graduate or postgraduate degrees and coming from most every denomination. For me as pastor, it offered all sorts of experience. It was in Crane that I had my first Adult Baptism, Dan J. Miles, age 30. We had an active, though very young, group of young people, and it was there I had my first professions of faith and baptisms for Carol Jean Birdsong, age 11, and Nancy Bower, age 10. A special event, with a notation beside the person's name in my book of pastoral records, "New Building", was the infant baptism of Richard Wayne Demler, 6 months of age, July 5, 1952. It was also in Crane I had my first weddings: a sailor in the U.S. Navy, age 25, and his bride, age 22, in the Crane Courthouse; and an oil worker, age 30, and his bride, age 25, in the Crane Manse. The couple that married in our manse insisted on giving a $15.00 wedding fee, which I in turn gave to Karin, following a tradition that any unexpected fees belong to the minister's wife. She bought a pair of shoes she had long admired in an Odessa store window.

Though Crane did not have an organized adult choir, music was never missing from worship. Mrs. Shaffer had a portable, rollaway organ and the church had a Junior Choir, which was led by three very musically talented daughters of Harold and Inabelle Garner. Two of the girls became members of the Crane Church while I was pastor, Anne at 12 years of age in the spring of 1950, and Nancy, age 10, spring 1951.

Somehow the word got around that Jack and Karin might be available for a move elsewhere once the new building was complete. The honeymooners gave serious consideration to an invitation from a pulpit search committee of a long established congregation in South Texas. Another committee came to Crane and invited us to visit San Antonio. This we did and I accepted a call to go to Crestholme Presbyterian Church. Our last Sunday in Crane would be that of the grand opening for the volunteer built building.

This was a time of sadness in leaving such a hard working and faithful group of people, but this was a time of anticipation. We were well aware that our greatest challenges lie ahead.

*"Presbyterian Church" sign points to the Crane Courthouse where I preached for three years from a Judge's podium.*

*New Sign at "Future Site" where I would serve as "construction boss".*

*Our Manse; our Ford; our first dog, Tessie from Odessie; Jack's sidewalk; small window above the kitchen sink known as Karin's Wonderful "Picture Window" featuring, each evening, the Methodist Church Steeple in Magnificent Sunset!*

*The Construction Boss and Volunteers.*

*Thirteen*

# An Unsettling Revelation
## *1953*

The moving van arrived in front of the Crane home the morning after the congregation's farewell party. Most of the furnishings in the small house had been provided by the congregation and would remain for the next pastor. We had purchased an ironing board, two folding lounge chairs and our electric stove, the only furniture we had bought during our year together.

One other item, an antique curved glass cabinet, had been given us by a minister friend, Matthew Lynn, later a General Assembly moderator. He had no room for it in his Midland home since some friends had given them a new dining set which did not fit and made the cabinet look out of place. Knowing the newly weds had no means of storing wedding china, he offered it to us if we could transport it to Crane.

I borrowed a truck. I drove it to Midland and with Karin's and Matthew's help loaded the fragile china cabinet into the vehicle's carrying bay. The priceless antique had been in the possession of several generations of Presbyterian ministers. The unique piece of furniture survived fifty miles of rough roads in spite of the inexperienced truck driver's inept maneuvering. As I think about it now, I marvel that Karin and I were able to transfer the china cabinet from the truck into the room in the manse, for we had no help when we arrived in Crane. I must have backed up the cement sidewalk I had laid to my porch, and both the sidewalk and cabinet survived what a new bridegroom will attempt.

The antique curved glass-front china cabinet was the only item the moving van operator had to take special care in handling. Our meager possessions were loaded into the van along with my books and the bookcases I had built myself.

Two furniture items, a lamp table, and a magazine/book holder had been given the newlyweds at the going away party. Both items were blonde since dark furniture showed West Texas sand all too easily. Neither would go with the antique breakfront or the items we had put on lay away in San Antonio. At the final interview in San Antonio we had selected a bed, a dresser, chest of drawers and night stand along with a sofa and dining table for delivery to the church owned house upon our arrival.

The van driver helped out by making an unscheduled stop at the Crane furniture store. The two light colored items, which were a parting gift from the Crane congregation, were exchanged for furniture of a darker hue. The store manager promised Karin that he would not tell the donors of the last-minute trade. Karin who had been a minister's wife only eleven months had already learned the wily art of refraining from hurting the feelings of well-meaning parishioners.

The moving van pulled up in front of 423 Monticello Court in San Antonio where they were greeted by bright sunshine and green grass, a contrast to the sand of Crane. As the doors of the moving van opened, up drove Ed Rock, Clerk of the Session, and Bert Ragsdale, member of the Session. Both greeted us and then their eyes fell on Karin's electric stove.

"Oh, Dear", sighed Bert who was a top executive with the Gas Company, "An electric stove!"

"No problem", said Ed Rock, an electrician capable of wiring a house for a stove but convinced gas was the only way to cook. "I can get a gas stove for a little of nothing."

This was the first time for Bert and Ed to meet Karin who was by this time attached to her new Hotpoint electric stove with a deep well. Though she had refrained from offending the members who gave furniture in Crane, she defended herself and her stove and the manse was quickly wired for an electric stove. Somehow she managed to survive our first crisis at Crestholme. Years later, at a Crestholme anniversary celebration she would mention and laugh about it in her public remembrances of her life as pastor's wife. However, it was serious business on moving day, no laughing matter.

The San Antonio home was large by comparison with the one in which we had been living for nearly a year: two bedrooms a bathroom with a full sized tub, a front room with a fire place, a dining room and a kitchen more than adequate once it was wired for the electric stove. The front of the house faced south on Monticello Court, only two short blocks from the thirty-year-old church building.

Elderly ministers had served the church for years. My immediate predecessor had been named Stated Supply. This was a temporary pastoral relationship, which could be renewed annually, a *temporary* pastoral relationship that he had held for a dozen years.

Although he was in his late seventies, he was in excellent health and lived in the San Antonio area well into his nineties continuing to pastor a small church within easy driving distance of Crestholme. He had endeared himself to the congregation by constant visitation. In addition, he had met personal needs that were well beyond the call of normal ministerial services. He had often driven across town to pick up a dozen tamales or a grocery item for a church member. I determined I would be as faithful a pastor as possible but not an order taker for tamale delivery.

A major problem became apparent. There was no realistic congregational roll, only a list of the members without addresses or phone numbers. I spent my first several months establishing a mailing list of the congregation. I then undertook the task of visiting as many of the members as possible. The church had claimed a membership in excess of four hundred for years.

After diligent efforts to locate as many living persons as I could, I asked the Session to move nearly two hundred names to an inactive status. When this report was sent to Presbytery, the cleansing of Crestholme's roll not only made me look bad but cost Western Texas Presbytery one less commissioner seat to the national General Assembly.

From the outset, Karin and Jack were both warmly received by most of the congregation, especially the younger couples. When I made pastoral visits to shut-ins and older members, Karin often accompanied me. She always charmed the grandmotherly types with her youthful appearance and obvious wisdom. The older adults soon became our most ardent supporters.

One long-time member was a woman nearly four times the age of Karin, known to us as "Mrs. Varga". She was deeply appreciative of Karin's efforts to fulfill her role as the minister's wife. On one occasion she came to church wearing a priceless crystal necklace given to her as a child by her father from Austria.

Karin had complimented her on the beauty of the necklace when she had seen Mrs. Varga wear it several times before. This night Karin once again complimented the beautifully sparkling jewelry and was stunned when Mrs. Varga took her crystals off and placed them around Karin's neck, declaring that they were a gift.

When Karin objected, the necklace donor stated, "I told a friend last week that if you ever noticed the necklace again, I was going to give it to you. This is a family heirloom and you are the one person above all others who should have it."

Karin accepted the gift realizing this was a genuine act of

love, an indication of a total acceptance of Karin.

The high school age class became a youth fellowship. Members of the group attended the Sunday evening service at the church and then went to the home on Monticello Court. Karin served refreshments and led the group in serious discussions.

From the first, we always found ways to involve the young people in practical ways to express their Christianity. I remember one time in the old *fellowship hall*, actually designed as a gymnasium, located behind the sanctuary with basketball goals at each end, one almost directly over the kitchen food window. The hall was a perfect place for fellowship suppers and the Boy Scouts enjoyed the basketball hoops. On the night I remember, the young people had stacks and stacks of old clothing that they had gathered and were packing to give to the needy. I do not remember taking off my shoes, but I do remember being embarrassed when I missed them and found the young people had put them in the *Discard Box*, too worn to be *givable*.

I later learned that one reason the pulpit committee, which had invited us to consider the San Antonio church, had sought us was because of Karin's former leadership position in the statewide youth program. It was not my preaching skills or my academic achievements that led the decision-makers to Crane. It was my youthful bride's reputation that prompted the committee' decision.

Karin did not disappoint them. Teenagers filled the front room of our home each Sunday night. When the group grew too large for the manse parlor, youth filled the spacious back yard.

Each October a haunted house party took place. Karin and I would locate a decaying farmhouse beyond the city limit; gain permission from the owners to use the uninhabited building and go to great lengths to find volunteers to help haunt it. As many as thirty young adults and parents of youth aided the haunting by constructing eerie scenes and squeaky coffin lids that opened in unexpected places.

Jim Beverly, a student from Scotland and ministerial candidate attending Trinity University, assisted me in the pulpit and helped Karin in her work with the youths. When Jim went on to seminary in Austin, Texas another future Presbyterian minister, Bob Poteet, helped with the program. At the time Bob was the church organist. He enthusiastically donated his services to Crestholme's youth activities. After one of the Sunday night youth meetings, Bob, Karin and I stood on the front steps of our house and talked for a long time. It was at that time that Bob confessed he and members of his family were Methodist, but he was considering changing in order to become a Presbyterian minister.

On one of the overnight events two-dozen youths spent several hours discussing justice issues. On the return journey through the rolling countryside the lead car of the caravan stopped to collect several clumps of bluebonnets that bloomed profusely beside the road. This act took place near a highway sign that made it clear the picking of the Texas state flower was strictly against the law.

Karin ordered the youths, who were traveling in caravan with agreed rules, to get back in their cars and remain silent until they reached the church. There, on the church parking lot they gathered around Karin and concluded their discussion. She left the decision to them and went inside the church to unload retreat supplies. Suddenly the young people brought all the bluebonnets into the kitchen and asked where the vases were kept. The next morning the sanctuary was decorated with bluebonnets, a lesson which none of those who participated in the event would ever forget. Karin's work gained the attention of Austin Presbyterian Seminary professors who sent students to San Antonio to work with and learn from Karin.

One of my most enjoyable activities was teaching a large communicant's class on a weekday after school. My first group of students at Crestholme included a slender girl in her early teens. She came to the class with determined regularity and participated enthusiastically in the learning process. When I sought an address for her, I discovered she lived in a run down tourist court outside the immediate neighborhood, one that was considered a site for immoral activity.

Although her clothing was quite simple, she always appeared at class and worship services neatly dressed. When she met with the church Session in preparation for communicant membership, her statement of faith demonstrated a profound sense of spiritual involvement. Her mother who was repeatedly in and out of the county jail had named her for a famed operatic star. Apparently she hoped for better things for her offspring than she could provide in the environment in which she lived.

When the young teenager needed serious dental work, Karin and I sought to assist her and even considered adopting her as our own. One of her mother's *boy friends* threatened me for my efforts in the youth's behalf. We took the threat so seriously that we left San Antonio for a trip to Sweetwater twelve hours earlier than we had planned. Eventually a distant relative became involved and secured a more stable situation for her in another part of the city. Although we eventually lost contact with her, we did hear she overcame the problems of her early environment. She was one of the youth we had helped gain spiritual and moral maturity.

My ministry included all ages. I was called upon to visit a seven-year-old youth who was dying of an incurable disease. I soon discovered that he was a profoundly spiritual person. He asked if he could become a full member of the church and take communion. I took the entire Session to his bedside where he made a deeply moving statement of faith. The elders of the church approved his admission to membership and the sacrament of the Lord's Supper was administered, using prune juice since grape juice was toxic to his medications. His death occurred a few days later on his father's birthday. The father, a high school football coach, declared that he would never again celebrate his birthday. This was a vow he never kept for a second son was born exactly one year later, on his birthday.

When we discovered that a half dozen of the older members of the church still wanted a Wednesday night Bible study, Karin and I met with them for the best part of our first year in

San Antonio. Karin finally suggested that they reach out to other members of the church with a weekly covered dish supper followed by an informal Bible study led by Jack. The group of elderly widows was delighted with the suggestion and became the primary promoters of the church suppers, which continued fifty weeks out of each year for the remainder of the Ramsay's ministry at Crestholme.

I spent as much of my time as possible in pastoral visitation, realizing that the former minister, who continued to live in the immediate area, knew who was hospitalized before I did. In time, my willingness to fulfill the pastoral role became known and I was able to win the race to the hospital bedside at least on occasion.

One of the families in the congregation had a thirty-year-old son who had been bedridden all of his life. Regular visits were deeply appreciated. On one occasion I was in the home of the handicapped man when his mother, his sole caretaker, asked if Karin knew "how to fix chicken."

I answered, "yes."

She left the room and soon returned with a live chicken in her hand.

"Mother, don't you think you should tie the chicken's legs?," asked the paralyzed son. She protested but at his insistence tied the legs together and I was on my way home with a chicken thrashing about on the back seat of the car. I left the creature with tied legs in the garage while I went in and sheepishly told Karin what had happened. We thought of letting the bird loose, but that would have resulted in the gift of another living chicken. In a quandary we went to the Wednesday night meeting where the half dozen widows seemed in an unusually jolly mood. Once the gathering was over, one of the ladies, a grandmother we knew as "Mrs. Prozanski", took Karin aside and told her she had witnessed the chicken event from across the street.

"My son could never wring a chicken's neck. Just bring it to me and I will take care of everything." She "fixed the chicken" and we had a delightful fried chicken meal.

This "chicken fixing" occurred shortly before the group

agreed to spearhead the family night suppers. The same lady occasionally brought fried chicken as her contribution to the evening meal. When she did, she would nudge Jack or Karin and wink in commemoration of our shared secret.

My Ford 6 began to develop a nasty habit of refusing to move even after the engine was running properly. Karin would have to get out and help me rock the car back and forth several times in order to get the gear un-stuck before we could get underway. On a trip to Sweetwater to visit the Kinseys, Karin's father, Kirby, told me about wonderful deals the local Studebaker dealer was giving on new cars. We fell in love with a sleek looking cream-colored sedan with a sky blue top that we could purchase within our means.

I had just filled the Ford's tank with gas. I did the logical thing: I siphoned most of the gas out of the old car into one of Kirby's emergency tanks. At the time new cars were sold with a minimum amount of gasoline in their tanks, usually no more than a gallon or two. When the new car was delivered I filled the Studebaker's tank with the salvaged gas. Not being used to the siphoning process, I inhaled when I should not have. For the next twenty-four hours, I belched so many gasoline fumes Karin was afraid to kiss me. Who knew what might happen when my angel kissed me? She feared she might spark an explosion.

The salvaged gasoline made it possible to extend our trip in the smoothly running new auto to Alpine and the Big Bend country before returning to San Antonio. The Studebaker was the best car we ever owned. We gave it a special nickname, "Studey-Sue". After all, the vehicle was an important part of the Ramsay household. Other than the furniture, the decision to buy the car was the first really major purchase the two young lovers made together.

A committee had long been at work planning the thirtieth anniversary celebration of the founding of Crestholme. They invited me to assist. When I learned there was little interest in asking the former minister to preach I proposed that they seek the founder of the congregation, Dr. P. B. Hill, who was living on a ranch west of the city. He was famous for his membership in the legendary Texas Rangers. I was told he would probably come dressed in western attire with his Ranger badge on his jacket.

I picked up Dr. Hill at the Gunter Hotel where he had been promised free lodging for life due to the fame of his former service. He was dressed like a ranger should be dressed, but there was no evidence of a badge or weapon. He wore his Texas boots in the pulpit and delivered a dynamic sermon. He reminded his hearers that Jack was then about the same age he had been when he helped found the congregation.

I was beginning to feel comfortable with my ministerial position when I received an unsettling revelation. I attended a meeting of Presbytery at which the New Church Development Committee requested funds for purchase of a site near the location of Crestholme.

I asked the chairman what this meant. He explained the details of the plan. Hal Hyde, the General Assembly expert on new church location, had conducted a demographic study of southeast San Antonio. This had indicated a change of location would be necessary for Crestholme. Funds from the General Assembly would be available if the congregation agreed to the relocation.

At first I was uncertain about the proposal since the church would have to raise matching funds to claim the grant, a sum well beyond the congregation's present means. That night in the motel I talked it over with Karin. She immediately saw the potential in the proposal. The present church building was hopelessly inadequate and there was no room for expansion on the small plot of land where the congregation had worshipped for three decades.

Why not attempt the impossible and build a church structure that would meet all the needs of the congregation? We both knew this could end our ministry in San Antonio should the plan be rejected by the membership of the church. With Karin's resolute wisdom backing me, I went to the Presbytery official the next day and told him I would do all possible to implement the proposition.

*Fourteen*

# "You and Jack Just Murdered a Man."
## *1954*

I returned from the meeting of Presbytery fearful of challenges that lie ahead. Only Karin's confidence brought me reassurance. I sought the opinions of as many members of the congregation as practical. Several of the elders I approached were enthusiastic about the proposal's possibilities. Surprisingly, some of the older of the Session members such as Mr. McGaughy in his eighties who sold candy from his small grocery store to children of the neighborhood; Mr. Bodie, a retired barber in his late sixties, and Mr. McDougall, who was forced to retire when another company took over the company for whom he worked, were the most enthusiastic. They saw the plan as a chance to strengthen the church and reach out to future generations.

At the next regular meeting of the Session, I shared my information with the church's Ruling Elders. All present agreed a Presbytery official should meet with us and answer questions.

Wendell Crofoot, the recently elected executive of the Presbytery was present at the next meeting. He gave a glowing account of the proposal's possibilities. One elder was strongly opposed, the long time church treasurer and Church School superintendent.

The telephone began to ring in my office. Word had spread throughout the neighborhood that the church would be closed and the property sold for some purpose that would be detrimental to the residential area. Most of those who called were angry and gave names that I did not recognize. I realized that much misinformation was floating about and that most of those who objected to the proposal were either non-members or persons who had been removed from the active roll of the church.

I asked the Session to issue a call for a congregational meeting as soon as possible. This they did. I requested a ruling from the Stated Clerk of the General Assembly as to who could vote on the issue, whether or not an inactive member was entitled to vote.

The ruling came back that both active and inactive members would have to be allowed full participation in the meeting soon to be held. This would make passage of a resolution to build a new church extremely difficult.

In the final week before the meeting, Karin and I visited twenty-seven families urging their support of the plan. These were among the most active members of the congregation. All gave positive responses. But during the same period, one longtime member called me at home and denounced me for what the objector considered "apostate leadership".

Apparently his wife had been aware of his frustration with me during that telephone call. As soon as he hung up, my telephone rang again. This time it was his wife, crying and pleading with me to stop any possible sale of the building. Stronger and faster her words came.

Finally she blurted, "You can't sell that building. You can't sell that building! After all, it is desecrated to the Lord!"

Wanting to laugh at the word she had misused, I managed to tell her I would pray about it and she was content to hang up.

## "You and Jack Just Murdered a Man."

Karin and I laughed and laughed at the word she had used. Somehow, laughter helped us to sleep well that night and occasionally we still remind each other of anything not meeting our approval by referring to it as "desecrated to the Lord".

The date for the decisive meeting finally arrived. The sanctuary was crowded as never before. We had communion at the close of worship and then I sought to moderate the meeting as calmly as I could. Executive Presbyter Crofoot spoke. He stated that Hal Hyde, the General Assembly's new church development consultant had made the recommendation for relocation. The executive mentioned the fact that Hyde had once worked for General Motors. He had conducted demographic studies that determined investment opportunities for the nation's largest corporation.

The gentleman who had so vigorously denounced me a few days earlier, who had his wife call me again, who had refused to take communion because I had presided, stood up.

"Are we going to build a church up on that hill or an automobile factory?" he asked and immediately slumped to the floor.

I halted the meeting and a registered nurse, Lillian Draper, went to the side of the protester. She rushed to the church phone and called the Robert B. Green, San Antonio's charity hospital, asking for an immediate emergency response. A family member heard the call and demanded that the request be canceled since she did not want the patient to go to a charity hospital where other races were treated.

A call was made to the Baptist hospital for ambulance service. When the ambulance arrived, the limp form of the objector was carried to the requested hospital where he was pronounced dead on arrival. The nurse who had attended the dying man later told me that she would not have considered the demand to cancel the initial emergency call had she had not been sure that death had already occurred.

I called the meeting to order. A prayer was voiced for the patient then on the way to the hospital. Soon after the meeting was reconvened, word came of his death. This was announced to the congregation. A motion was made to take an immediate vote on the issue at hand and conclude the meeting.

A ballot had been given to everyone who had their name on either the active or inactive roll. These were quickly counted. The vast majority voted "yes" and the meeting was adjourned.

As the crowd left the sanctuary, Karin was still standing on the church steps near the main door where she had stayed; listening as best she could during the vote.

"You and Jack just murdered a man", said one of the opposition as she pushed past Karin.

Some, who had not been actively voicing any opinions before, were leaving for their cars when they overheard the comment. They immediately came to Karin's side. News of what had been said to Karin spread like wildfire. We suddenly had more friends than we realized.

When Wendell Crofoot heard, he was concerned, not only as a Presbytery executive, but also as a pastor for another pastor and his wife, and he insisted that he take us across town to his home where we could have lunch with them. Not only did we need lunch, we needed to be away from the whole situation for a period.

Five member families, a total of twelve communicant members, gave notice to the Session they were leaving to join another church. One family would later return to Crestholme but the other four would continue to live in the area and worship elsewhere.

I heard rumors of a petition being circulated in the neighborhood that would be presented to the next Presbytery meeting. This document would request that the congregation's action be overturned.

At the next meeting of Western Texas Presbytery in Kingsville, Texas, the church's long time Scoutmaster appeared. He presented the rumored document. This was relayed to a committee for consideration. When I had a chance to see the actual petition, I was able to assure the chairman that most of the signers were not members of Crestholme. I then recounted the care that had been given in following the constitution of the denomination.

The committee reported to Presbytery the next day that there was no reason for overriding the church's action. Their report cleared the way and gave approval necessary for the construction of a new building on a two-and-a-half acre lot on Goliad Road, a site just over one mile from the original building.

A few weeks after the rejection of the petition by Presbytery, the Scoutmaster appeared at my front door after midnight one night. A man of few words, he simply made the statement, "Preacher, your church is on fire."

I believed him when I heard the fire sirens. I pulled on my pants and a jacket over my pajamas. I ran the block and a half to the church. By the time I arrived, the San Antonio Fire Department had doused the flames. There was no damage to the building as a whole. Only the interior of the men's restroom had been damaged.

The church's fire insurance paid off without question when it was determined that the fire had been caused by a burning cigarette beside the toilet in the men's room. The Scoutmaster who lived next door saved the rickety wooden church from total destruction. Somehow during Scout meeting, a lighted cigarette had found its way beneath a pile of paper mâché Bible School maps and smoldered there until late in the night when the Scoutmaster saw an orange glow in the men's room window and called the fire department. Although the Scout leader had spent countless hours seeking signatures for his petition against Crestholme's relocation, he acted responsibly when he realized the old building was in danger of being totally destroyed.

Karin and I knew we had our greatest challenge ahead of us. I organized neighborhood meetings in several homes in which everyone who attended was asked to give suggestions for the new building.

Another congregational meeting was called by the Session to elect a building committee. The mood of this gathering was very different than that of the first. Several names were proposed for the important task. All accepted enthusiastically and the committee began work using the home meetings as the basis of their planning.

An able architect who specialized in church construction, Henry Steinbommer, was employed. He drew up plans for a first unit, which would include a large fellowship hall and adjoining kitchen, an office wing and three educational wings. A national fund raising organization was named to assist the committee in gaining the money necessary to build. Ruth Chapman as a Volunteer Secretary had helped me find addresses for the list of members I inherited. René Ofton realized that in order to raise funds we would need to have a means to keep people correctly informed. She suggested and helped create *The Crestholme Crier*.

The on site fund-raiser set a goal of three times the church's annual budget. The campaign was an exciting time in the life of the congregation. Some families including Karin and Jack decided to double tithe.

One family had established a savings account for the purpose of remodeling their home bathroom. They pledged most of this to the building fund and did the work themselves, a project that resulted in a plumbing mistake that connected the hot water line to the toilet. They were willing to put up with cold showers for a time knowing they could warm up elsewhere.

A father and son plumbing company pledged the gift of their services for the new church building. I later heard that the *free plumbers* for the new building did take time out to solve the cold shower problems for their fellow church members.

The campaign was oversubscribed and the building committee called for a groundbreaking ceremony in which everyone was asked to bring his or her own shovel. That Sunday two hundred spades dug into the ground on the hilltop lot.

Building inspection became a favorite pastime of many of the church members. Each evening there were almost enough Crestholme members gathered at the site of the evolving building to constitute some sort of inspection committee. The favorite time for Karin and me to check on the building was just before sunset. As we drove up Avondale we could see the building rising higher and higher above the end of the street that dead-ended at the site of our new church.

One day we noticed that in the tall framework rising to new heights there was a small child also rising to new heights. Rickie was a small child whose mother and father, Ruth and LeRoy Price, had left the meeting where we had been introduced to the congregation to go to the hospital for his birth a little over three years earlier. Somehow young Rickie had managed to find a way to climb almost to the top. We drove up as quietly as we could and told his mother where Rickie was, thinking any loud sound might frighten him.

I can still hear Ruth, "Rickie, come down here right now." He did.

When heavy rain came on the night the foundation had been laid, pastor and members thought the building would float away. I was so worried that I called Bob Colgrove who was in construction and asked him to go look at the foundation. The next day he called and said all was well. He later became a very active Deacon.

In the spring of that year, I was elected by the Presbytery of Western Texas to be a commissioner to the General Assembly that was scheduled to meet near Memorial Day 1955 in Richmond, Virginia. Karin and I made the trip east to the site of the national meeting in our Studebaker, Studie Sue.

After the close of the Richmond Assembly we drove to Newark, New Jersey where we lodged in a motel convenient to downtown Manhattan. Each day we explored the city by bus and subway.

On our last night in New York, strangers picked us out of a line waiting and hoping for some free tickets to a television show. They were schoolteachers and gave us tickets to the Copa Cabaña, explaining that they had to return home earlier than they had originally planned and wanted us to have tickets they could not use. We were not sure the unexpected free tickets included a full meal so we ate Chinese food early and then went to the club. The waiter was quite upset that we turned down the free meal. We ate only a desert but we saw a great show.

When we returned to San Antonio, the work on the new church building was complete. The old structure with a refurbished men's room had been sold to a Pentecostal minister who wanted to start a congregation of his own. We were fascinated that ministers of Pentecostal churches make their own decisions without boards and they themselves purchase and own the church building where they preach. He was eager to move in; we were equally eager to move out and on to the church that was clearly visible at the end of the street and at the peak of the hill.

There was one slight delay for both congregations. There was a strike by the lock makers, and we were locked out of the new building. The Pentecostal minister could not hold his enthusiastic congregation back and they started moving our furnishings out to the sidewalk. Fortunately Karin and I happened to drive by and found our piano sitting on the sidewalk along with all the nursery cribs. We had to make a deal with the new owners of our old building, and we had to rent back the building. One of our members who had a truck rescued the piano until the locksmith strike was over about two weeks later and we were given keys to the new church.

Moving day was an occasion to celebrate. No professional movers were needed. The whole congregation turned out with a parade of cars, trucks, trailers and jubilant children and adults, all helping transport all moveable items to the new site and set up for our first worship. Things were a bit confused that first Sunday, but by the formal grand opening several weeks later, everything came together. Presbytery leaders, ministers and members of other churches and some former members were present for the big event.

*The Sanctuary, Gym in the rear, Classrooms to the left, 1953.*

*Offices, Fellowship Hall and Classrooms, 1955.*

*The Gymnasium where we first met the people.*

## Fifteen

## Five Percent of a Chance

### 1956

The congregation's move in the summer of 1955 to the new site was an immediate success. The dramatic concrete cross with a colored ceramic seal was visible to all who passed by. Finishing touches had been put on the building in late September and formal opening was held in October. Each day, hundreds of vehicles drove by the new building on Goliad Road. None of these would have had any reason to view the old building on Hermitage Court.

Attendance at worship increased dramatically in 1956. One year after the formal opening, 100 new members had been added to the congregation. Even though the new building had twice as much floor space as the old building, when the attendance for Sunday Church School began to average around 230, an increase of over 100 over the previous year, even the new Crestholme building began to look a bit cramped.

The Wednesday night suppers became the focal point of

the congregation's weekday activities. After the meal in the large hall, tables were put away and chairs arranged close to the speaker's stand where Biblical themes, Bible studies, and justice issues were discussed. Occasionally Scottish church history and the existence of the Ecumenical movement were a part of the presentations.

Following the general gathering there were choir rehearsals, committee meetings and other church activities. Wednesday nights at Crestholme no longer involved only a half dozen faithful souls. Instead the mid-week event brought forth sixty to a hundred or more persons most Wednesday nights.

The year featured many special events. In February there was a formal Valentine banquet for the Senior High Youth Group, later in the spring a Youth Council Retreat and many Pioneer parties. The Women of the Church entertained 150 members of area Evening Circles and over 200 Day Circle women from throughout the San Antonio District for a two day event in February. Andrew Club visitation in March introduced a number of new faces to the Crestholme family. In April an all-member visitation and special pre-Easter Service of Communion prepared for Easter Sunday when over 400 people attended church. In June Crestholme welcomed new members with a special supper and in October 50 young people attended the *annual* Haunted House party for the senior high group. November saw the most successful Every Member Canvass in Crestholme's history when over $17,000 was pledged to the budget and building funds. Men of the Church had many meetings, including a dove fry. The men began a building for Boy Scout Troop 16 that they sponsored.

One of the unexpected results of the relocation was an increase in requests for my services as a performer of weddings. Karin had served as my consultant for several ceremonies in the old church building, all of which involved long time Crestholme members. I accepted requests for weddings from couples that were not members of Crestholme if both persons were willing to participate in pre-nuptial counseling sessions. Some of these later joined the congregation. In all cases I extracted from those I married a promise to find a church home near the place they planned to live.

Although Karin and I had worked out the logistics of weddings of all sizes in the old building, the new, much larger structure created unique problems. One of the first such events on Goliad Road was a wedding for a non-member couple who found the new church and thought it would be the perfect place for a wedding. They had invited a large number of guests. The worship area had already begun to fill, when the bride asked Karin if the organist was present.

"I don't know, who is your organist?"

"Ann Ragsdale, your church organist, " she replied.

Karin realized she had not seen Ann. Karin left and called Ann's home. Margaret, Ann's mother answered, and when Karin asked if Ann had already left for the wedding, Margaret replied, "No, she's gone to the ball game." Ann had put the wrong date on her calendar not realizing there was a conflict with the ball game.

"Hang up the telephone," said Karin. "I have to find an organist."

When Karin kept rushing back and forth between the organ and the office telephone, one of the guests realized there was a problem and offered to play the organ. Karin was delighted, but when she took her to the organ they found it locked. Karin came to me for help. I could not believe that the organ was locked. Nobody had ever mentioned to me anything about locks on the organ. Already in my robe, I went out and tried to open the organ keyboard.

Karin called Dorothy Prozanski, another organist, who often served as a substitute. She admitted she had a key, to which Karin said, "When I drive by, you have the key ready to hand me."

Karin arrived, no Dorothy and no key! When her preschool daughter opened the door, Dorothy had a vase full of keys scattered on the table and was frantically sorting through them. She could not find the key to the organ.

In the meantime, the wedding guest and I were both on

the fellowship hall stage where all could see I was trying to pry open the keyboard. When we gave up, the groomsmen rolled a large piano from a church school classroom into the side hallway of the new worship area. There the instrument became hopelessly stuck.

The would-be guest organist said, "Leave it here, I'll play from here."

We notified the bride that she would have piano music.

Even though the guest-pianist could not see the minister or the wedding party, she would begin the wedding march and then listen for my cues. The bride could hear her music and Karin would help her know what to do. The ceremony began almost on time. All went well until the volunteer musician who did not know my usual ceremony started the recessional before I had pronounced the couple husband and wife. I raised my voice, finishing the ceremony as she soft peddled until she heard, "Amen" and started the recessional again. Though I got all the necessary words into the ceremony and signed the certificate affirming that the two were properly married, the County Clerk of a county out of our area mailed it back for me to sign again. I had signed it in the wrong place.

Another wedding, while the building was still new, was delayed by nearly thirty minutes. I used the groomsmen for communicating with Karin on the other side of the building complex. When I realized something was wrong, I sent an inquiry to Karin. She replied that the bride had equipment problems. At last I was told all was well and I could give the organist the signal to begin.

The needed equipment was the bride's girdle. She had been fitted for her magnificent gown wearing a girdle and could not get into her dress no matter how hard she tried. A member of the wedding party went to her home, located the essential accessory, and brought it to the bride's dressing room. I had to explain the delay to the assembled crowd without mentioning any of the embarrassing details. After this, Karin and I believed we could handle almost anything, even difficulties with bridal equipment.

Although the church grew in spirit and size, Karin and I were well aware of the fact we were the sole residents of the home on Monticello Court. The one great void in our life together was the fact that after five years of marriage there were no children. We had almost decided we were destined to remain childless.

One evening in attending a citywide church event at the downtown Presbyterian Church, I recognized my Davidson College roommate, Ed Currie. I had not seen him for over a dozen years. I had helped Ed load his bags on a Greyhound bus that took him to an Air Force induction center. Ed had joined the war effort on the promise the USAF would eventually help him complete his education including medical school. At the time Lieutenant Currie was on temporary duty in San Antonio.

The Ramsays and the Curries got together on several occasions. On one such event, we mentioned our situation. By what Karin and I considered as more than a coincidence, Ed Currie had special medical training in this area. He suggested some preliminary tests and put Karin in contact with a civilian doctor, a Doctor Foster, who specialized, in reproductive therapy.

Karin became a patient of the specialist. Several more complicated tests took place. Dr. Foster recommended surgery for Karin which he believed would give her "five percent of a chance" to bear a child. The surgery was performed at San Antonio's Nix Hospital. Soon afterward, Karin became pregnant.

On June 5, 1956, I rushed Karin back to the Nix hospital where she gave birth to our first born, Annetta Jean, namesake of Annetta Jones, wife of Dr. Robert F. Jones, the pastor of First Presbyterian Church of Fort Worth. Both Dr. Jones and Annetta were sponsors who traveled with Synod's Youth Council when Karin was on Council. Everyone in the congregation seemed delighted. Although Annetta's birth took place on the first day of the annual Vacation Bible School, Karin was not expected to take part as she had on all previous events of this type and I was excused for being late on the very first morning of Vacation Bible School. The head nurse of the hospital's pediatric division, a Mrs. Grassley, was a part of the Crestholme family. She brought our daughter to Karin's room very soon after her birth. I was present and she allowed me to hold our newborn daughter in my arms for a few minutes. This was a breach of acceptable procedure for this was an age when fathers were expected to make themselves extremely scarce throughout the birthing process. Nurse Grassley gave both mother and baby very special attention during their stay at the Nix.

Even before Dr. Foster's surgical procedure, Ed Currie had been transferred elsewhere. The Ramsays lost contact with him and were never able to tell him of the amazing miracle that had resulted from his recommendation. Years later, I was able to gain an address for Ed from the Davidson Alumni office. I sent him a letter of thanks for his all-important medical advice. At this point, I still have not heard from Ed.

The church's youth group gave the Monticello Court home a complete house cleaning during Karin's brief hospital stay. The president of the Youth Fellowship, Sue Hohner, organized the cleanup. When I brought Karin and Annetta home, the manse was spotless as never before. We were not really surprised at how clean it was though we do like to wonder who Sue had doing what. The groups who met in our home before Annetta's birth were special groups. We noticed our scrapbooks have lots of pictures of them and we can still point to the pictures in our scrapbook and name them: Lee Allen McDougal, Joan Hermann, Gene Rimmer, Ruth Ann Gibson, LeRoy Haws, Walter Goodenough, Johnny Ragsdale, Bob Mooty, Carolyn Allison, Beverly Harris, James Magee, Bennett Todd, Beverly Todd, Tommy Mercer, Patti Lee and Wayne Watson, Lois Stappenbeck, Jimmy Birkner, and more, a whole scrapbook! In 1957 the Young People no longer met at the manse, the Women of the Church began preparing supper for both Senior High and Junior High Youths. After youth meetings, adults and young people (and those young children who had been there while parents helped with meal and meetings) joined together for Eventide, a time of singing and vespers. While we celebrated the growth of the program, we missed the times at the Manse with the Young People on Sunday nights.

The birth of Annetta at that time only added to our excitement about what was going on with the Crestholme Church Family. Easter attendance 1957 of 525 with 25 people joining as members that day, over 60 new members during the year would be inspirational to any pastor. Family night activities continued every Wednesday night, sharing food, fellowship, and inspiration. Every member canvas reporting $19,000, added to the attendance records, proved that the move had been the correct decision.

Statistics of the next year, 1958, showed even more proof: Easter attendance of 550; Andrew Club visitation with 33 decisions for church membership in 3 nights; 92 new members for the year, 15 more than any previous year; Women of the Church growing to eight Circles. Presbytery met at Crestholme in 1958, something that would never have been possible in the old building. Men of the Church were meeting regularly for exciting activities. However, I do have to admit that I cannot remember what the program for Men of the Church was in February. I had gone to the new building for the meeting when Karin called and asked me to come home. There was no emergency. She simply wanted me there.

I left the meeting without giving an excuse for my early departure. When I got home, Karin simply said she had to get out of the house. This we did by going to the Rodeo. We sat through most of the performance until Karin said she thought it best for her to go home. It was a cold night, the beginning of one of San Antonio's rare freezes, an ice storm that lasted nine days.

When we reached Studie Sue, we found our car sitting in a frigid puddle of water with a flat. I went to work changing the tire. When I had the last lug tightened, I realized I had lost my wedding ring. I knew a trip to the hospital was imminent, one time I wanted to have evidence of my marriage. Both Karin and I got down on our knees in the icy water to search for proof of our wedding. Finally Karin found my ring and we headed home. We called the doctor and picked up the bag Karin had prepared for the trip to the Nix and left Annetta with our neighbors, the

Fords. We arrived at the hospital barely twenty minutes before Robin's birth. I was the last one into the father's waiting room and the first one out.

Twenty months after Annetta's birth, February 11, 1958, our joy was doubled by the birth of a second child, a boy, Robin Andrew. Although Annetta was on schedule, Robin had arrived a bit early.

Word spread through the congregation of a second birth to the Ramsays, but some found it hard to believe. Several had seen us at the Rodeo and had concluded I had simply been shirking my ministerial duties on a night when I would have usually been with the Men of the Church.

All was forgiven when it was known my peculiar behavior on the night of the church meeting was because I needed to take Karin to the hospital for the birth of Robin, though taking a detour to a Rodeo does seem a bit strange.

In all of the nearly four decades of Crestholme's history, Annetta and Robin were the only two births that took place in the family of any of the various ministers while they were actively serving as Pastor of Crestholme. Mrs. Bodie, life-long member of Crestholme, introduced herself to Karin by telling her she felt especially close to minister's families because the only *child of the manse* for Crestholme had been her best friend. Papa Green's daughter, Evelyn Green, who became one of the most respected Directors of Christian Education in the General Assembly, was her childhood playmate, a *Preacher's Kid* (sometimes called a *P.K.*) a *child of the manse* even though not born while her family lived in the Crestholme manse. Karin had learned to love *Miss Green* who had been her counselor at Karin's first church camp experience in Cisco, Texas.

Children of the Manse were a new experience for the Crestholme congregation. Karin was delighted that they loved the children, but she quickly learned not to "let the children sit in church" with members who so loved them. It was only two weeks after Robin's birth that Karin and both children attended the Sunday night service in the new church building, a fellowship hall with a high stage, hallways on each side leading to restrooms and kitchen. Margaret Ragsdale asked if Annetta could "sit with me" that night while Karin and the baby remained on the back row. Margaret allowed twenty-month-old Annetta to go to the restroom while I was preaching. I was in the middle of a sentence when I heard a voice coming from the foot of the stage, just outside the hall leading to the restroom.

"I can't pottie because the light is not on," came the voice. I paused.

"I said, I can't pottie because the light is not on," came the voice a little more loudly. I lost my train of thought. I hoped Karin would do something. I wished Annetta had not learned to speak so plainly and so loudly at so young an age. Nobody did anything. The hall was deathly quiet.

I am told that I said, "Will someone go help the young lady? There are knives in the kitchen." Why I said that I don't know.

Karin remained in her chair, pretending to be attentive to Robin. Margaret finally went to rescue Annetta. She turned on the light and asked Annetta if she could help her. Annetta replied, "No thank you, I never fall in." Karin never again allowed any member to take Annetta to sit with them during church.

When it came time for the denomination to vote on the question of the reunion of the two major branches of Presbyterianism, I was elected as Presbytery Moderator. This was more than an honor. It was recognition of the fact that I was known as one who would treat both sides of a controversial issue fairly.

Presbytery met in Kingsville. There was a vigorous discussion before the vote. I was able to calm some of the rancor that was obvious in the heated debate. Western Texas Presbytery voted to reunite with our separated brothers and sisters in the north, but the proposal failed to gain enough votes across the denomination to pass. This was a decision that would stand for another quarter of a century. At the end of the daylong argument, I was given a standing round of applause for my conduct as moderator.

**128** *Angel Kisses And My Beating Heart*

When there was a reorganization of the U.S. Presbyterian Synod of Texas, it was agreed that the Presbytery I had moderated, Western Texas, then the largest in geographical size in the General Assembly, should be divided. The area around San Antonio became John Knox Presbytery. The first meeting of John Knox Presbytery was held in the First Presbyterian Church of San Antonio. I was elected as moderator of the newly formed governing body in spite of the fact the same person was seldom if ever named to serve as moderator more than once. This meeting had no issues before it that called for vigorous debate. My service as elected head of Presbytery for the second time around proved to be a delightful experience, all honor and no argument.

Sunday Night at the Manse
423 Monticello Court
San Antonio, Texas

## Five Percent of a Chance

Karin & I on the steps of Crestholme Presbyterian Church, Hermitage Court, San Antonio

Robin & Annetta Ramsay, To This Date, The Only "Children Born To The Manse" Of Crestholme Presbyterian Church.

## Sixteen

## "Nobody Is Home"

### 1959

Our final five years at Crestholme were both pleasant and productive. In 1959, search committees began to show up at Sunday worship. One member of the San Antonio congregation believed she could always spot visitors who were present for the purpose of luring the pastor elsewhere. In early December, a pulpit nominating committee eluded her vigilance. They met us after Sunday morning worship. They followed the Ramsays back to our home on Monticello Court, on the way passing the Allisons who were in their front yard and waved enthusiastically to the Ramsays. We often wondered what they thought when they saw the Allisons, for after they arrived at the house the committee quickly presented their case: Karin and Jack were needed in a recently organized congregation in the North Dallas area. One very forceful member of the Committee, Lynn Lawther, a Dallas County Commissioner, would not give up until he extracted a promise from us to visit Dallas. He assured us that the committee had already decided whom they wanted for their pastor. They were confident that we would agree to move northward once we had visited the area.

A few days later, in the midst of the always busy Christmas season, all four Ramsays boarded a Braniff Turbo Jet bound for Love Field. We were met by the committee and given a whirlwind tour of the Carrollton Farmers Branch area. That night we returned to San Antonio by a turbo jet which was running late. Once in the air, the plane flew at top speed. It was exactly six o'clock when we left the Love Field central lobby. The aircraft arrived at the San Antonio airport in time for us to reach our parked car by 6:30 P.M.

A similar plane to the one on which we flew, also a turbo-prop, had met disaster, exploding in mid-air shortly before our return flight. A few days after our flight, a second turbo-prop disaster took place. A member of Covenant Presbyterian Church had died in the first Braniff explosion. The final pastoral act of my predecessor, Joe Rand, had been that of identifying the broken body. Investigation established the fact that both crashes had been caused by excessive speed. From all indications, our safe return should be considered a miracle.

The decision to leave Crestholme had to be made in the midst of Christmas activities and was not an easy one. Easter attendance in 1959 had been 800 with three services necessary. Bob Poteet, a youth in high school employed as our organist, had invigorated the entire congregation when he and the youth group built two cinemascope movie screens and showed movies, *The Robe* and *A Man Called Peter*. The Pioneer (Junior High) group hosted a Presbytery Youth Rally and the Women of the Church made new choir robes for the Adult Choir. Memories of good times and hard times; laughter and tears; memories of people with whom we had shared weddings, births and funerals all entered into emotional ties with a congregation we loved. Mrs. Geigenmiller never allowed us to forget that I had officiated at the weddings of her three granddaughters: the Wilson sisters,

Dawn and Sandra at age 19 and Janis at age 18. The last wedding I performed at Crestholme was for Carolyn Allison, a member of the youth group who met at the manse and often drank spiced tea after a program and business meeting.

Even though the two-bedroom house was no longer adequate, the home held countless memories. It was difficult to bid so many good friends goodbye on the Valentine Day move after the challenging events we had experienced together. The move northward was difficult in itself. This time, the movers broke several pieces of our wedding china because they "did not pack it because it was in a china cabinet", a new piece of furniture. Although the distance from San Antonio to the Dallas suburb of Farmers Branch was less than that of our first move, it was a relocation that represented an even more drastic change.

Once the usual formal reception in the church hall was over, we began the difficult task of adjusting to a completely new situation. The church building was located between two communities, the rapidly growing city of Farmers Branch and the older town of Carrollton. The church had been organized four years earlier and the building had been in use less than a year. Few people knew their fellow church members. By the time we arrived at Covenant there was nothing other than a new building and a group of people who had not yet coalesced into a body of faith. The challenge before us was even greater than that which we had originally faced at Crestholme.

I began by visiting every family as soon as possible. This was my only means of understanding the needs of the congregation. The church was over-organized. In my previous pastorates I had been responsible for setting up as many working committees as possible. When I arrived at Covenant, which then had 196 communicant members, I was told that the six-member Session had approved sixteen different committees. When I asked how such a complex structure had come about, I was told Highland Park Presbyterian Church, a several thousand-member congregation from which most of the Covenant leaders had come, had 16 committees.

I had the difficult task of weeding out the non-essential committees and enlarging the official governing bodies. At first, my efforts were little understood. Turf wars had already sprung up between strong-minded individuals who dominated certain committees that acted without regard for the total mission of the church.

One event that broke the seriousness of the tensions we faced took place only a couple of weeks after our arrival and before my installation as pastor. Robin received a second baptism. While we were still adjusting to the relocation, the two-year old preacher's kid was re-baptized by an almost full container of baptismal water. It was a windy and icy day late in February. In order to empty the excess water from the portable baptismal bowl used for a baptism in the makeshift sanctuary designed as a fellowship hall, I took the bowl to the church's back door. I think I scarcely looked since a fresh *norther* had descended upon us and my back door faced the north wind. I quickly opened the door, tossed the water to the wind and slammed the door. Robin and his mother were crossing the icy lawn. He took the full discharge in his face, mystifying his mother as to where water had so suddenly come.

Karin immediately appeared at my inside study door, holding in her arms a sputtering child, freezing icy water on his face, she complaining to me, "Somebody threw water on Robin." I finally admitted I was guilty. Only now do we laugh.

During July of that year a church picnic, held at a nearby Presbytery owned campground, demonstrated the lack of community in the congregation. Each family brought their own food and no one was willing to share what they had prepared with anyone else. Karin suggested that a new format for the next year's picnic be considered, one in which all would be invited to come and bring only what they wished to share whether it be a small bag of potato chips or an ample batch of fried chicken. One of the committee chairpersons was certain this would not work, but Karin and I had enough experience with church suppers to know it would and it did.

Other than Sunday morning activities and countless committee meetings during the week, the church schedule had not been locked into a set schedule. As is so often true in a newly established church, high school young people are often not organized and there is not leadership eager to reach out to them. Elizabeth Rodriquez, age 16, was the first member to join Covenant after our arrival in February 1960. Soon to follow were Ted McCabe, age 17; Clayton Pledger, age 16, Sandra Speigel, Sandra King and, in September, Sandra Kelly. We had only been there a month or so when we drove into the driveway and found the whole group planting grass and raking our front yard. Karin and I invited the young people into our home for Sunday nights. Soon we had another group of young people "going to the Ramsays for Sunday night." We enlisted Leone and Bill Sampson to help us when the group rapidly grew. Ginny Maddox, Billy Sampson, Robert Schecter were already members when we came, and the group soon included others such as Arthur Keywood, Jr. in 1961, Connie Burns and Winston Cooper in 1962, and Al Wood in 1965.

It was this group of young people who was able to inspire the church to reach beyond the walls of the church building. One night, a woman from another Presbyterian Church, came to the manse and told the young people about the migrants who lived each winter in a former POW Camp for Germans in Princeton. After she described children who had never even played ball, the group, spearheaded by Sandy King, visited the camp and made friends with children there. They took balls and bats to the camp, played baseball and volleyball with them and left the equipment in care of some of the children who learned to play ball that day.

This soon developed into an all-church project. Each year after crops had been harvested, camp inhabitants were without work or adequate food during the Christmas season. Members of Covenant took food and *adopted* every person stranded there, a project that was a massive project almost from the start in 1962 and lasted through 1967. For six Christmases in a row, a caravan of cars traveled from Carrollton to the migrant campsite. The few motorists on the road on Christmas Eve morning were startled to see a red suited figure directing traffic at intersections on the way. Santa Claus, alias Mel Jensen, dressed in a suit made by Vivian Cozby, saw to it that every family had adequate food. Local merchants donated groceries and supplies. Every person in the camp had a white box of wrapped gifts chosen specifically for that individual. On the final trip in 1967 a Carrollton company provided four large delivery trucks for a Christmas day delivery for two hundred persons.

On the first Christmas trip to the Princeton camp, Robin Ramsay *adopted* the name of a child his age named *Corny*, short for Cornelius. When Corny did not appear to receive his Christmas gifts, five-year-old Robin went to investigate. He found Corny in one of the small cabins unable to walk. The bedridden child, who was lying on a pallet on the floor when Robin found him, was later placed in a Masonic children's hospital and, in 1968, in a foster home where he eventually gained the use of his legs. Covenant members, especially Arthur Keywood, Jr., visited him through a series of surgical procedures and kept in contact with him through the years.

When the town of Princeton decided to close the migrant camp, members of the church sponsored *Operation Bootstrap*, a program the church designed to help find work and housing for any of the displaced families who wanted to remain in the area. Elizabeth Rodriquez, who spoke fluent Spanish, aided this portion of the project. Two persons, who had been raised in migrant camps, were married in Covenant's new sanctuary. Another family with several children was anxious to settle in the area. Members of the congregation helped the father find work. A house available for rent was located and furniture was provided.

In 1968, there was no migrant project because Princeton had closed the Migrant Camp. That year the church collected gifts and toys for the 1700 students at the Denton State School.

In November 1961, my second year at Covenant, I was able to use my experience as a firefighter. I had been working late in my office. When I came out of the back door, I saw a column of smoke rising above the church building. A bystander told me the Carrollton volunteers were on their way. When the pumper truck arrived, I led the crew into the church hall. I then took the red line hose to the ledge above the office. I had once carried a similar hose to the top of a blazing Gulf Oil Company tank in Crane County. The local firefighters soon joined me and quickly put out the blaze. Later investigation indicated the fire had been caused by the improper installation of a gas heater. The whole building would have been destroyed within minutes had not water reached the base of the flames immediately.

The 1961 General Assembly met in Dallas and after the meeting on one of those nights Karin and I were able to host an after-the-meeting party in our home for our friends who had come to Dallas from across the General Assembly.

Presbytery had been watching what was happening in Covenant and began to urge that we consider a building program. From March to December of 1960, ten-and-a-half months, we had added 62 new members, giving us a membership of 213. Easter attendance had been 296, and 23 leaders had attended the leadership school at Preston Hollow. Sunday evening family nights were averaging 60 to 80 people, young people were meeting for Afterglow at the Manse, and the Every Member Canvas pledges had been $25,000. In twenty-one months, by 1961, we had added 122 new members and the education program had reached a plateau. Presbytery had recommended, and we were holding, dual services for both worship and Sunday school.

We invited the Congregation to the manse for a New Year's Eve Party in 1962, a holiday tradition we continued for most of our years in the Dallas area. Later Karin hosted a spring party for the Women of the Church. Robin who had to stay in the back room during the party said it sounded like we had crickets in the house that day. Dr. George Mauzé, pastor of First Presbyterian Church in San Antonio, was a guest who used Annetta's room while he conducted A Pre-Easter Preaching Mission. Annetta liked that because Dr. Mauzé, who had baptized her as an infant, smoked a pipe and she said he made her room smell like a hotel.

In March I represented the Synod of Texas at a meeting of the Texas Conference of Churches in Corpus Christi. After the meeting we joined my mother and father for a brief vacation at the seashore. As it turned out, our delightful visit with them was only ten days before my father, John C. Ramsay, Sr., had a sudden heart attack and died. After his death my mother moved to Dallas to live in an Oak Cliff Apartment with my sister, Liz, who was a Director of Christian Education in the Oak Cliff Church. Mother lived in Dallas with Liz until Liz married and moved with her husband to California. Then mother moved into Presbyterian Village.

In May the Synod of Texas met in Midland and Karin and I were able to go while the Kinseys kept the children in Sweetwater, a rare time for us to be without children and one of only two times they were able to play grandparents without us. We traveled with them to the Grand Canyon for a camping vacation that year.

In 1963 the tragic shooting of President Kennedy shocked the area. Covenant was the first church in the metroplex that made a spiritual response. Karin called the top name on each page of the church directory. She asked that person to call all others on the same page urging that they attend a special worship service at six p. m. as people came home from work. That evening the church was filled with people for a service of prayer for a nation in crisis. Other churches also gathered, their services scheduled later than our six p.m. time of prayer, theirs for seven, seven-thirty or eight p.m.

The next summer all four Ramsays traveled to New York where I took continuing education at Union Seminary in upper Manhattan. After learning all I could in morning seminars, I joined Karin, Annetta and Robin for a subway trip to the World Fair on Long Island. Whenever asked where we were from, we always gave our mailing address, Dallas. This usually brought forth comments. Many assumed that anyone from Dallas must have been in on the plot that took the life of a president.

During this period, I was invited to take part in a program designed to aid ministers in understanding the problems of the Sixties by riding beside officers on patrol. I signed on for both the Carrollton and the Dallas Police Departments. On two occasions I rode with a Sergeant Lassiter. Nothing more exciting took place other than bringing a drunk driver into the Police Station and finally taking him to the Dallas County jail. My companion had been able to spot him as a drunk because he was driving too slowly on Interstate 35.

When I rode with the Dallas Police, my host for the evening was an able officer who was greeted by those who knew him as "Johnnie". He was determined to explain Dallas nightlife to a naïve minister. As soon as it became dark, he took me to several clubs in the downtown area of the city. One had a topless black dancer with unbelievably large breasts that she was able to move in rhythm to her dancing. Johnnie explained that such was legal under the current city code because she wore a Band-Aid on each tit. We did not linger long there since this was not the dancer he wanted to show to me. We were cruising several blocks away from the club area when he brought the patrol car to a stop.

"There she is. That's the one I wanted you to see in motion."

He pulled us beside a young lady of much more slender proportions than any of the dancers we had seen.

He asked, "What are you doing in this neighborhood?"

"I am just meeting a friend", she replied with a coy smile.

"I bet you are", replied the officer.

At that point he received an officer assist call that had to be answered immediately. We left the scene but Johnnie later told me I had met the highest priced prostitute in Dallas. After that brief encounter, all else proved to be quite routine.

One of the issues that confronted many Protestant congregations during these turbulent years was whether or not a particular church would welcome persons of color to Sunday morning worship. Shortly before my arrival at Covenant this issue had been discussed at a meeting of the Session. Lynn Lawther, who had played a significant role in our decision to move north, had declared he would be honored to have any Black person worship beside his family. Other elders made similar declarations and the ushers were instructed to act accordingly. This was the year in which Martin Luther King, Jr. made his magnificent "I Have a Dream" speech. Shortly after this I had an opportunity to hear Dr. King in person when he spoke before the Dallas Minister's Association. He predicted his own martyrdom. This was a deeply moving experience, one that I shall always remember.

Children are a wonderful way to keep a pastor from taking life too seriously. One such event occurred while Robin was still pre-school age. We were rushing to get to the church when the phone rang. Neither Karin nor I answered it. Robin did. He announced clearly: "Nobody is home".  When we reached the church, the Deacon in charge of finances was chuckling. He had made the call and readily accepted our explanation. Fortunately this was not the Presbytery Executive calling to see how the recently arrived pastor was doing.

*Seventeen*

# A Cross Hanging On A G-String
## *1965*

Other than Sunday night youth meetings at the manse for our first year or two, most of the activities that had been successful in San Antonio did not work at Covenant. There was little interest in my version of Scottish history or my knowledge of the ecumenical movement. Weekly covered dish suppers were out of the question. One activity that did succeed was that of involving as many persons as possible in outreach visitation. Using a program that was endorsed by the national denomination, I organized an Andrew Club. This was an activity that used trained visitors to seek out families without a church home in the area. This continued throughout my ministry. Not only did this aid the congregation in numerical growth, but it also demonstrated this was a church, which was anxious to receive other persons into its fellowship.

Our trip to New York and the World Fair was only possible because my mother, Lilian, helped finance the event. Vacations of less expensive nature would be necessary in the years to come. We bought a forty-five dollar tent. The first night out, we set up in a campground in East Texas where the heat made sleeping almost impossible. The next night we found a campsite in the hills of western Arkansas that proved to be ideal. The nights were pleasantly cool and there was a beautiful body of water nearby called Shady Lake.

The first morning in our new campsite, the children explored the nearby shoreline. Robin came back with a water line mark across the middle of his T-shirt. Karin admonished him for going into the lake. "How did you know?" he asked. Once he dried out and promised to take reasonable care beside potentially dangerous water, all four Ramsays thoroughly enjoyed their days at the isolated site. Although we had planned to explore other campgrounds, we remained in the shade of Shady Lake for most of our remaining vacation days.

The next summer we added to our camping equipment by purchasing a large tarp, which could be set up on aluminum poles, near the tent entrance. On our first night in a Colorado campground, we carefully staked out our canvass assemblage. Karin got up early to cook breakfast using our small butane stove. Suddenly a wind gust came down from nearby heights. Karin, stove and breakfast were doused with a huge sheet of water from rain that had collected in the tarp during the night. We quickly broke camp and ate our morning meal in a nearby café. Although we soon learned where to set up and not set up our canvass, we decided to improve our gear beyond that of a forty-five dollar tent and a ten-dollar tarp.

The next year we purchased a used tent trailer. This was a unique device that opened in accordion fashion to provide a large sleeping area above a carpeted floor. The Presbytery Executive, Jeff Garrison, had raised his children with this trailer by towing the device each summer to the Presbyterian conference center in the Smokey Mountains of North Carolina. Since our improved camping equipment knew the way to Montreat, we hooked it to the bumper of our station wagon and made the long journey east. Once set up in the conference's campgrounds, Robin's gregarious nature led him to visit our camping neighbors. Having lived in Dallas, *The Bible Belt*, where even at his young age of five he was aware Presbyterians were not in the majority, he was amazed to discover that all in the campground were Presbyterians and most of the youths were Preacher's Kids.

On other excursions we went to New Mexico and Colorado. We finally purchased a pop-up camper with sleeping quarters on each end, a table, butane stove and an icebox in the middle. Our equipment eventually included a freestanding curtained shower bath with an overhead water tank that could be heated by sun light during the day. This device provided four pleasant showers before bedtime. For several summers we visited a wide variety of campsites making use of our upgraded equipment.

During her early years of elementary school, Annetta surprised her parents by performing a hula dance for the Janie Stark elementary school PTA. When we asked where she learned to hula, she replied she learned from a book. When we asked the teacher why she performed solo, the teacher replied that Annetta made the others look like amateurs. We were able to afford ballet lessons for her that later led to a membership in the Dallas Civic Ballet Company under a nationally known director, George Skabine. She remained with this organization until she realized that continuing a career in dance required absolute dedication to a single art form. She took a permanent leave of absence from the company when she reached high school. She learned to play her flute and expressed her artistic ambitions as a member of the R. L. Turner marching band and also sang as a member of the R.L. Turner Choir. Of course, I was proud March 26, 1967 when she was a member of my communicant's class and officially became a member of the church.

Robin became a member of the Texas Boys Choir headquartered in Fort Worth. For several years, Karin drove Robin to the Choir rehearsals five or six times a week. Anneta's rehearsals were in the opposite direction from Fort Worth. I took her to her dance lessons on weekdays. I found I could often make a hospital visit or two while Annetta danced. When we had no Covenant members who were hospitalized in near down town medical facilities, I could take sermon preparation materials with me and make much more progress toward next Sunday's message than I could in my office where the telephone rang constantly. Annetta was on stage for several premier ballet performances. On one occasion she danced with internationally known Dame Margo Fontane at SMU's McFarland auditorium.

Robin's boy choir concerts were usually in Fort Worth. Summer rehearsals were held in New Mexico. Three Ramsays spent two summer vacations camped in the rugged mountains nearby while Robin was in summer camp with the Boy Choir. On one occasion we saw and heard Robin and his fellow choir members on the stage of the Santa Fe Opera. That winter the choir traveled to New York where they made a nationally televised Christmas program.

Karin made use of her time during Robin's rehearsals by making good friends in Fort Worth. One friend was the Monsignor of Holy Family Catholic Church. Robin was asked to sing in the Church choir. He received a modest stipend for this activity although other choir members who were Catholic received no payment for their services. The Monsignor was fascinated with the fact the son of a Presbyterian Minister was singing for his church and a minister's wife was a regular visitor to his parking lot. He asked Karin to help him redesign a basement area where the youth of the congregation met. Karin used her creative talents and successfully changed an unattractive basement area into a warm and useful room.

Occasionally I was able to go with Karin and sit in on a rehearsal. On a Saturday before Easter, I was among the parents who were present during the choir's preparations for the following day. I was the lone male present. A woman came out of the area behind the altar and asked me to help tighten the spigot on the baptismal urn so there would be no chance of a leak. I did the best I could. I heard later that the woman was surprised to learn she had selected a Presbyterian pastor to secure the water blessed by the Monsignor. Apparently, my tightening job held. If it had failed, ecumenism might have been set back for years.

One other program in San Antonio did succeed at Covenant: this was the challenge to build. For four years, two services of worship and two sessions of Sunday School were necessary. In 1962, when the plans for a six-sided sanctuary instead of the traditional oblong building were presented, there was skepticism. Karin and I hosted gatherings at the manse on ten consecutive Sunday afternoons where people were able to dream about whatever they wanted in the way of buildings for Covenant and the concept of a six-sided sanctuary soon took hold. The congregation approved a plan that would exceed all budgetary expectations. Most churches at the time were using professional fund-raisers for building. Crestholme had done so, but the Covenant committee refused to consider outside assistance. I pulled up all of my files from the building program of my previous pastorate. I sold the committee on a proposal that followed the San Antonio plan in every detail. The fund raising was a success and Covenant was on its way to the construction of a unique place of worship. Ground was broken October 3, 1965 and the foundation was poured.

New families were moving into the area. Both the Church Session and the Board of Deacons were enlarged each year. Bob Poteet, who had worked with me in the San Antonio church, had become a student at Austin Presbyterian Seminary. He spent the second summer of his theological education at Covenant. The new church sanctuary was under construction. When the building was finished in June of 1966, one of the early major events was that of the ordination and installation of Bob Poteet as Associate Pastor of the church.

Bob immediately added enthusiasm to all we were doing. In July the congregation gave a carnival for the migrants in Princeton. We had hot dogs, hamburgers, cold drinks, dunking booths, prize booths, pony rides and clowns with tickets we sold for five cents so that the migrants could roam around and *buy* whatever they wanted and win all sorts of things. We allowed them to purchase for five cents something worth at least fifty cents or more value. Many purchased burgers and took them to their home to eat in privacy.

All summer, people were painting and cleaning the building and grounds for the formal opening in September. On the Saturday before the September grand opening service was to be held in the new sanctuary, Karin and I, along with Bob and several church members made preparations for the big event. All shared a concern that there was no religious symbolism other than the attractive slab-glass windows on each side of the building. The church hall had been adequate as a site for worship because a large wooden cross was attached to the wall above the choir and pulpit area. Since the steeple had been moved from the roof of the hall to the top of the new sanctuary, those present decided that the cross inside the hall should be relocated in an appropriate place in the new structure. Removing the cross from the church hall was easy enough, but it required a bit of ingenuity to hang it properly in the new place of worship. Large eyelets were purchased and securely screwed into the cross and the inside of the roof. Piano wire could support the weight of the cross. Karin sent someone out to get the necessary wire. She was asked what kind should be bought.

"G-string is the strongest piano wire", she replied.

Once the symbolic object had been securely hung, there was another problem: the cross was exactly the same color as the sanctuary ceiling. This made it almost invisible. Karin once again came up with a solution: paint the inside beveled portion of the cross jet-black. No one wanted to take the cross down since it was already safely in place so Karin, who was desperately afraid of heights, bravely mounted a tall stepladder and did the job. Still another difficulty remained. Since the Church Session had granted no official permission for such a change, something had to be done to cover the metal studs angrily sticking out of the wall of the former place of worship. I was able to solve this one.

I found two pieces of edging left over from carpeting the sanctuary floor. These I set over the studs forming an impromptu cross. I decided I would apologize and replace my cross, made of edging, with something else if anyone complained. To the best of my knowledge the edging is still there, though it once formed a foundation designed by the young people years later when they were planning a special musical production for the hall, a Celtic cross made of broken pieces of mirror.

In 1967 a homemade ice cream social was planned for a late summer evening, an event that would be held in the Church Hall. A large banner was prepared to advertise the occasion with these words: "Operation Scoop". One of the more active couples in the church, Jim and Vivian Cozby, invited the Ramsays to go out to dinner with them at their favorite fish restaurant, *Duck Inn* located what seemed miles away from Covenant. Before we accepted the supper date for the night of the social, we made the Cozbys promise to get us back to the church well before the hour the homemade ice cream would be served.

The fish dinner took much longer than I had expected. Jim and Vivian seemed full of reasons for delaying our trip to the church. At last the Cozbys and the Ramsays arrived at the church hall where a large crowd had already assembled. A single letter had been changed in the advertising banner. When we were ushered into the hall, the banner read "Operation Snoop". Associate Pastor Poteet announced the pastor and his family would have to wait for their ice cream while they heard of the results of a special investigation. For the next hour or so, persons from Jack and Karin's past appeared and presented their part on the program, *This Is Your Life, Jack and Karin.* Since all said only complementary things about us, we found the "snooping" a thoroughly enjoyable operation. After all had eaten homemade ice cream, we were presented with a gold-plated ice cream scoop. Our gold scoop is mounted in a display box that has become one of our treasured trophies, an indication that the congregation of the north Dallas Area church had finally accepted us.

# Angel Kisses And My Beating Heart

## Eighteen

## He Lay Limp On The Floor

### 1968

Covenant continued to grow. As the turbulent years of the 1960s neared an end, the congregation had more than doubled in numerical size. In spite of all efforts to maintain a clean roll, the church continued to report communicant membership in excess of 450. I felt the local church had grown in an even more important dimension. The congregation had become a viable body of faith. As pastor and congregation we had met the challenge of a necessary building program and survived several minor crises.

We continued to run a full schedule of activities showing concern for the world about us. However, I noticed that somehow our congregation had ceased singing with joy. *Operation Crisis Stop*, a Sunday night program with a thirty-minute time of hymn singing followed by speakers chosen by a youth-adult council and programs given by the youths themselves, was designed to fill this gap. Attendance surprised all.

At the beginning of each New Year, a church officer's retreat was held at the Presbytery Conference Center near Argyle, Texas. All elders and deacons including both incoming and those who had completed their term of office were invited. This event provided time for reflection. There the work of the church was reviewed. Goals were set and objectives were outlined. These gatherings gave unity to the life and work of the congregation as a whole.

Always we found youth work rewarding. We enjoyed the 1968 Haunted House party in which sixty adults took part in the haunting and nearly 130 youths attended. Perhaps the success of those parties instigated the commercial Haunted Houses of today and left church youth work to take new directions.

One advantage of the Presbyterian Church is the fact we are a connectional church, sharing conferences as well as Presbytery and Synod meetings to mutually encourage each other. In 1968 I graduated from two years as Bible Teacher at the Mo-Ranch Women's Conference to Director for the two events held at Mo-Ranch for Presbyterian Women: a week-end event and a week-long conference. It was a refreshing duty and I was delighted to be asked to serve more than once as Director for such capable women.

Karin and I were aware that we had our critics. Karin was sometimes criticized for either doing too much or too little, largely by persons who did not want to confront the minister himself. When criticisms did reach her, she simply responded with the observation that the minister's wife was expected to do only what no one else in the congregation wanted to do or she was supposed to sing alto in the choir. She was not an alto and she had serious doubts about her ability as a soprano.

One person did spend an entire morning telling me of my areas of incompetence. This was an individual who had been involved in the turf wars of the early 1960s. She asked me to sit on a front row in the new sanctuary, a sanctuary that was a little too cool for my comfort, where she spent four-and-a-half-hours describing my failings. Since most of these criticisms were in the area of my lack of administrative skills, I simply agreed with most of what she had to say. This left my confronter a bit frustrated. I tried not to argue, believing though not saying to her out loud that I was called as pastor to my people and expositor of the Word of God, rather than executive secretary of a social club.

After this confrontation I sought, more than ever before, the help of elders who were experienced administrators. By this time the Session included several persons who excelled in executive acumen. One who was particularly helpful was Newman Smith, longtime Superintendent of the Carrollton-Farmers Branch Independent School District. His wife, Pauline, was a stalwart advisor. Eventually she became one of the first women to become an elder of the congregation. Dr. Percy Pentecost, an Assistant School Superintendent under Newman Smith was one of those I sometimes consulted. There were others among the elected officers who were willing to work with the pastor in designing organizational procedures. Larry Herriot, a specialist in efficiency administration gave me free advice. He was a paid consultant for commercial and governmental reorganization programs. When the Session committee structure needed an overhaul, he helped me redesign the church's organizational chart.

One of Larry's practical comments was, "Just remember, it is easier to apologize than to ask permission".

Karin was concerned over the lack of prayer in much of the church's decision-making. She suggested that I invite Covenant's officers to a prayer breakfast. I did this by having most of the elected leadership of the church meet in the back room of a Carrollton restaurant. The group decided to approve a prayer session for anyone willing to pray each week before Church School and Sunday worship. For the remaining years of my ministry at Covenant, half dozen or more persons ate breakfast together at a local restaurant and then prayed for any causes or special needs known to the pastor or to any person present. I will never know how much these prayers may have meant to the many persons for whom we prayed. I can only affirm that I often felt uniquely sustained by a Power beyond myself as I attempted to prepare for the awesome and frightening task of proclaiming eternal truth.

One major problem was the heavy indebtedness caused by the building of a sanctuary. This left little budgetary support for program. Bob Poteet continued to bring energy and strength to a wide variety of activities. Katherine Tait who had been church secretary since early in my ministry once told Bob that he had changed the tempo at Covenant. Before his coming, the office clock did no more than calmly say "tick, tock, tick, tock." Once he became Associate Pastor, the clock sounded more like "tickety-tick-tickety-tick-tickety-tick". She emphasized the clock sound by moving her finger slowly at first and then rapidly in order to describe the vigor of the energetic young minister. He remained with the church as long as possible. When a larger church in Dallas with a stronger program budget, invited him to join their staff, Bob accepted their call.

Although the large sanctuary created a budgetary problem, the new facility deeply enriched the Sunday morning worship experience. There were other benefits that the building provided. For the first time in the life of the congregation, there was an adequate site for celebrating the rite of marriage. There had been few requests for weddings in the bleakness of a church hall. Once again Karin and I found ourselves back in the marriage business. Small and intimate ceremonies could take place in front of the table of communion. Yet the worship area provided space for an event that might draw a crowd of several hundred guests.

I remember one wedding in which the groom was a guitarist. He wanted to sing of his love to his bride. Karin figured out the logistics. One of the attendants held the guitar until the groom needed the instrument. He then sang to the young woman looking into her loving face. There were few tearless eyes among the assembled guests.

On another occasion the groom fainted. This was the second wedding for the couple. After a year or two of marriage, they had divorced. Several years of separation convinced them they could not live without each other. When they came to me with

## He Lay Limp On The Floor 153

their request for re-marriage, I asked why they thought they could make it on a second try.

"We bought a porch swing", they replied.

I had to ask what that had to do with the whole process?

They gave me an answer that made sense: "We have agreed to sit in that swing touching each other when we have a disagreement. We will stay there until we work it out."

I agreed to marry them once more. Halfway through the ceremony, the knees of the groom buckled. He leaned toward his bride and then, like ice cream melting down a cone, he lay limp on the floor. I helped him get up to a nearby pew. Karin came to our assistance and asked if the fainted groom needed some water.

He answered weakly, "No, but I would like a coke."

This was unexpected, but Karin realized the church had a new coke machine in the fellowship hall so she grabbed her purse, found enough quarters for two cokes, one for the groom who had fainted and one for the bride. The grateful bride and groom shared their cokes as the bottles were quickly passed down the row each way and then back to the bride and groom who finished them off. When the groom indicated he could make it through the ceremony he then took his place beside his second time bride, Karin took the empty bottles, and I hastily finished the ceremony. Some who knew me said they did not realize I could read with such speed.

Stewardship was the major challenge for Covenant. Karin suggested to me a unique approach to the problem. Rather than begging for funds based on financial need each year, she suggested that the committee propose and present to the congregation a budget based on goals of the church and that the congregation be challenged to give in faith, trusting God to provide. Pledge cards would no longer ask for an exact monetary amount. Instead, members would merely sign a card indicating that they intended to give as the Lord blessed them personally. Officers and congregation would adopt what they believed was a realistic goal, with no padding, to meet the cost of what the church felt they as people of faith needed to accomplish the goals to which God was calling them. The Session approved her proposal.

For years at stewardship season, a *Palestinian Supper* had been served in the hall that had been named *Rand Hall* in honor of the congregation's organizing pastor, Joe Rand. The menu consisted of food available when Jesus walked the pathways of Galilee and Judea. There were two sessions and all were invited to make a reservation in advance. On most years the hall was full to capacity for both sessions. Participants entered in silence. The main dish as described in *The Biblical Cookbook* was a large bowl of what came to be known as *Palestinian Stew*. This carefully seasoned stew had to be prepared in large caldrons and had to be cooked all night. Members of the congregation worked all day assembling ingredients and then took turns in stirring the heavy cooking vessels during the evening and night before the stew was to be served. At the conclusion of the supper, all were invited to make a spiritual commitment of life and possessions by signing a pledge card for the year ahead. Originally this included a dollar amount indicating what they planned to give to the work of the Church. Officers would then adjust the upcoming budget to fit the dollar amount as pledged.

Once the Session adopted Karin's suggestion for a *Faith Budget*, the name for the centerpiece of the stewardship program, *Palestinian Supper,* was dropped. Though we continued the supper for a while, there was no longer a need to dramatize the element of the spiritual since a pledge based on a realization of God's blessings was highly personal, a *faith budget*. This approach, which made no promise of an amount to be given, resulted in a real case of jitters for the budget planners. They had always based their financial requests on the sum total of the dollars that had been pledged. The *Faith Budget* concept changed this, forcing officers to concentrate less on a dollar amount, which seldom matched the amount pledged and concentrate instead on planning to spend what was necessary to accomplish what a faithful church should be doing, trusting God's promises to lead. This worked in spite of all the fears the proposal engendered.

Finances ceased to be a problem at Covenant once there was no longer an artificial limit to individual giving or an unnecessary cap on the church budget.

Children of the Manse were growing up. Robin had joined the church April 3, 1969 when he was 11. July 1970 saw Annetta, Karin and Jack traveling to New Mexico to meet Robin where he was finishing a month of singing with the Texas Boys Choir and Santa Fe Opera. The three of us found a lovely campsite sixteen miles from Las Vegas, NM where the choir was training and camped there for a week. Then on to Santa Fe and another site in the Black Canyon where we camped until Robin joined us. In Santa Fe, after Robin was again part of the family, our car was ransacked. Three dollars and Karin's watch was taken. Fortunately the robber was caught, partly because Robin helped identify him, but the watch and money were never found. Robin enjoyed being the only Ramsay witness the police called. We later learned our robber was wanted for more than robbery, he was wanted for murder. Robin identified him first from a mug shot picked out of the police book, then from one-way glass in a police line-up!

For five weeks in 1970 I was bedridden with a serious illness, Hepatitis. During the months that followed, my activities were drastically restricted. For the first time we cancelled the Christmas Open House at the manse. During this time able elders led the worship services and preached. Church members assisted with pastoral responsibilities. Women of the Church organized a taxi service to take the Ramsay kids when Karin had extra nursing duties. Christmas and Advent activities, choirs, and youth groups went forward as usual, officers seeing that no activity was dropped from the schedule. Gifts were collected for the 1700 Denton State School residents and food provided for West Dallas. I don't think I ever was able to thank the congregation sufficiently for all they did during my illness.

August 31, 1971 (our wedding anniversary) I entered the hospital for tests after continuous infections and hepatitis suffered in the fall of 1970. Miraculously, the tests showed no permanent damage and mainly the doctors prescribed exercise every day.

Karin organized a garage sale and earned enough money to purchase our second bicycle-for-two, hoping to push me into getting exercise and so the four of us might ride as a family. Her scheme worked, for I became an avid rider, sometimes, on my day off, riding as much as 50 miles a day. After the speedometer on my original bicycle turned 9,999.0 miles, she bought me a fancier bicycle and found other things to do while I enjoyed my exercise. I took the speedometer off my bicycle so it would not flip from 9999 to 0000 and hung it on the wall of my office.

In 1972 an exciting event occurred: a trip to witness the Apollo 17 blast-off. Covenant members, Dr. Jack Maxfield, a noted cancer specialist, and his wife Sugie, arranged for Karin and I to be a part of a group that flew to Cape Canaveral. We boarded one of the planes chartered by the Maxfields at Love Field. Once at the Cape, we sat in the VIP section next to the massive building in which space vehicles had been built. We witnessed and felt the tremendous power of lift-off. The next day we were given a tour of the area. Our guide told us that we were allowed to enter portions of the project that few other persons were permitted to see because we were guests of the Maxfields who had been part of every space mission, Dr. Maxfield and his brother available as consultants for the possibilities of cancer developing for those traveling in space. Not only were our hosts associates of astronauts and space officials, they also were in contact with some of the leading scientists of the century including Werner Von Braun and Edward Teller. I do not remember speaking with either of these men, but both were a part of the entourage. One of them helped the Maxfield's daughter with her math assignment during the flight from Dallas to Florida. On the return trip I sat next to the Senior Captain of the Texas Rangers. He was a person of genuine spirituality and profound religious belief. Later Suggie gave me a paper written by Von Braun on the subject of "Immortality". This was a personal statement of deep and abiding faith.

*Nineteen*

## Sparkling Rays Across The Water
*1972*

Sometime, I don't remember where, when or to whom I mentioned it, but I must have told someone that I dreamed of visiting the Holy Land. The congregation must have been listening, for they held an ice cream social after I recovered from Hepatitis and announced they were giving us a trip to the Holy Land, enough money for all four Ramsays to make the journey of a lifetime.

We left Love Field on Christmas day of 1972, flew to Cyprus where we boarded a ship which then became our floating hotel. Each day bus tours took us into Turkey, Lebanon or Israel. In Galilee we took a boat ride on the sea where Jesus and his disciples had once sailed. The day was calm and beautiful. The sky above was blue. The hills of Golan Heights rose above the mirrored surface of the lake in purple splendor. Once out in the waters of Galilee, the leader of the tour group requested that the ship's motor be silenced. For a brief time, the vessel seemed suspended in space. He then read from an appropriate passage of Scripture. He allowed sufficient time for silence, an experience the Ramsays would never forget.

We later toured the Jerusalem area, saw shepherds in the field near Bethlehem, visited the site where Jesus was believed to have prayed shortly before his arrest. On the final day in Israel, the guide took us to the Garden Tomb where again there was time for meditation and prayer. One mishap occurred on the return flight after we arrived in the Bangor, Main and were preparing to exit our plane for customs inspection: a service vehicle, with the ladder already fully-extended for our exit, struck the wing of our charter DC-8. We still visualize the pilot's animated body language as he inspected the ladder welded to that wing! This made it necessary for the entire tour group to spend the night in a partly heated hanger while we waited for a replacement aircraft to be flown from London. Yet this was a perfect trip, one that could not have taken place a few years earlier or at any later time without a serious potential of danger.

Once back home, I made my report to the church by showing the color slides I had taken during the journey. On four Sunday nights Karin, Annetta and Robin helped fill in details of the trip while I managed the slide show, the only times Sunday night services were truly successful at Covenant.

A major problem arose during this period. A young adult came to me and declared she was going to see to it that Covenant would leave the Presbyterian Church. She had joined the congregation after being raised in the Northwest Bible Church, a faith community that had come together in North Dallas among persons who had left Presbyterian churches over the issue of Dispensationalism. Although this was a Biblical interpretation that had been rejected by the General Assembly of the Presbyterian Church in the U. S., this concept had regained popularity in the Dallas area. Those who promoted this belief claimed they would be *raptured* out of human existence leaving all of the rest of us in a devilish hell.

My confronter told me she had already set up plans for a home Bible study group to which she was inviting all members of Covenant. Karin and I decided we had best be on hand for this particular study, the two of us qualifying as members of Covenant. Ten or twelve people showed up for the event that was scheduled to continue meeting each Tuesday.

Karin and I gave a more reasonable interpretation to the Scriptures than that provided by the Dispensationalists. After six sessions, the group agreed to disband. All who had participated seemed satisfied except for the original organizer. When I learned she had invited a Dallas Seminary student to meet in her home each Tuesday to correct my theology, I asked the Session to establish a Bible Study at the church which would be led by the pastor on Tuesday nights. The Ramsays canceled a vacation we had planned. I sought to answer the questions that had been raised by the controversy. Well before the end of the summer all who attended my studies of Scripture agreed they were not ready to be *raptured*. A less radical interpretation of the Bible was sufficient for Covenant.

The church had a strong staff. Arthur Keywood, Sr., a recently retired professional bookkeeper, became business manager. His son Arthur Jr., was Youth Worker and Church Visitor. Both received very small stipends, but Arthur Sr., spent most of his waking hours planning and supervising church activities. During the Keywood era the church was well administered. I was able to devote more of my time to the all-important task of being a pastor.

Katherine Tait continued to serve as church secretary, a position she held for a total of twenty-two years of faithful and dedicated service. Troy Duval became Covenant's custodian, bringing far greater talents to this important task than any of the several persons or cleaning services that had preceded him. Marge Edwards joined the staff as the first Weekday Kindergarten director. She enlisted Karin's expertise in determining what such a program should include. Together they toured several successful pre-school programs and then asked the Session to approve the plan and establish a supervisory committee. Later, a day care program known as Mother's Day Out was added with Jean Bunteen as the original Coordinator. Covenant has always seemed way ahead of the trends in child and nursery care. I remember that when we first arrived we had two children of nursery age. At that time, 1960, George and Mozelle Mills were both working as teachers in the Nursery. We were impressed that a male was in the nursery, and even more impressed that a couple was working together in that age group. After the addition of a Weekday Kindergarten and Mother's Day Out were added as a service to families in the area, over two hundred children were in the building on most weekdays.

The needs of adults were not overlooked. For a time a square dance group met regularly in Rand Hall. Later a Scottish dance organization used the facilities that the church provided. Karin and I occasionally dropped in on that group. Although I was far from being an accomplished dancer, I could remember some of the simpler routines I had learned when I was an Assistant Minister at Richmond-Craigmillar in Scotland. When it became known that Karin and I were moving on to new challenges, the leader of Covenant's Scottish dance group wrote and her group performed a special dance program that honored Karin and me. She had her group perform the dance and then presented us with a plaque commemorating our Scottish heritage. We still display the unique Scottish gift in the entrance to our home.

Covenant became a part of the Mariners, a national Presbyterian program that provided fellowship for couples. Members met in homes. An airline pilot had become familiar with the program while living in California. When he explained the purpose of Mariners to a group of interested adults, he was elected Admiral of the fleet. This gave him the authority to organize seven home groups known as "ships". During his years as leader of the program, he continually recruited new "sailors" for what he described as "Seven Stalwart Ships Sailing Seven Salient Seas." The ships continued to sail for the remainder of my ministry at Covenant.

## Sparkling Rays Across The Water 161

Older adults were not neglected. Each Friday afternoon as soon as the children involved in Weekday Kindergarten and Mother's Day Out left the building, Rand Hall became full of senior adults. Informal social activities such as card games and the consumption of light refreshments became a well-attended community-wide activity.

Business Manager Keywood reviewed the varied range of programs and meetings with me on a regular basis. Suddenly I realized that a whole week was blank on my calendar. I was surprised when an elder told me he needed to make an important announcement before Sunday morning worship began. He invited everyone to a special meeting in Rand Hall to be held immediately after worship that morning but did not explain why. As Karin and I were on our way to Rand Hall, we were told we must wait to enter until the entire congregation could assemble. Upon our entry, we were presented with a money tree that contained more than enough to send us to New Orleans the very next day for the blank week on my calendar. The event planners had learned from Karin's wedding book the exact number of the room we had occupied in our honeymoon hotel and had reserved that very room weeks earlier. This investigative feat had been accomplished with the help of Annetta and Robin. Most unexpectedly, we hastily packed and left the next day for New Orleans.

I promised we would do everything we had done on our first honeymoon. I purchased a corsage of six pink roses in the hotel flower shop where I had bought similar corsage years earlier. Karin wore the roses to Brennan's that evening. The headwaiter asked what was the occasion for such beautiful flowers on a lovely lady? When we admitted we had been there exactly twenty-five years earlier, the whole staff helped us celebrate with special deserts and champagne. Later that evening we walked hand-in-hand along the banks of the great river as the moon broke through the clouds and sent sparkling rays across the water.

Early in the Covenant years Karin had been active in organizing a program for young people, starting with meetings at the manse. As more and more people became interested in the education program, and as Annetta and Robin became old enough for youth programs, Karin stepped back and allowed others to take the lead. However, in the early 70s, across the nation, less and less people wanted to work with young people. In Covenant the youth group dwindled to only a few, five to be exact. Karin didn't mind.

She said, "I think I can design a program capitalizing on the reality that a group of five will fit in my car."

She began a study of what people believe, studying the Bible, various creeds and interpretations of the Bible, and seeking leadership from other faiths who were open to sharing with those who wanted to learn and understand faith in God. The group followed up each section of study by visiting people of that faith: Jewish, Orthodox, and Charismatic.

For years Karin led the way in practical projects, especially youth projects that demonstrated the importance of Biblical teaching. The migrant project, which had resulted in Princeton closing the migrant camp, had started with the young people who met at the manse. Actually, it was one of the young people who convinced the congregation of Covenant to build a sanctuary, pleading that she wanted to worship in a sanctuary rather than a fellowship hall. In the 1970s, young people seemed to be suffering from images painted of young people, images that had been created because of previous generations of teens, teens that had rebelled during the years of race riots, Vietnam and unrest on college campuses. Few people across the nation really wanted to work with young people. Karin felt young people simply needed to regain self-confidence. She organized a summer of travel for the group beginning with a retreat to a home in Shreveport owned by C.D. and Mary Kelly. The purpose was group-building and for the group to plan what they wanted to do that summer. The Kellys had been one of the families that followed us to Covenant from Crestholme to the Carrollton-Farmers Branch area. C. D. had served as Church School Superintendent at Covenant and

## Sparkling Rays Across The Water

was also an active member of the Andrew Club. Though they no longer lived in the area, they were still available to help when Covenant needed something.

Karin's success with youths resulted in a jealous response from some that had not participated in the Migrant Project. One individual contended that only a specially trained person should oversee youth activities. He questioned her unique approach. Her critic was unaware of Karin's background, believing she should be no more than a very submissive wife. Karin heard of the criticism and asked the Session to grant her time on the governing body's agenda. She remained out in the hall until her scheduled time when she was ushered into the meeting. There she related the extensive training she had received in Christian Education at Trinity University. She then eloquently described her vision for working with youth. She asked the Session to grant her the opportunity to continue to serve as Youth Coordinator. The vote was unanimous and never again were Karin's qualifications questioned.

*Twenty*

## God's Spell At Covenant

*1972*

Covenant Presbyterian Church discovered a new activity during 1972: sleeping in church! *Explo 1972*, a Campus Crusade Event, brought 100,000 youths to Dallas and Covenant responded to the unusal need for housing by offering our classrooms and fellowship hall to house and feed 50 of the 100,000 youths in town for the event.

As a follow-up to *Explo 1972*, a youth group in West Texas Midland was invited to visit Covenant and then the Midland Church hosted our suburban group. A trip to Six Flags in exchange for playtime in the Sand Dunes; discussion between the two groups who each thought their world different from the other; time for discussion and shared worship. Our group found a service held in the Sand Hills of West Texas especially meaningful.

The next journey was a four-vehicle caravan to the Texas border where the Covenanters repainted a church building in

Nuevo Laredo, sleeping on the floor in vacant apartment housing in Laredo. In spite of the best intentions of the painters, Covenant's youths ran afoul of the South of the Border police when freshly painted church pews were placed on the sidewalk to dry. Local merchants objected, fearing access to their businesses would be impeded. For a time the group wondered if they would be hauled off to a Mexican jail. The local pastor finally explained the importance of the help he and his people of Mexico were receiving from the "Norté Americano gringo" workers. Once the project was understood on both sides of the language barrier, the objecting merchants helped in returning the freshly dried pews to the proper place. After a hard day's work on the church building, the youths toured the market before re-crossing the international border. One of the youths innocently purchased a pocketknife. The U. S. Border Patrol confiscated this item since bringing any weapon into the United States was a violation of U.S. law. That evening Karin led the group in a serious discussion of the issues their experiences had raised: international relations, cultural differences, police and the law, the language barrier and the necessity of understanding and respecting the culture of persons of another race.

The next day, Sunday, the Covenant youths returned to Mexico and worshiped with the congregation in the newly painted sanctuary. Their fellow Presbyterians appreciated their efforts and warmly received them.

The caravan made one more stop before heading home: an overnight visit to the Presbyterian Pan American School in Kingsville. Though the Covenant young people were hoping to learn a few words in Spanish, students from Mexico attending Pan American School were on a crash course to learn English for use in Christian service in both Mexico and the United States and were not allowed to speak Spanish. Eating a meal at tables with them and playing volleyball were unique experiences. It was possible to play and laugh without speaking absolutely perfect English.

At the end of the summer, a musical theater report was

presented to the congregation. The youths wrote words describing their travels for the songs they sang. Vicki Tucker, an able pianist, joined the church staff as Youth Choir Director. She directed the music for the presentation that was called *Cov-e-nant*, music adapted from the musical *Camelot,* words written by the young people. The minister and his wife played a bedroom scene in which Karin dreamed up the summer youth program. Rand Hall was packed that evening when word got out that a bedroom scene would be included in the production.

The success of the summer and the end-of-the-summer show called for an encore. Karin heard some of the songs from the off-Broadway musical *Godspell* and realized that the original script for the show was taken directly from the Gospel of Matthew, "a perfect way to present the scripture to a youth group"! She consulted Vicki, asked if Vicki could buy the music and determine if it was possible for use with our group. Karin then wrote Nan Pearlman who owned the copyright on the music and asked how much of the music she could use and what the cost would be. Nan Pearlman granted permission for the group to sing four songs with no movement for a fee of twenty-five dollars per performance. Karin developed a shortened reading of the scriptures from Matthew and Vicki taught four songs to the young people and Barbara Jordan played the piano for the *Youth Choir*. At the end of the summer the group took their first Greyhound charter bus trip to New Orleans, staying in the guesthouse of a Presbyterian Church on Canal Street and working on their new music, which they planned to present twice, first for the Chinese-speaking church in New Orleans and for their end of the summer program at Covenant.

At the end of the summer Karin and Vicki put their heads together, realizing there was much more they could do with *Godspell*. Though *Godspell* was new and very controversial in some conservative circles, it seemed to have exciting possibilities for Karin who saw possibilities for really practical Bible study, for Vicki and Barbara who loved the music, and for the young people who thought the modern musical belonged to their generation.

At first the Covenant youths had been granted permission to sing only four songs with no movement. Karin was intrigued by a story, which was circulating that the music for *Godspell* had been originally written as a master's thesis, and, when the deadline for submitting it to the masters program approached, there were no words. In desperation, or as Karin says, in a moment of inspiration, the Book of Matthew fit the music. Karin checked it out, word by word, and she vows, there is only one short line added to the Book of Matthew as recorded in the Bible. All the accounts of Matthew follow in exact sequence: an educator's dream teaching tool! She then discovered she could use the Gospel of Matthew as a script, directing three of the youths in reading from the New Testament as other youths acted out and sang their roles on stage. Young people not interested in being on stage were organized into a Sound Crew and a Wardrobe/Stage Crew. Robin played the lead. He was the only member of the cast who had undergone formal vocal instruction. Annetta played her flute and sang and danced in the chorus. Karin directed the show and I tried to lend as much moral support as possible.

When God's Spell at Covenant evolved into a two-and-a-half-hour production, Karin decided to pay the full royalty for each performance, giving her the right to all the songs and the script. She used the music, retaining her adapted script from Matthew for the three readers, a script that included a resurrection scene not in the copyright version. This was an expensive decision but one which was in keeping with the principles she had taught the youths. At first she employed musicians from Highland Park Church who did not seem to understand the Covenant approach. Vicki Tucker came in contact with professional musicians, two of who had been in the original *Godspell* production. They agreed to help for one performance. Invitations began to come from far and wide. A summer tour was in the making. The professionals could not go on tour, but they helped make a tape that could travel. This resulted in twenty-seven performances over a three-year period in Texas and eighteen other

# God's Spell At Covenant 169

states, twenty-seven performances to help a youth group memorize the Book of Matthew. Karin was delighted a year later when a minor disagreement among the group erupted on the bus and, almost instantly, the remaining group members, with one voice and no prompting, quieted the situation with lines from *Godspell*. Her goal of teaching the Bible was being achieved.

Originally, *Covenant's Godspell* was to be a one-time performance, for the congregation of Covenant. Nuns from a Catholic Church in Fort Worth were in attendance and were so impressed that they invited the group to come to Holy Family Catholic Church and give a performance in Fort Worth. From that performance came another invitation from Mary Walker, one of the Catholic members, an invitation to Klamath Falls, Oregon: a major tour far beyond any imagination.

Finances for *Godspell* were unique because the young people agreed that there would be no tickets sold and no fund raising for the performances or tours. The success of *Godspell* would depend on the efforts they put into practice and performances. They would travel only as far and as long as free will offerings taken by Stage Crew in buckets at the doors after performances took them, each young person contributing only $50 each summer, scholarships available.

Betty Runkel, a Covenant elder, was essential to *Godspell*. When the first multi-state tour was in the planning stage, Betty and Karin visited the Greyhound depot and carefully measured the baggage compartment on the bus that would be chartered. Hubert Laney, parent of one of the singers, built two-dozen heavy boxes that served as containers for all of the stage sets, lighting and wardrobe. The boxes were designed of various sizes to fit snugly into the bus baggage area. Upon arrival at a performance site, the cast was asked to stay on the bus until the Stage Crew had unloaded the boxes. The Cast then met to go over staging changes that would be made for that particular performance while the Stage Crew emptied and turned over the boxes to create a stage that would fit that hall or sanctuary. Each box was labeled with the name of a book of the Bible beginning with Matthew.

One very small box remained after the boxes were named. Hubert painted the name of his daughter *Holli* on it. Once Betty's Stage Crew learned the New Testament books in sequence, Matthew through Revelation plus *Holli,* they could unload and set up in less than an hour, a performance by the Stage Crew which always attracted an audience.

The first major tour began in the parking lot of the Covenant Presbytery Office that was then located in North Dallas. In their parking lot, thirty youths and three adults, Karin, Betty Runkel and I, loaded our personal gear on the chartered bus and formed a prayer circle before boarding. Our first performance was for a church in Denver, Colorado. The pastor was Billy Baine, my first year seminary roommate and Taft High School classmate. Betty's stage crew quickly set up and the cast performed like seasoned professionals. This first far from home performance was a resounding success due to the enthusiastic applause the Denver congregation gave Covenant's youths. Billy Baine who was still recovering from an illness, was seated on the front row. He led his people in a warm round of applause at every appropriate place in the evening's presentation.

The tour continued north into Wyoming, to Jackson Hole and Yellowstone Park. Although it was mid June, much of the area was still covered in snow. A spirited snowball fight on a slope in the national park resulted in the breakage of the bus driver's dark glasses. The youths immediately took up a collection of their own money that provided funds for replacing Dwight Dwight Fortier's eyewear and purchasing a backup pair.

Two performances were scheduled for the state of Oregon. The first was in a small ranching community where almost all of those who attended the evening show lived on ranches. Since they had been told a group of Texas youths would visit their area, most assumed their guests would be the sons and daughters of ranchers. There was some disappointment when local citizens learned that none of their visitors shared their ranching heritage. Yet there was no lack of appreciation for the performance that evening. Although the shape of the building made stage set up very difficult, Betty's crew managed to get all necessary equipment into an area in front of a beautiful stained glass window. This was one that portrayed Jesus praying in the Garden before his arrest. All were concerned about the extended daylight in the North Country. The resurrection scene worked best in total darkness. Stage lights could be suddenly turned on for the final scene. This had worked in the Casper, Wyoming show since the whole event was in a basement. But in Oregon there was no basement and the show began hours before sunset.

The first act went well but even though Karin extended the intermission a bit, the sun still rode high in the sky. Then the impossible happened. When the cast began the prayer scene in the garden, sunlight fell directly on the stained glass window. It lingered there until the scene was completed. Moments later the sun dimmed as a dark rain cloud drifted across it, darkening the sanctuary just in time to allow a dramatic ending to the presentation. The cast left the stage in complete silence, stunned by God's dramatic lighting effects. Although all the remaining shows were highly successful none could top that which took place in the ranch lands of central Oregon.

The next day the Godspellers moved on to Klamath Falls, where Mary Walker, the Catholic friend, had invited them for a performance in the state university student center. This well-attended show brought forth enthusiastic applause. This was the apex of the trip, the point at which the travelers were further from home than at any other portion of the tour. Karin had promised visits to known natural wonders. By this time the Colorado Rockies and the majestic mountains surrounding Jackson Hole had been viewed and Yellowstone toured. All looked forward to a visit of famed Crater Lake after completing their Oregon commitments. Karin realized there was a lot of territory yet to be covered. Something had to be eliminated in order to reach all performance sites on schedule without pushing the tour beyond the limits of physical and mental endurance. As leader of the tour she had to make a difficult decision. The side trip to Crater Lake had to be eliminated. Everyone including Jack complained.

Crater Lake was the one natural wonder my family had bypassed on our western tour thirty-seven years earlier. Nobody sat beside Karin on the bus that day on the trip to San Francisco. Dwight Fortier, the bus driver, was the only person who agreed with Karin. He knew he would run into much heavier traffic once he reached California.

When the group finally returned home, they learned that Karin's decision had been wise for a reason other than time and traffic considerations. Parents and friends had heard of an outbreak of a serious illness attributed to the drinking water at Crater Lake. This information, not known to anyone on the *Godspell* bus at the time, had been nationally broadcast and published in newspapers everywhere. The first question asked by parents when the group returned home was, "Did you drink any water at Crater Lake?" All of the parents gave a sigh of relief when they learned Karin had insisted they avoid the famed natural wonder.

The tour continued to San Francisco. After an outstanding performance arranged by faculty members of the San Francisco Presbyterian Seminary, the bus turned toward the east. The group traveled across Utah; performed in Durango, Colorado, Albuquerque, New Mexico and in the Theater in Amarillo, Texas on a set of a ship used the previous evening for a production of *HMS Pinafore*. It was only in Durango that they had a small crowd. The circus was in town and other events overshadowed the visit of the *Godspell* group. But even this turned out to be a unique success. A Minnesota family was present that evening. They were camping near the Colorado town. After Karin arrived home she received a letter from Jim Babcock's family saying, "Bring *Godspell* to Minneapolis the next year".

Jim Babcock had been one of the *Explo 1972* youths the Covenant group had entertained. He had stayed in touch with some of the Covenant members and had convinced his family to camp in Colorado so they could see *Covenant's Godspell*. When a check for five hundred dollars and a promise of more to come later from Minnesota and an official invitation from the Session of the Minneapolis Church was included in the letter from Minneapolis, Karin began to plan another major trip for the following summer.

Top row: Annetta Ramsay, Alycyn Lorenzen, Melody Mooty, Jeanie Pitchford, Burt Burton, Jennifer Hinkle, Sylvia Pitchford, Robin Ramsay.
Kneeling: Jack Stalder, Valerie Goering, David Blackney, Holli Laney.

"We Can Build A Beautiful City" – Covenant's Godspell
Annetta Ramsay, Robin Ramsay.

*Twenty-One*

# We Cried, We Laughed, We Prayed
## *1974*

Each time a tour became a possibility, Covenant members, proud of their youth group, submitted names of churches with which they had previously been associated as possibilities for lodging and/or performances. Some were parents of young people in the traveling group: Liz Hendricks a performance in a North Park Christian Church in Dallas; John and Orletta Goering, a performance for their Mennonite Church in Newton, Kansas; Dr. Clyde Larrabee, a performance in his mother's church in Durango, Colorado. Others merely wanted their home churches to know about the group: the Knutson family arranged housing in a Methodist Church in Sergeant Bluff, Idaho and Bob and Jane Ingebritsen, a performance in Albuquerque, New Mexico.

Jimmy Cozby, who had been part of Karin's five-member-fit-in-the-Ramsay-car traveling class, which explored various religions, was now the priest for a Greek Orthodox Church near

Clear Lake, Wisconsin. Generally, Orthodox priests are not permitted to marry unless they marry before they are ordained. Jimmy married Susan Ramsey, a member of the Covenant youth group before his ordination, and they became "Father" Dimetri and "Matushka" Susan and were happily serving a very active Orthodox Church in a lovely building in a picturesque setting of Wisconsin. They organized the whole area around Clear Lake and arranged for an interdenominational performance in a school auditorium. We slept in the Greek Orthodox Church and were treated to a Greek hospitality breakfast the next morning, a breakfast featuring dishes that were so delicious that even the young people were requesting recipes.

By the next spring, plans for the requested trip north were in place. This time they would tour the midwestern states. After their first performance in Kansas, interpersonal relations broke down. Karin called the group together and declared she would turn the bus around and go home unless those who were at odds with each other could work out their differences. They could not portray the life and mission of Jesus Christ without a spirit of love among themselves. Karin asked all to come to the sanctuary of the church in which they were staying. This was to be a time of silent prayer that finally produced words that sought forgiveness. Once forgiveness was both requested and received, the group could return to their bedrolls and look forward to continuing the journey. The next performance reflected a new understanding of the forgiveness the woman being stoned found. Once again both the cast and the audience experienced new depth in their understanding of *Covenant's Godspell*.

The apex of the northern tour was two performances in a Minneapolis church sanctuary for Jim Babcock and the group of youths Covenant fed and housed during *Explo 1972*. The final showing was a Sunday evening when *Godspell* replaced a traditional worship service. Several persons walked out in protest when the stage lights became bright red flashes, which dramatically accompanied the less than sanctified portion of the musical score preceding the "let the one who is without sin cast the first stone" scene when the adulterous woman was brought before Jesus for judgment. In spite of the objections of a handful of individuals, the vast majority of the audience remained and gave the players a thunderous applause at the conclusion of the scene.

That evening the entire group slept in bedrolls on a gymnasium floor. Karin and I had our sleeping pads in the middle with girls at one end and boys at the other. After the performance, the youths were in high spirits. I reminded them of a busy schedule ahead. I begged them to settle down and get as much sleep as possible. For a time after each of my requests, there were a few moments of silence. Then there was renewed conversation and giggling, beginning softly and escalating as the volume on an out-of-control radio. I hoped Karin would soon come to my rescue. She remained in the girl's locker room, taking her time until everyone else had left.

Suddenly she appeared and walked quietly to the middle of the floor. She spoke only one word: "Listen".

There was complete silence. I dove into my bedroll to avoid making any sound and used my pillow to smother the giggle I wanted to make. Absolute quiet reigned for the remainder of the night and no one arose before Karin did. All got the sleep they needed to continue the journey.

Bus driver Dwight Fortier was as much a member of the leadership team as anyone else. Karin had always made sure he was available for any bus trip outside the Dallas Metroplex. On the tour of the Midwest states, Dwight had difficulty securing lodging. Greyhound required that all charter drivers get eight hours of sleep in a proper bed, not a bedroll on a church hall floor. On several occasions Karin sent one of the older boys to assist Dwight in securing a place to sleep. Six-foot Clyde Larrabee would go to the Motel desk and ask for a room. When he was told to sign in, he would say, "This is for my friend Dwight." Usually the uniformed driver would be granted lodging without difficulty. On one occasion when the group spent the night in a Missouri town, Dwight had more of a problem than usual. Later the group discussed the phenomenon. One of the youths asked why this was. An adult gave the obvious answer: "I am sure it is because he is black."

"Oh," replied the Godspeller who had been with the tour from the beginning, "Is Dwight black?"

Would that all could be as color blind, as the *Godspell* players had become.

Kirby Kinsey, Karin's father who had been an encourager to me when I was vigorously courting Karin, would have enjoyed *Covenant's Godspell*. Sadly, he died June 4, 1974, the day of Annetta's graduation and the day before her birthday.

Mrs. Roy Gwyn, his sister-in-law and Karin's Aunt, age 95, who lived only four houses up the street from us for 14 years, died two weeks before Kirby. A proud lady of German heritage, she had been in perfect health, ate her last meal at her table and then slipped into a coma and lasted only a week. Karin was alone with Aunt Wanda, sitting with her and holding her hand when she died. We found it amazing that the manse bought by the church was on the same street where Aunt Wanda and Uncle Roy (Kirby's brother) had lived for several years. Though she never saw any of our performances, she often slipped Karin some money to take care of extra expenses when she thought no one would know.

Soon after the *Godspell* experience, Karin was asked to design a chapel for Brookhaven hospital in Farmers Branch. A memorial fund honoring the son of Dr. Quary, a physician who practiced in the hospital, underwrote the cost of the Chris Quary Chapel. Karin was given the authority to act as a committee of one, with complete freedom to create. Her only challenge was that she was given an odd shaped room to work with, one that could not be used for anything else. She drew up plans with recessed lighting both overhead and behind stained glass windows. The chapel in the small room included comfortable seating for individual or small group meditation and prayer. Imperial Furniture of Waco built special pews and used the basic design of the hutch we had bought as our first piece of furniture to create a lighted worship center. The focal point of the light within the worship center would fall upon a tapestry made to order by Georgia Moncada, a friend of Karin's who was an artist in New Orleans. The tapestry displayed a ray of light falling on troubled water, an idea that had come after Karin's interview with the family of Chris who loved the outdoors. She commissioned Manlio Cavallini in San Antonio to design stained glass windows that would portray scenes with Old Testament symbols of hope. All of the symbolism would be equally appropriate to adherents of both the Jewish and the Christian faiths.

Karin found she could cover the bleakness of the area's walls by placing blue linen that cost $6.50 per yard, wholesale, a high price even at that time, over the room's stark interior. This hue would match the background of the picture of the deceased son that would be on display. The workmen who were given the task of covering the walls complained.

They insisted, "you do not put fabric on a wall, only paper".

They created wrinkles on the wall when they failed to get the seams straight. Karin had to call on friends to help her salvage the project. After hours of crying first, then praying and painting with diluted Elmer's Glue, stretching and straightening she saw to it that all seams were correct.

The chapel was visited by an unbelievably large number of persons who found comfort in the serenity of the unique facility. Peter Wolfe, famous for staging Dallas Musicals and who designed the door and window frames, wrote Karin thanking her for the experience. Fred Schilling, the hospital chaplain, wrote Karin thanking her for her work. He reported that he had conducted several weddings in the chapel and frequently used the worship area for services of communion. Later, when a large hospital corporation took over, the area was destroyed. The stained glass windows, the tapestry, and the wood carved doors and frame that stated the chapel's name were moved elsewhere. These features were placed in a small room without the advantage of Karin's careful planning. Although the Farmers Branch chapel ceased to exist as Karin had conceived it, similar therapeutic meditation facilities came into being in other Dallas area medical institutions. In my hospital visiting, I found several replicas of Karin's chapel, none of which even began to measure up to her original concept.

June 13 of 1976 both Karin and I were at the bedside of my mother, Lilian Cook Ramsay, when she died. Presbyterian Village called and we raced across town and it seemed as if she was waiting for us. She died early that Sunday morning. We returned to Covenant and I preached the sermon I had planned, "When Does God Hide His Face?" based on Psalm 102:2, just as she would have wanted.

My mother had discussed her death with me and with her grandchildren. She had especially discussed it with Karin, over the telephone. Over the years the two of them discussed many things over the telephone. Karin still speaks of her as "my best friend". My mother had given Karin strict instructions that no heroic efforts to extend her life be allowed. She stated repeatedly her purpose was "to GLORIFY God and ENJOY Him FOREVER". A Seminary Classmate of her husband, Dr. Eugene W. McLaurin, held memorial services in Dallas at Glendale Presbyterian Church adjacent to Presbyterian Village where she lived and had made many friends. Annetta and Robin sang "Now the Day Is Over"; Robin sang "Abide With Me", both songs from their Grandmom's own hymnal which she had marked with her favorites. I conducted burial services at the Laredo Cemetery.

My sister, Elizabeth, was in Laredo for the graveside services and returned to Dallas for her last visit in our home. By Thanksgiving she developed a malignancy. October of 1977 Karin and I attended a Youth Specialties Convention in Chicago and had an unforgettable afternoon's visit in the Nursing Home where she was a patient.

I can still remember the wonderful, long conversation we shared which began as Karin said to her, "Liz, I am angry with God for all that is happening to you."

We cried, we laughed, we prayed!

A month later, on my birthday, we returned to Chicago for her funeral. The night of her funeral it was snowy and foggy in Chicago and planes could not fly. Suddenly all hotels were full of people who were tired and hungry and really wanted to be some place else. Karin and I were among the fortunate. We found a room and watched as others were turned away from the Inn. And then, it seemed as if time was suspended. The snow scene from the hotel window was strangely peaceful. It was almost as if we felt the brush of angel kisses. It was somber preparation for Christmas 1977.

# Angel Kisses And My Beating Heart

*Twenty-Two*

## A Bit of Urban Witchery
*1977*

The death of my mother in 1976 and my sister in November of 1977 left me with a small family, growing smaller. The four of us now can claim only Karin's mother and Karin's two sisters and their families as immediate family.

Covenant fit the usual description of a newly organized church, few elderly and infirmed. There are only seven funerals during 1976 and 1977 in my book of records, yet all seven of those seemed to affect me personally: Bob Durk whose wife, Mickie, called me when authorities notified her that her husband had died aboard a flight; my Mother; Louise Dowdle and Sarah Smith, both lived within two or three blocks of us and each of them left husbands not much older than I was; Col. Dick Broadhurst who was retired, lived immediately behind our house, somehow sensed when I needed encouragement and would drop by my office; Arthur Keywood, staff, followed three months later by

Jeanne Bunteen, another Covenant staff member. Jeanne was a young single parent who began working with Covenant in the Nursery and was the first Mother's Day Out Coordinator, jobs to supplement childcare in her home. She had no family and left an orphaned son, only slightly younger than our son. Less than a week after Jeanne, my sister died in Chicago.

The death of Arthur Keywood, Sr., August 25, 1977, was a real loss for me as his death ended a nearly perfect church staff. Not only would replacing valuable staff create a new crisis in the church, I had lost a dear friend. Once his death was known, efforts to find the pastor failed. No one answered the phone at the manse and even my long time secretary Katherine Tait, did not know where I could be reached.

One of the elders called a High School friend of Robin seeking help in finding the Ramsays. The friend jokingly suggested that the sheriff of a nearby county be contacted. The elder took the High School youth seriously. The sheriff who was known for protecting a house of ill repute was called. His support of the "best little" facility of this type had been publicized through the media. He was later portrayed in both a Broadway musical and a popular movie. The notorious sheriff called back and reported to the church elder that no one matching a description of either Jack or Karin had spent the night in a well-known house in his County. Since the Ramsays had been unable to have a family vacation that year, all four had gone to an Arlington motel and spent the following day at Six Flags Over Texas. I did not think I could possibly be missed for so short a time.

In 1977, soon after the loss of Arthur Keywood on my staff, I received a telephone call from Dr. Roy Zuefeldt, pastor of Northminster Presbyterian Church in northeast Dallas. He asked if I would be offended if he offered my wife a job on his church staff. His congregation was larger in numerical size than Covenant. In addition it was a member of the United Presbyterian Church in the U. S. A. It was then, and would continue to be for the next half dozen years, a completely separate denomination from the one in which Karin and I had labored for most of our lives. One of the last performances of Godspell had taken place in the Northminster sanctuary. The pastor had been deeply impressed with both the musical show and Karin's ability to work with young people.

I simply told him that decision would be very much up to Karin, but I would be quite supportive should she be willing to accept his offer. A day or two later she received a call from Dr. Zuefeldt asking her to consider a paying position as youth coordinator for the church where he served as pastor. She agreed to work with the congregation on a trial and a part-time basis, stating she wanted to get back to Covenant for 11 A.M. worship. She would have lunch with me and then return to Northminster for the afternoon and evening. It was possible for her to keep the morning activities at Northminster running, leaving Plano Road in far northeast Dallas, cross Dallas, taking 13 minutes on LBJ in Sunday traffic, and arrive in Carrollton in time walk into worship not more than a minute or two late. Try that today!

Since Karin had been so much a part of the life and work of the congregation I was serving, I asked the Session of Covenant Presbyterian Church to approve her decision to become a staff member of another congregation. They approved her decision, though one elder wanted to know what credentials she had to qualify her for a paying job.

Soon after Karin began her work at Northminster in 1977, a Covenant committee was appointed to study staff needs. The committee established the fact that my work schedule included attendance at forty meetings or events each month requiring a workweek, which sometimes totaled seventy hours. John Cunningham, my Presbytery executive who had a genuine understanding of the needs of the local church, helped the committee determine future staffing for Covenant. This study concluded that the church needed a business manager to replace Arthur Keywood and a church educator to take the place of what they had failed to realize Karin quietly had done to assist me with the education program. He recommended that Vesta Ruffin, the widow of a Presbyterian minister, be invited to serve a dual role as Educator and Manager. She accepted both positions and effectively juggled her responsibilities with poise.

During Karin's tenure as Director of Christian Education of Northminster, she developed a unique clown ministry, 21 clowns of all ages working in mime, drama, music, dance and deaf sign language. The idea for a clown group came after Karin invited the first woman to ever graduate from Barnum and Bailey Circus Clown College to give a youth program. Karin really expected merely her story. Instead, she took some of the young people and demonstrated how each person has their own unique clown face. Karin noticed that when clown make-up was applied, each young person came out from the mask they usually wore and was able to be more themselves than they had been before the make-up. Both *Thee Holy Fools* and the participants' ages of fourth grade through age sixty-seven years became well known in the Dallas area before either the terms *clown ministry* or *intergenerational* were used and understood. Several adults assisted Karin, one of whom was a sixty-seven year old retired schoolteacher, George Kriehn, who taught the young people deaf sign language and performed as a clown with them. The group worked in nursing homes and performed for a variety of Dallas groups, some social, others church-related, sometimes turning down invitations because of previous commitments. On one occasion, in a nursing home, working in absolute synchronization in deaf sign language, the clowns mimed Malotte's *Lord's Prayer* and broke through a catatonic patient. Nurses were ecstatic. On more than one occasion they appeared in Thanksgiving Square in downtown Dallas, once featured with Roger Staubach of Dallas Cowboy fame.

I remember a time when I went to Northminster, to contact Karin. I saw a youth in the church parking lot.

He proudly told me "I am one of Mrs. Ramsay's clowns".

Several years later when Karin had completed her work at the church, the father of that young person gave Karin a framed gift of appreciation for what she had done for that particular youth. The father had made incomplete and destroyed the monetary value of his complete collection of First Day Issue Stamps that included envelopes addressed to him by giving Karin the one page of stamps honoring clowns. That framed invaluable page of clown five cent 1966 stamps with the address pasted over, now addressed, "To Karin with love from your 'Holy Fool' David E. '81", still hangs on the wall of Karin's office. Even though *Covenant's Godspell* traveled across the nation and was eventually seen by over 9,000 people with expenses totaling nearly $18,000, it was Karin's clowns, *Thee Holy Fools,* which were best known in the Dallas area.

Another time I was waiting in the Northminster parking lot where Karin was completing arrangements with adults and young people for an elaborate *Drive-Through Advent* event featuring a costumed Nativity scene complete with live animals. I was talking to one of the adults and casually mentioned that I hoped it wouldn't rain.

Beulah Strange, Director of the all-day child care facility at Northminster, laughed and responded, "God wouldn't dare let it rain this weekend! Karin Ramsay is in charge of the *Drive-Through!*" The next year Karin organized an elaborate *Festival of Trees* in the Northex of the Church and Karin proved to the church that the Northex was a unique architectural design and an ideal location that could be used for all sorts of activities, including luncheons.

With both children attending SMU and no longer living at home, we sought every possible opportunity to enjoy each other's company in non-church activities. One Sunday evening after a full day of activities for each of us, we had a slight case of "Sunday night Blues" and so we visited what our son had told us was a fraternity initiation site in a grove of trees between two office buildings near downtown Dallas. He told us that freshmen were brought there to watch the three stone figures that appeared to dance as light filtered through the darkened overhanging tree branches. This illusion was most apparent when there was a breeze blowing through the grove. On this particular evening conditions were ideal for a bit of urban witchery.

As we watched, a car appeared. The vehicle contained college age young men. At Karin's suggestion we quickly moved into position with the hooded figures of stone, creating the illusion of five dancers instead of the expected three. We hastily pulled raincoats up over our heads making it appear that we were as hooded as our stone counterparts as lights of the car headed for us. The car drove through the parking area once, then paused, then turned around and headed back toward us for a second look. The two added figures made sudden and dramatic moves. The car took off at high speed. Sparks flew in all directions as the vehicle bounced over two double curbs. The car did not return for a third look. We went home and giggled for hours. What did the driver tell the pledges who must have been curious as to why he left the initiation scene so quickly? The "Blues" were gone. We slept well.

In April 1979 tornadoes cut a nine-mile path across the city of Wichita Falls. Karin contacted the Mennonite Disaster Service. She asked how churches in the Dallas area could help. Accepting the advice of the relief experts, she mobilized both the Northminster congregation and Covenant. Within six days of the devastation, a charter busload of thirty-five workers from the two churches reached the disaster site. Karin was appointed crew boss for the task of clearing a mobile home area that had been totally destroyed. We were warned that we might find bodies beneath the mass of debris since two persons believed to be residents of the area were missing. Relieved to find no cadavers, we were disappointed when the boxes containing the meager salvageable items we collected at each site were robbed while we left the area for a brief lunch break.

Several weeks later the group returned to work under Mennonite direction for reconstruction work. On our second trip, we brought with us mobile kitchen equipment and power tools that the long-term workers desperately needed. Karin and the young people had sponsored their own carnival to raise funds to pay for this equipment. Church members who could not go to Wichita Falls in person contributed generously to the fund started by the carnival fund. She later secured donations that financed a trip to Dallas for about thirty Mennonite relief workers who had made commitments of volunteer labor for three to six months. We saw to it that each had a chance for Rest & Relaxation and to see important sites such as the Dallas Apparel Mart, have a day at Six Flags and enjoy a good meal before returning to their difficult tasks of rebuilding. When the Mennonites held their disaster relief conference February 1981, Karin was invited to speak. She was told later that she was the first female crew boss and the first woman to make a presentation to an international Mennonite gathering. Before the day ended, they had requested, printed and distributed 500 copies of Karin's speech.

For several years, Karin and I attended the Youth Specialties conventions. These events were national workshops for church youth leaders. We took part in intensive youth worker training in Chicago, Atlanta, San Diego, Dallas and Portland. At the Portland conference, we were honored as the couple that had attended more times than any other pair. These conferences were enriched by two unique individuals: Tony Campolo, a Baptist minister who taught sociology at Eastern College, and Craig Wilson, who made an unusual presentation of the life of Christ called *The Fifth Gospel*. We invited Craig to Dallas where he gave his version of the gospel at both Covenant and Northminster.

We both enjoyed going to the National Youth Conventions where we always came back inspired with new visions for both Covenant and Northminster. The first one we attended was in San Diego and after the Convention we went to Disneyland, without kids! We stayed in a motel almost at the door of Disneyland where we could walk to the park. When Sunday came we asked the motel owner where Dr. Schuller's Church was.

She told us it was, "Not far, just over there."

We asked about buses or taxis and she said that they didn't run on Sunday. We really wanted to see the church that had started in a Drive-In Theater, so we decided that since it was "Just over there" we could walk. We intended to go to the early service, but since "just over there" turned out to be 41 blocks, we were relieved that we arrived in time for the last service that morning! That was one time the service could have lasted longer, for it was barely enough resting time for our feet to recover before we had to walk 41 blocks back to the motel, Karin in high heels! (We counted the blocks as we returned to the Motel!)

For the 1980 Convention in Portland, Oregon we flew over Mt. St. Helens and noticed that smoke was coming from the volcano. We were safely back home in Dallas before the big eruption.

After nearly five years, a period that included at least a couple of years or more with Dr. Zuefeldt, two interims and a portion of the ministry of an installed pastor, Karin resigned her position as Director of Christian Education at Northminster. During her time at Northminster she had completed her certification procedures for the General Assembly as educator, been interviewed on TV about *Thee Holy Fools*, and a Dallas newspaper had featured her philosophy of "teaching through drama". She sought a job closer to home. For a time she was bookkeeper and bill collector for a cardiologist in Farmers Branch. Her physician boss had been on call at Parkland when the lifeless body of President Kennedy was brought to the hospital. Although this was not her favorite job, her experience with the medical profession led to one that challenged her creative capabilities. She became the Lifeline Coordinator for Lutheran Social Services. This position made her responsible for providing emergency response for handicapped or infirmed and physically house-bound persons who might need immediate medical help. Each of her clients could touch an electronic button that used the telephone line to send an emergency message to the hospital switchboard. Karin not only learned the technical aspects of installing and maintaining the Lifeline units, but she trained over 200 volunteers to assist her. She went to Boston for a national Lifeline Convention, met the inventor of Lifeline and returned home to promote this important life saving device. In two years, she proved that the Lifeline concept would allow elderly and physically handicapped to remain in their homes unassisted and was viable for the Dallas area when maintained by the volunteers she had inspired.

Thee Holy Fools
*At Thanksgiving Square*

Standing: A Friend, Ajay Dass, Jay Turner, Evan Secor, Geoff Cox, Alex Thornburg, Stephanie Cox, Kareem Iliya, Lynn Vanderpool.
Seated: Karin Ramsay, Melinda Volker, Karen Vanderpool, Tiffany Nelson, Burke Henley.

Robin, Karin, Jack, Annetta
May 25, 1979

*Twenty-Three*

# A Decorum Broken By Applause
*May 1979*

On May 25, 1979 Annetta married Randy Hunt. They met during their years as students at Southern Methodist University. Annetta as a Junior at SMU was already serving a second term as Student Body Secretary, was on the Judiciary Level III, was President of Zeta Tau Alpha Sorority and had been elected to Who's Who. She had been active in the cause of Women's rights, for a time as president of W. I. C. (Women's Interest Coalition). In this capacity she challenged the existence of the college's all-male band. For years the smartly dressed students had taken the field at football half-time shows with nearly one hundred male students with instruments led by a scantily clad female twirler. They advertised their performance as "Ninety-nine Guys and a Doll". Annetta found this display of male chauvinism offensive.

  She did a bit of research and was able to gain the attention of the University's administration by pointing out that the college could loose federal funds unless they admitted females to the only musical organization that could prepare both sexes for positions as directors of high school marching bands. The band leadership selected the bass drummer, Randy Hunt, to confer with Annetta. That meeting not only made possible the admission of female students to the college band, but also proved to be the beginning of a romance.

Randy's father, Dr. Richard Hunt, was a Methodist minister who was teaching sociology at SMU. He would later become a professor at Fuller Seminary in Pasadena, California. The wedding took place in Covenant's sanctuary. Richard Hunt and I shared the responsibilities of officiating at the event that drew a full crowd. Members of the *Covenant's Godspell* provided music for the event including *Sunrise, Sunset* from *Fiddler On the Roof*. After the ceremony Annetta and Randy lived for a time in a SMU dormitory, Randy as the only male in a dorm full of women, while Annetta was Dorm Director. When staff positions at North Texas University, opened up, they moved to Denton. For several years Annetta worked as a staff member of the Denton University while she completed both a Master's degree and a Ph. D.

In 1980, I was elected as a commissioner to the General Assembly of the United Presbyterian Church, U. S. A. The national Assembly met that year in Detroit. Although I was a Southern Presbyterian minister, I was entitled to participate in the Detroit Assembly since I was a member of a Grace Union Presbytery. I was probably chosen for this responsibility because I made one of the speeches before Presbytery, a speech that supported the reunion of the denominations.

During the years Karin worked outside the home, we had little opportunity to see each other during normal work hours. Nonetheless, we managed to get together most days for lunch or supper. Beulah Strange once introduced me for a speech before the Latin American Auxiliary as "the last of the romantics, an inspiration to Northminster young people who watched with fascination as I would come pick up Karin for a date." She followed that statement, saying that even though Northminster no longer employed Karin, when she walked through the Northminster Northex she still sensed the sweet aroma of Karin Ramsay.

After completing his college degree at S. M. U. Robin was accepted into the Texas Tech School of Law in Lubbock, Texas. I well remember the several week period in 1983 between graduation from law school and announcement of the names of those who had succeeded in passing the rigid bar examination that would grant them the right to practice law in Texas. Karin paid for a week in Cancun, Mexico where the three of us went during this difficult waiting period. Robin had a classmate who had a job in Austin where the examination results would be posted. Robin called his friend on the day the names of those who had passed the test would be known. He asked his friend about the posting.

"Well", said his classmate, "One of us passed".

Robin proceeded to congratulate his friend. He was immediately interrupted with the words: "Robin, you passed."

Robin went to Austin and was sworn in as an Attorney-at-law. He was installed as a Deacon in Covenant Presbyterian Church in January 1984, the same year he was hired for his first full-time paying job as Attorney and Legal Advisor to Students at Denton's University of North Texas. His secretary was a charming young lady named Kathy. The two eventually married and Robin had a ready-made family since Kathy had two children, a vivacious daughter, Jena, and a son named Jared. Robin joined a Denton law firm where he specialized in family law. He then became Municipal Judge for the City of Denton.

A genuinely enriching event took place at Covenant when a Cerebral Palsy handicapped person named Jim Barton wheeled into the building. That week I received a letter from him asking if he would be welcome at Covenant. Karin and I visited him in his apartment and assured him that he was more than welcome. I saw to it that by the following Sunday, a handicapped parking sign was in place beside the main sanctuary entrance. Jim quickly became known to most of the congregation. He was invited to be Church School Superintendent. Jim's smile and enthusiastic grin endeared him to everyone as he rode his wheel chair about the building seeing to it that each teacher had their proper materials and attendance records. Jim was an IBM employee who had won a $25,000 grant from them to develop computer hardware that would be user friendly to other handicapped persons. In his spare time he rode horseback in Special Olympic events, winning within six months an event that qualified him and his horse for a trip overseas for international competition. He brought Covenant members a deeper understanding of the problems of the physically impaired.

Both Karin and I were elected to presbytery responsibilities. She was a member of two important committees: Candidates for the Ministry and Examinations. Matthew Lynn had become the General Presbyter of what was then known as Grace Union Presbytery. On one occasion he commented to me that Karin had the best theological mind of any person he knew that had not received a formal degree in theological studies. He believed she had reasoning capabilities in this area that were far superior to that of most Seminary graduates.

I served as chairman of the board of Good Shepherd Community Center, an outreach and service program for Hispanic families in West Dallas. During the early years of the Center's operation, Covenant members prepared and took meals to West Dallas to assure each child in the program had at least one hot meal each day. When the Dallas Health Department decided to discourage volunteer meal preparation, Covenant helped raise funds for an on-site cook that would guarantee both safe and healthy foods. In later years Covenant's volunteer cooks took part in a citywide food program for the homeless. They joined several area churches in serving meals at the downtown Dallas overnight shelter known as Stewpot.

For seventeen years I was deeply involved in the Ecumenical movement. During the 1960s, I was chairman of the social action division of the Texas Council of Churches. This was a statewide ecumenical organization that included over a dozen Protestant denominations. I was on the Council's board when we persuaded the Roman Catholics of Texas to join the organization. We then became the Texas Conference of Churches. This was the first Catholic-Protestant state program in the nation. This responsibility required regular trips to Austin, Texas.

On one trip to the Texas capital city, I found a turtle outside my motel. Since Karin and I had often saved such creatures from being crushed when Karin spotted them on the roadway, I picked up the turtle and carefully carried it back to my room. I will never forget the expression on the face of one of the more dignified conference members who observed my turtle saving effort. Once back home, I added the Austin turtle to our collection in a large enclosed area just outside our back door. The salvaged animals thrived on peanut butter, even coming to the glass door to beg with open mouths for us to feed them peanut butter on crackers. The satisfied expression on turtle faces after each cleared its beak of peanut butter, one claw at a time, first with the right, then with the left, more than made up for the look of anguish on the face of my fellow conference participant.

Although I considered myself a moderate in both theology and politics, I was once publicly called a "flaming liberal" by a prominent member of the church for my involvement in ecumenism. This was a dangerous thing to be in the politically conservative climate of North Dallas. My position of moderation was affirmed when the Carrollton-Farmers Branch Rotary Club elected me to the highest honor they could bestow, that of naming me a Paul Harris Fellow and paying the initiation fee of one thousand dollars from club funds.

When Vesta remarried and moved to another part of the state, she resigned, and Covenant called the Reverend Kathy Idol to serve as Associate Pastor. Sugie Maxfield, a long time member of the church and an elder, became Business Manager. For many years to come she would provide expert administrative assistance to the congregation. Marty Wohkittel became church secretary after the retirement of Katherine Tait. During the 1960s the music program was under the leadership of one person, Warren Zorn. When he left Covenant, we gained the services of a young couple, the Borens. The male member of this duo, Ted, was a seminarian who was completing his studies at a nearby seminary. He became the choir director and his wife Janet was church organist. This combination proved so successful that for the remaining years of my ministry, we would have at least two musicians on the staff. Peggy O'Neill, the high school music teacher, became Choir Director and Barbara Jordan her organist. Bill Gardner, a professor of Music at North Texas University, became music director and served in this position for a longer period of time than any other choirmaster. Several organists served with Bill at various times. Both Sue Smith from Denton and Doris Macphearson, a member of Covenant, worked with Bill, though Doris was the organist who worked with him longer than anyone else.

As Covenant's Choir director, Bill Gardner helped Karin surprise me during morning worship in May 1981 with a formal presentation of a silver cross and chain to wear with my pulpit robe. The cross was a gift from Karin in honor of the thirty-fifth anniversary of my ordination as a Presbyterian minister and in lieu of the fact that I had been unable to attend the reunion of my Seminary Class in Richmond, Virginia. Roy Sherrod and Jim McCrary did go out with me for a mini-celebration.

Schedule conflicts also prevented me attending the 100th anniversary of the my home church in Laredo, the 100th anniversary of Karin's home church in Sweetwater as well as homecoming in our former church in San Antonio. Our disappointment was eased a bit when Crestholme missed us and scheduled a special day just for us. We will never forget that day, November 1, 1981.

When the constitution of the Presbyterian Church in the U. S. was changed to allow the election of women elders, Covenant was one of the first to take advantage of this means of strengthening the Session, nominating from the floor and electing Pauline Smith and Connie Adler as elders. In December 1980, the same year Karin became a certified educator in the General Assembly, making her eligible to attend Presbytery with voice without vote, she was also asked by the elected Officer Nominating Committee to accept nomination as elder on the Covenant Session which would give her the right to attend Presbytery, and when so elected, give her the right to vote as well as have voice. In January of 1981 when a new class of elders was ordained before the congregation, I gave the right hand of fellowship to each in turn until I reached Karin.

I kissed her.

I then stated, "I can assure you, that is the first time I have ever kissed an elder of the church."

For a few moments the usual decorum of worship was broken with both laughter and applause.

Though she was working as a bookkeeper for a janitorial service, several appreciated Karin's ability to teach Bible and went to her, requesting she lead them in Bible study. Karin agreed, providing she could use her lunch hour to teach in a location near to her work. Karin asked the hotel manager of a multi-story hotel near her work if they would permit a Bible study on their property. Although the management was agreeable to any location that Karin and her students selected, the group found an open area that was both attractive and convenient, the hotel bar. For the next several years, Karin led a study for a half dozen to sometimes over twice that number. I had my Rotary club meeting at the same time, Thursday at noon. The bar Bible study continued for each Thursday for the remainder of our ministry at Covenant.

We had long sought to build a Senior Citizen residence on the two-acre plot behind the church. The U. S. Department of Housing and Urban Development (HUD) granted a four million-dollar loan approval. After thirteen years of planning by a committee elected by Covenant's Session, Washington politicians decreased the funds available. This made an adequate facility impossible. The plot was sold to a local developer who hoped to construct the home without government funds. The profit from the sale of the back lot did make it possible for Covenant to build additional classrooms, offices and a large parlor.

I don't remember the reason why Karin and I went to the church that afternoon in 1982. I do remember the outside doors were locked, but, once inside, I found the door to my study was open and the desk and closets looked as though someone was cleaning. The man at the secretary's desk was busily looking through the drawers. Boldly I walked right up and asked if I could help. With one jump and a loud yell, the man was over the desk, through the door and down the hall before he realized he was trapped. He reversed and ran back past the secretary's office, rounded the corner and headed for the door Karin and I had entered. This time he was face to face with Karin who greeted him with a big "Hi!" His response was to push past her, through the door and disappear outside. Police arrived and deacons came to fix the broken windows, but the series of burglaries at Covenant stopped. Karin and I were cordial and hope that if he ever came back it was to attend worship, not for another robbery.

I had worked for years researching the life of Mirabeau Lamar. In 1985, Eakin Press of Austin, Texas published my work under the title *Thunder Beyond the Brazos*. This book received the Fehrenbach Award for the best biographical work in Texas history that year. Much of the research for this book was done in the state archives in Austin. My trips to the state capital accomplished more than occasionally saving a turtle.

In the same year the congregation raised funds sufficient to send Karin and me to Scotland. Since I was a graduate of the University of Edinburgh, I was eligible to receive University housing at a fraction of the cost of a hotel, leaving money for extending our trip plans. We flew from DFW airport to London. Karin met her World War II pen pal, Pearl Maunder. For years Karin had corresponded with her but had never met her face to face. Pearl had helped me adjust to British life when I was a student and she had been equally gracious to our son, Robin, when he visited England during his semester of study in Paris. Karin and I were given magnificent tours of London and Oxford by Pearl and her University Regent husband. After an overnight visit with the Maunders in their spacious cottage on the Thames, we took the train north. Although we arrived in Edinburgh in a heavy rain and had difficulty in finding our way to our Edinburgh lodging that night, the rest of the trip went well. After we dried from our drenching, though it did take two days for the clothes we were wearing to dry, we were able to get about the town on public transportation with little difficulty.

On our first day in the Scottish capital, we went by the New College Library. I discovered my thesis on the Darien Scheme was no longer stashed away in a remote part of the building. We were told that the bound volume was frequently requested for call up by persons who were interested in learning about the legality of the British union.

I enjoyed showing Karin the beautiful land in which I had lived and worked for two years. We purchased a Brit Rail pass. On the days we felt like traveling we went to the Edinburgh rail station and took the first train that came into the station. This form of travel took us to Stirling, St. Andrews, Inverness, and a host of smaller towns in northern and eastern Scotland. Unfortunately we were unable to visit the western isles since a conductor's strike was taking place. We visited the Richmond Craigmillar Church on a Sunday where there were about a dozen people who remembered me though it had been more than twenty-five years. There we were given information on how to locate Alex Hutchison, the minister with whom I had worked during my years in Scotland. He had a retirement home in the highlands. We took the train north and spent a full day with Alex and his wife, Nanette who took us on a tour of the Highlands. Alex drove us around the famed Loch Ness, but Nessie the Monster, failed to show herself that day. That evening we spent the night in a Bed and Breakfast operated by a woman who had been one of the Richmond Craigmillar youth group. Later I was able to introduced Karin to Ronald Selby Wright who was retired and living in The Queen's House in Edinburgh.

We bought tickets to the famed Edinburgh Tattoo, heard bagpipe bands at their best and watched the seamen of the British Navy display their talents in rigging high above the stone esplanade. Later we learned that the seamen who performed so magnificently would never again scale the tall masts. Even the tradition bound British Navy had to cut costs. We were among the last to view this unique display. We ate Scottish food in the cafes and bars near Princes Street. We shopped in the stores on the High Street and browsed in the bookstores near the Old College Quad. Our shopping required frequent use of the Master Card that had my name upon it followed by the words "Dallas, Texas."

On one occasion I was asked: "Do you know J. R?"

I replied: "Look at the card. Notice my name, Jack Ramsay. I was J. R. long before that Dallas television show was invented." We got excellent service in every place we used a credit card.

From Edinburgh we took the train south to the White Cliffs of Dover. We boarded a hovercraft that took us across the English Channel to France. We spent several days in Paris before our return trip to Dallas.

Once back home, Karin and I began to look for even greater adventures.

*Alex and I celebrated seeing each other again. It had been 25 years since I worked with Alex in Richmond Craigmiller.*

*Alex Hutchison, former pastor of Richmond Craigmiller Church in Edinburgh, retired and now living in the Highlands, and his wife, Nanette, are seen here after taking us completely around Loch Ness.*

*No Monster sighted!*

*Twenty-Four*

## Spouse Trailers

*June 1987*

The time for a major decision had come. As the fateful date approached, Karin and I discussed possibilities. By my sixty-fifth birthday November 1987, I would have served as pastor of Covenant Presbyterian Church for two months short of twenty-eight years. No one in the local congregation had mentioned the word retirement, but the General Presbyter had questioned me about my plans for my final years.

Karin had served the Church as a professional. Having gained her certification as a Church Educator while working at Northminster, she had standing in both denominations. Each Sunday morning she had traveled across North Dallas, set up her classes there and returned to Covenant in time for the eleven A. M. service. During those years she was an active elder of the Southern Presbyterian Church while serving as a staff member of a United Presbyterian congregation. In this she was a half dozen years ahead of the actual reunion of the two branches of Presbyterianism.

In 1987, Karin and I had only two choices. We could remain in our comfortable home on Lavita Lane or seek some other place where we might be useful. If we chose the first of these options, Presbytery officials would expect us to avoid anything but the most casual contact with our former churches. This would be extremely difficult to do if we elected to continue to live in Farmers Branch.

The concept of *spouse trailering* had become an option for two married individuals with unique skills. Both look about. When either one finds a position that fits their particular abilities, that person accepts the job, *drives the cab*, while the other follows and finds something to do in the location of the other's job, *becomes the trailer*. For three-and-a-half decades Karin had trailed me. After rejecting the offer to teach in Crane, she continued to be the trailer in San Antonio and North Dallas County. We agreed that it was time to consider a new driver. We would look at all possibilities.

I had already published my first book and I was interested in continuing my career as an author. Karin had established herself as a capable administrator both in her work at Northminster and her service with Lutheran Social Services. We were both in good health and anxious to find new challenges.

On the night of the June Session meeting at Covenant we received an answer to our dilemma. I had gone ahead to the church to set up for the meeting. Karin would come later. She arrived earlier than I expected. As other members of the Session were arriving, she called me out into the hall to tell of a telephone call she had received at home a few minutes earlier.

The Chairman of the Staff Search Committee of University Presbyterian Church in Chapel Hill, North Carolina had phoned. He told her they were very impressed with her résumé. One statement bothered him. Karin had written that she was interested only in work that was "within commuting distance of my husband".

The chairman asked, "Is Chapel Hill in commuting distance of Dallas?"

"I don't know, tell me more about Chapel Hill." she replied.

She was asked to fly to Chapel Hill for an interview, "tomorrow, if possible". She told them that was too soon but did agree to fly there on Friday. A few days after her interview she was offered the job. The impact of what was about to happen hit Karin, so she told them she wanted to be fair both to them and to us. She proposed that we go to North Carolina in August. She would work for Chapel Hill for a month on a mutual trial basis for both Karin and the Church. I would attend a two-week session of classes that were offered at Duke while she worked and then return to Covenant while she completed her month in Chapel Hill. The Church surprised her by accepting her proposal.

At the end of the month of August in North Carolina both Karin and Chapel Hill Presbyterian Church wanted to continue the relationship. They then granted a two-month leave of absence for Karin to return to Texas and help me with the fifteen hundred-mile move east. After all the years Karin had been the trailer, she would now become the driver.

After forty years as a full time pastor, I was ready to take the back seat. During that time, I had been involved in major building programs for four churches and had served as Chairman of the Board of a presbytery owned community center that required my leadership for an extensive remodeling program.

Members of my first pastorate, the Roscoe congregation, had given me a bound volume that provided space for recording a lifetime of pastoral work. I had carefully listed all of my ministerial acts. At the time of my technical retirement, my records show the following:

3,121 sermons
707 baptisms
344 weddings
228 funerals
38, 856 pastoral visits
1,994 members received

I had always hoped I would have time to write, but the intense schedule of the pastorate had provided very little time to do so.

My publisher, Ed Eakin, had reviewed a preliminary draft of what would eventually be my second book. Believing I needed more data on Cynthia Ann's situation during her prairie years, he recommended I continue my research in major libraries beyond the bounds of Texas and Oklahoma. He suggested that I visit the Library of Congress and investigate the records of the Department of Indian Affairs.

Chapel Hill was an ideal site for historical study. Three major university libraries were in the immediate area and the town was only a few hours drive from the world's greatest library in the nation's capital. When I made my first research trip to Washington, I gave my North Carolina address. The Curator of the national library's Manuscript Division noted this and told me that I could find materials in the resource centers in and around Chapel Hill that would be equal to the holdings he supervised in Washington.

Karin and I decided we would tell no one about our plans until we were certain the move was right for both of us. I went with Karin in our small red Honda loaded with everything Karin might need for her four weeks away from home. I flew back to Dallas to quietly begin closing out my ministry at Covenant. We would not announce our plans until Karin had found a satisfactory place to live. I stayed in North Carolina long enough to survey the possibilities before I returned to Farmers Branch wondering if anyone at Covenant had caught on to what was underway.

When a close friend asked about Karin, I said as casually as possible, "Oh, she is working this month in Chapel Hill."

At the time I feared our secret had been discovered, but I learned later my questioner had assumed Karin had a summer job in a North Dallas church named Chapel Hill Presbyterian.

Another question had to be answered. I told a friend we had gone to North Carolina together and Karin had stayed there to work two more weeks than I could stay. She did accept that, but knew we had driven the Honda to North Carolina. When I slipped and mentioned the fact that we both would fly to New Orleans to meet each for another of our honeymoons, she asked how we planned to get the little red Honda back to Dallas?

I gave a very evasive answer, "Oh, we will have to figure something out on that."

In spite of my evasiveness, no one at Covenant guessed our intentions. In late August I received a call from Karin. She had found a beautiful town house amid tall pine trees that could be purchased within our means. I knew from the sound of her voice that this was the place for the two of us. I signed my name to the documents Karin's realtor had prepared and enclosed a check for the required initial payment. We would meet a few days later in New Orleans.

I announced our plans to the Session the first Sunday of September. Two hours after I relayed my decision to the congregation, I was on my way to my meeting with Karin. My plane landed at the Crescent City airport only minutes before Karin arrived from North Carolina. There we began our great adventure in the city in which we first honeymooned. Once again we visited the restaurants and sites of the romantic city. We walked hand in hand beside the silver waters of the Mississippi.

*Our Family 1960*

*Our Family 1987*
*28 Years minus two months*

*Installed Pastor, Covenant Presbyterian Church, Carrollton, Texas*

*February 1960
November 1987*

*Spouse Trailers 1988*

*Switching Drivers*

*In late August I received a call from Karin. She had found a beautiful town house amid tall pines that could be purchased within our means. I knew from the sound of her voice that this was the place for the two of us.*

*Our Honda and our Nissan in front of our Town House, 138 Channing Lane, Chapel Hill, North Carolina.*

# Angel Kisses And My Beating Heart

*Twenty-Five*

## Eastward to the Sea

*Fall 1987*

The retirement announcement caught everyone by surprise.

Annetta and Robin said, "You are going to do what?" Followed by, "You are going to sell our house?"

It certainly had not been an easy decision. By faith Covenant had done so much: sponsored migrant projects; moved from a pastor and a part-time secretary to a paid staff of 18 people; begun a kindergarten as a service to the community; sponsored missionaries to Brazil; helped Good Shepherd in West Dallas to move from a kindergarten and chapel to a full-service community center; allowed their young people to step out in faith and with only $50 per person to tour twenty-nine states on Greyhound buses to spread the message of God's Spell of Love. By faith Covenant had completed three building programs and May 1987 had rededicated a sanctuary.

Even the General Presbyter was caught off guard, despite

the fact he had once indicated he expected me to retire on schedule. One Elder, Jim Macphearson was so shocked by my announcement that he went to bed for several days claiming his illness was due to my decision to leave Covenant.

In late July, just before Karin's month in North Carolina, we met with the committee, which planned another Scottish heritage event. The committee once again set a Scottish event for the last Sunday of October. Only Karin and I knew this might be our last day at Covenant. We exchanged glances when the committee decided a full bagpipe band would be invited for the occasion. When the final Sunday of my pastorate arrived, October 1987, the pipers were on hand. The two of us, I in my clergy kilt bought for me from a Roman Catholic Priest by the Jim Macphearsons and their friends and Karin in the Ramsay tartan, marched with the bagpipe band into the sanctuary. On our trip to Scotland, Bill Innes, an elder and a Scot who was in the fashion business, insisted I buy a jacket and every possible accessory to make my outfit complete. I did. I felt truly handsome.

The Scottish pageantry gave a dramatic conclusion to my last sermon at Covenant. How unexpected that an event so spectacular should fall on the Sunday dictated by my birthday, the technical date that the General Presbyter had told me I should consider retiring. After worship, Karin and I followed the pipers around the building, a parade we would never forget and the conclusion of our time at Covenant and the beginning of a new life for both Covenant and for us. With bagpipes and drumbeat we had no other choice except to march out with our heads held high.

That afternoon, the large new church parlor was full to capacity. The crowd included both present members of the church and visitors from the community. In addition some past members were present. The hall was renamed *Ramsay Parlor* in honor of Karin and me. Both the Mayor of Carrollton and the Mayor of Farmers Branch read proclamations honoring us and presented plaques of both statements that still hang on my office wall.

The next morning a large orange moving van pulled up in

front of 3015 Lavita Lane, Farmers Branch. By late afternoon the van was loaded and on the way eastward. We spent the night on the bedroom floor and the next day packed a few leftover items for shipment by UPS. By mid afternoon we were ready to close the home in which we had lived for such a long time, the place where we had raised our children, the house that was filled with countless memories.

Although it was late, we decided to begin the journey after one last meal in a favorite Mexican food restaurant on Forest Lane. When we told the manager we were moving far beyond the bounds of Texas, he gave us complementary meals.

That night we reached the Texas border. The next morning we said goodbye to the state in which Karin, a seventh-generation Texan, had lived all of her life and I had lived for over half a century. We journeyed across Arkansas where we heeded a sign that claimed to have "the world's greatest catfish". We ate there and decided there was ample justification for the claim. At least, we were extremely satisfied certain there would be no catfish any better ahead. We crossed Tennessee and stopped in Nashville where I bought a western style shirt since I didn't own one. I wanted to look somewhat like the Texan North Carolinians probably expected in our new place of residence.

We arrived in Chapel Hill one day ahead of the van and slept on the floor of our new home, a beautiful two-story house in the tall pine section of the town. Karin had found the perfect place to live after exploring dozens of sites with her realtor, P. B. Adams. The house was on a hillside that sloped down to a dry streamed bed.

A back deck looked out on a green valley filled with trees, shrubs, and flowering plants. Because of the contour of the land, we had a *crawl space* of over sixteen feet in height. This provided ample storage area for work tools, my nearly new Trek bicycle and our bicycle-built-for-two. The Trek that Karin had given me was the best possible bicycle, built to my size with all of the latest on board devices. I rode in the beautiful hilly forests of North Carolina thankful for the eighteen-speed system that made steep up slopes reasonably comfortable.

Karin and I were in an environment far different from any we had experienced before. Karin found her new job both exciting and challenging. She was responsible for developing programs for all ages in a university setting. She had been told she would have difficulty working with her senior pastor, David Hoffelt, a brilliant young minister who was one of the best preachers of the entire denomination. He very quickly understood the unique talents of his new Church Educator and she in turn recognized his. Karin told him they would probably disagree on some issues but they would do that privately and the two of them agreed neither of them would ever voice an opinion contrary to the other in public. She soon learned they both shared a common vision of what the church could and should be.

Though Dr. Hoffelt, a Princeton graduate, filled the Colonial Sanctuary Sunday after Sunday with preaching which was stimulating both to long-time Presbyterian members and typically skeptical college students, he was aware he had critics on the Christian Education Committee. It was not David who made Karin aware of this, committee members saw to it only two days after she was back from her trip with me to accomplish our move.

When it came time for the Confirmation Class that would include his own daughter he urged Karin to take the responsibility. She refused and suggested that the two of them *team-teach*. In order to give David confidence that they would cover all aspects which should be included as curriculum, Karin designed handouts, which would be discussion guides to use each session, and a schedule of study which would conclude with a charter bus trip to Union Seminary in Richmond where professors there would complete the course. She sent the curriculum study sheets and the schedule to Dr. Isabel Rogers who enthusiastically endorsed her materials. It would be a curriculum and basic plans that David would follow long after the two of them were no longer working together.

Each communicant was assigned two partners, one an adult member of the Session and the other an older youth of the church who was already a member of the Church. The charter bus trip to Richmond included the communicants and their older youth partners, plus Karin, David and I, two other adults and two small children. We stayed in a downtown Richmond Hotel and took a trip to the area theme park after we had some very special sessions at the seminary. It was a course of study I don't think anyone will forget. I enjoyed everything in which I participated except the miserably cold and wet underwear I had to wear all afternoon after I rode in the front seat of the log flume!

    I became a member of Orange Presbytery and accepted the position of Stated Supply at Yanceyville. This was a small church in historic Caswell County, fifty-two miles north of Chapel Hill. The area bordered on the state line that separated the state from the one in which I had been born. Only a few miles beyond the Dan River were the two towns where I had preached during my final year as a seminarian. Three years later, on the weekend when Karin was in Minnesota considering a position there, I drove north after conducting my service of worship at Yanceyville. I found the church building in Victoria. It was there that I was asked to consider a call to full time ministry. Although the sanctuary was much like it had been forty-five years earlier, a small educational building had been added behind the worship site. Little had changed in the intervening years.

    Four-and-a-half decades later, my duties were much the same as they would have been if I had chosen to begin my ministry in Virginia. My post-retirement responsibilities included preaching, leading worship and visiting the seriously ill. I had little difficulty in completing all of my pastoral work. The major hospital of the area, Duke, was only eight miles from the two-story house in the tall pines. The medical care facility was immediately adjacent to the University Library. This made it possible for me to combine ministerial tasks with my work as historical researcher.

    I made trips to the Library of Congress on several occasions in order to complete my second book, *Sunshine On the Prairie, The Story of Cynthia Ann Parker,* which was published in 1990 by Eakin Press of Austin, Texas.

I helped Karin whenever I could. I took seriously the fact she was now driving the cab and I was the trailer. When she took a group of youths on what was for all of them their "first ride on a train" to Orlando and Disney World, I went along. The group from Chapel Hill and I slept on the floor of a new, unfurnished home of a Baptist minister, Clyde Larrabee. He told me that one night in Jackson Hole, Wyoming while he was on the first of the *Godspell* tours he had made his decision to become a minister. Clyde was one of the three readers essential to *Covenant's Godspell*. When I told Karin this, we began to think of the young groups with whom we had worked, especially five people: Jim Beverly, a Presbyterian minister from Scotland; Bob Poteet, a Presbyterian minister in Houston; Jimmy Cozby (now known as Father Dimitri), a Greek Orthodox Priest in San Antonio; Clyde Larrabee, a Baptist minister in Florida; and Alex Thornburg, a Presbyterian minister from Northminster who has already published two books sold by the Presbyterian Book stores.

Karin's work at Chapel Hill meant that we did not have to lose contact with young people who kept us alive with fresh ideas. When a violent hurricane swept the Atlantic coast, a Presbyterian Church on Sullivan Island was completely destroyed. Karin made contact with the pastor who was determined to stay on the island and rebuild. Karin kept in contact with him throughout the months that followed the disaster. At first there was little a team of volunteers could do to aid recovery. When a remnant of the original congregation returned to their battered homes, a mobile building was established as a center for worship. Karin learned in early winter that life had resumed on the island with a reasonable lack of inconvenience except for one problem: natural gas lines had not yet been restored. As the Holiday Season approached, none of the inhabitants would be able to bake Christmas pies, cookies or pastries. Karin challenged her Chapel Hill friends to bake special goods, which she and I would deliver to the Sullivan Island congregation on Christmas Day. On Christmas Eve Karin collected a Nissan load of boxes of seasonal goodies.

Early the next morning, Karin and I drove south to deliver the generous response of the volunteer bakers. Christmas morning dawned bitterly cold. A rare ice and snowstorm battered the coast of the Carolinas. This would not be a white Christmas that would be remembered in song.

I checked with the Auto Club as to the safest route south. Even though I had to drive through slippery ice and several inches of snow, sometimes at five miles per hour, Karin and I made it to the Island by midday. There we delivered enough goodies to make a Christmas that might have been bleak for the islanders had it not been for the delivery that we made to the Presbyterian worship center.

After completing our mission, we returned to the mainland where we had made reservations to spend Christmas night in a Charleston hotel. We checked in and then discovered that the rare cold spell had broken water pipes making water in the bathroom, coffee urns in the room and hotel toilets inoperable. We were desperately thirsty and had not eaten any breakfast because we had been in a hurry to make the delivery of baked goods in time for Christmas morning. We decided to go out and eat breakfast. We had to try several places before we found one place open. They were cooking on sterno burners and using bottled water to make coffee. We decided the situation in Charleston was even worse than we had realized and were ever so glad Chapel Hill had sent baked goods to them.

We went back to the hotel and asked the desk clerk about the situation in the hotel. He shrugged his shoulders and offered us the option of checking out without staying the night for which we had reservations.  We checked out of our hotel thinking we would drive a few miles down the highway and find some place to spend Christmas night. Trees along the highway were bare and bent to appear as if a terrific wind was still blowing. For miles we drove beside the ghostly trees. Suddenly we had driven so far that we could as easily finish the journey as find a place to stay. We returned to our forest home in Chapel Hill. It was a Christmas to remember.

    I helped Karin on Sunday evenings when she had the University Church basement full of sons and daughters of members of the academic community. I assisted her in teaching a Kerygma Bible Study for adults. We reorganized this material to fit the scholastic schedule. We gave assignments to the participants that included Duke and North Carolina professors, college administrators, a College Dean, a Duke Chemistry Professor and a District Judge.

    I later would accompany Karin to the Courtroom of the District Judge Trish Hunt. I wasn't there the Sunday night it happened, so I still can't really imagine how it happened. Somehow, Karin had gone upstairs to get some supplies while the youth group was meeting in their basement room. Entering one door of a double door classroom to secure the materials she needed, Karin came face to face with a robber who had somehow entered the building. He quickly exited out the second door of the classroom and entered the room directly across from the double door classroom. Somehow she thought quickly enough to pull out her keys, locked the door he had entered and trapped him in, of all places, the second-story men's restroom! While he was trapped, she called the police, and, before the young people even knew anything was going on, police had arrived and arrested a person Karin was to later learn was wanted for murder! She was subpoenaed and I was there when she testified so convincingly that his attorney turned his head to look at his client, audibly said, "God!" and got up from his table, leaving his client sitting there glaring at Karin. She had identified his client as "wearing the same sweater today in court as he was wearing that night". When Prosecutors had shown Karin keys the prisoner had in his possession when arrested, Karin had dramatically reached in her pocket, pulled out her keys and matched key for key. All his attorney could do was to appeal the ruling that day to District Court. Karin was again subpoenaed and thought this time she would get to see Judge Trish Hunt at work. However, after we appeared and took our seats in the courtroom we were aware of much traffic back and forth to the Judge's Chambers. The Bailiff then appeared and said we were dismissed. The Attorney for the Defendant had spotted Karin in court and decided to plea bargain.

One of my efforts to assist Karin was unsuccessful. This was my attempt to help her plant an entire hillside with beautiful blooming shrubs. I kept digging out small roots that turned out to be poison oak. After I secured treatment from a local physician who specialized in treating allergies peculiar to the area, I recovered from my gardening efforts. From that time on, I left planting hillsides to Karin.

The two lovers took advantage of the area's charms. On three successive Thanksgivings, we visited Colonial Williamsburg. There we enjoyed early American foods prepared from menus familiar to our nation's founding fathers. One spring we traveled to Washington D. C. in cherry blossom time where we reveled in the magnificence of the famed blossoms. One winter we journeyed to Asheville in North Carolina's Smoky Mountains. We toured the Vanderbilt Mansion decorated for Christmas by candlelight and stayed in the Hotel that sponsors the most famous gingerbread house-building contest in the nation. The hotel itself a unique structure was adorned with Nineteenth Century Christmas decorations.

Beautiful Emerald Isle on the Carolina coast was another vacation get away. Karin's personnel chairman owned a share in a magnificent four level condo on the isle, which he made available to us when he could not take his family to the coast. Karin and I walked the beach, gathered shells, occasionally swam in the surf, and often watched both sunrise and sunset from our condo window. The island ran due east and west making such viewing possible. On every trip we enjoyed the beauty of the Carolina coast. The wonder of the ocean's vastness convinced us that our journey eastward to the sea was well worth the effort.

220 *Angel Kisses And My Beating Heart*

Jack in his office the week of his retirement.

Jack with Karin in his Clergy Kilt

Our daughter, Annetta, with us on our last Sunday.

*Eastward to the Sea* **221**

At University Presbyterian Church, Chapel Hill, Karin was responsible for developing programs for all ages in a university setting. The church pre-dated the University of North Carolina, the pastor bringing some of his Princeton friends to be part of the original UNC faculty.

When the present sanctuary was built, the land was actually dug out so that the steeple would not be higher than UNC buildings.

I became a member of Orange Presbytery and accepted the position of Stated Supply at Yanceyville. The Historic Church with its balcony for salves and the cemetery pre-dated the civil war.

*Christmas Day after Hurricane Hugo.*

*Sunset Presbyterian Church, Sullivan's Island, South Carolina, Christmas morning 1989*

*Twenty-Six*

## The Great Adventure

*July 1990*

When the Senior Minister of the Chapel Hill congregation accepted a call to a college church in Ohio, Karin put out her résumé once again. Always the rumor among educators had been that when the senior staff member leaves, the educator should begin preparations to leave. The rumor also was that it was best if the educator made a move before the next minister arrived. Karin and I were learning the secret of why the educator should consider the advisability of moving on: the success of an education program depends even more on the support of the senior pastor than it does the support of the education committee or the official governing body of the church.

This time, circulation of Karin's résumé led to an invitation to become the Director of Christian Education for the Oak Grove Presbyterian Church of Bloomington, a suburb of Minneapolis, Minnesota.

This presented a new aspect to our great adventure. Once again we placed our home on the market. We packed enough for two months in the little red Honda and traveled north to Minnesota, spent two months finding a place to live and to begin to learn about Oak Grove before our final move to the North Country. We flew back to North Carolina where we said good-bye to friends in Chapel Hill and Yanceyville, packed once more, loaded a moving van and then drove our Nisson to Minnesota, ready to live and work in a vastly different portion of the nation.

The job at Oak Grove Church presented Karin with a completely different set of challenges. She soon sensed the uniqueness of the Minnesota culture. Learning to speak Minnesotan is no joke; being understood when you speak Texan is not easy. Some words we never mastered! It is more than a matter of pronunciation: some words have completely different meaning. For instance, in Texas, when we wanted to be gracious and offer a cold drink to a friend, we should offer a "coke". That doesn't work in Minnesota; you offer a "soda". When you need to pick up something you forgot to buy when you bought groceries, you do not go to the "ice house"! If you did, you would be in the middle of one of the frozen lakes talking to a friend who had built a house on the ice over a hole where he was fishing! You do not tell the church staff that you are staying late at work because, "Jack is stuck at the bank and can't come after me." If you said that, they would become alarmed and want to send a snow rescue with extra blankets and supplies. You do not order barbecue though you quickly learn that the Jolly Green Giant product you bought in cans, the Land of Lakes, Pillsbury and most of the food products you bought in Texas other than barbecue originated in Minnesota! We learned why *sweet* corn is called *SWEET!* It is NOT because sugar has been added: it is because it is sweet when it is plucked off the stalk, and you haven't lived until you have gone to a church picnic where they feature corn on the cob. A native of Minnesota will not eat corn on the cob unless it has been harvested for less than two hours. As Texans, back in Texas, we eat it any way we can find it, with fond memories of Minnesota, though we do go to the market hoping to find some that will almost pass the Minnesota fresh test.

As to barbecue, you learn that every state has their own idea of what Texas barbecue is; most of their ideas don't match my idea. In North Carolina, they definitely had their own idea of barbecue: always pork, cooked on a revolving spit, picked off in shreds and then served with a sauce definitely not of the Texas type. It was delicious, different, but delicious. Karin had great fun adapting her events to match the area where she was working. In Chapel Hill, she had a grand end of the year teacher recognition: she had a *Pig Pickin'*. Because University Church had minimal grassy area not in use as a play yard, she had her *Pig Pickin'* on the front yard of the picturesque Colonial Church building which was on the main street of Chapel Hill and faced the front entrance to the University of North Carolina. It was a grand event, which I had to miss because of my duties in Yanceyville. However, she had a photographer who was equipped to take group pictures come take a picture of the whole group on the front steps of the church that *Pig Pickin'* day, another of the treasures which hangs on her office wall. In Minnesota, she looked forward to education events featuring Minnesota corn and brats, an essential sports accompaniment, which we had never eaten.

Karin had grown up as one of three daughters. Kirby, her father, had insisted that if he were to be the father of only girls, his daughters (and his wife) would learn the rules of football well enough to converse with any football fan. However, football fan that she is, she quickly learned there are other sports just as exciting and she adjusted her education program to fit the area. In North Carolina, NEVER, never schedule any event on the day of the Duke–Chapel Hill basketball game! We have a friend who specified that her funeral was not to occur on the same day as a basketball game for either team. Her husband was a professor at UNC. He did as she specified. In Bloomington, Karin honored the schedules of both the Minneapolis Vikings and especially the Twins who won the Pennant the year we were there. We thought about renting ourselves out as fans because when we lived in

Chapel Hill, Dean Smith's basketball team won the Final Four; when we lived in Bloomington, the Twins won; and when we lived later in Green Bay the Packers won the Super Bowl. We had lived in Farmers Branch (Dallas 75234 zip) when the Cowboys had won.

In Oak Grove in Bloomington, Karin organized an educational program that met a very different set of needs than any she had experienced in her earlier positions. I again transferred my Presbytery membership. I found myself in a strong ecclesiastical unit, the Twin Cities Area Presbytery. This governing body had long served the heavily populated areas of Minneapolis and St. Paul. Reorganization had enlarged the Presbytery's bounds to include most of the southeastern part of the state.

The Executive Presbyter recommended me for a staff position in an ultra conservative congregation. He assumed I would fit in the conservative church since I was from the South. After two intense interviews, I was told I was not *evangelical* enough for the job. The executive then referred me to a church considered more moderate in outlook, Bryn Mawr Presbyterian in near downtown Minneapolis. I served there as Pastoral Associate for a year. During this time I continued to teach informal Bible studies in three Presbyterian owned Senior Citizen homes. This was an activity that I thoroughly enjoyed, one that began with teaching one group in a home for elderly residents next door to Karin's church, later evolving into a teaching schedule for three groups.

I was then invited to become interim minister for a congregation in southern Minnesota, Claremont. This was one of the highlights of my post retirement years. The round trip from the apartment in Bloomington to Claremont required one hundred-and- forty miles of driving, sometimes driving through ice and snow. Yet once I arrived in Claremont, my presence was always appreciated.

I will always remember one night I had to return to Bloomington from Claremont in the face of dangerous weather. The January Session meeting had a full agenda that included the adoption of the congregation's annual budget. I called the

Session to order at the scheduled hour, 7:00 p. m. Suddenly the town's Chief of Police, who was also an elder of the church, rushed into the meeting room. He announced that he had just received information about a threat of icing and snow accumulations that would make my trip home difficult.

"We have to get this thing over fast so Jack can get out on the road".

The motion was made to adopt all items on the agenda. This was passed without the usual questions and discussion. Within minutes, I was on my way north. When I reached the main highway, two enclosed snowplows with flashing blue lights appeared. I followed the fast moving vehicles into the Minneapolis area at highway speeds. I arrived safely back in the Bloomington apartment at least two hours ahead of schedule.

On another occasion I decided to check the oil level on my car that I had parked in front of the Claremont church building. I raised the hood and reached for the dipstick. Suddenly the town's lone police car appeared beside me. The Elder-Police Chief had heard a report that I might be having car trouble. He resumed his appointed rounds after I assured him all was well.

Karin and I enjoyed the beauty of the northland. We reveled in the magnificence of the hoarfrost that glistened on tree branches in the morning light. We found the brilliant hues of the early fall fascinating. Even the heavy snows, which followed, were excitingly beautiful. Tall, graceful trees that presided over vast fields of glistening white became objects of endless wonder for the two lovers who had lived their lives in much warmer climes.

One evening we were treated with a rare light show. I had driven to Karin's church on a crisp winter night. I found her on the parking lot among her fellow elders looking at the sky. There were bursts of light in all colors spreading in magnificent waves. This continued for several minutes, halted briefly and began again and again. Even those who had spent all of their lives in Minnesota admitted they had never seen such a display. Television that night featured the fireworks show in the sky, an unusually spectacular sighting of the Aurora Borealis in the city, a sight usually visible in the country away from city lights. This beautiful sight was one that we believed may have been a part of a providential welcome to us, a compensation for the extreme cold which on occasion seemed to penetrate our very beings.

Even the blizzards, which occasionally came upon the land, fascinated us. We were present for the most severe snowstorm ever to strike Minneapolis, a storm memorialized in the front page headline of the *Star Tribune* Saturday, November 2, 1991: "It fell and fell and fell." with a line above the masthead, "Great Halloween Snowstorm, 28.4 inches, Oct. 31-Nov. 2, 1991". We treasure our cup featuring that headline.

Karin had been working in her basement office that Halloween very warm afternoon when the fluorescent light above her exploded. No programs were planned for that evening since it was Halloween. Fumes from fluorescent gases were giving her a headache, but she kept working. It was not long before staff members from upstairs came down to see what was the odor that was making them sick. When they discovered the cause, they suggested she leave her office window ajar and go home for the rest of the day. She did.

We had the new experience of being snow-bound, and were perhaps only two of a few who enjoyed the experience. Two days later, I drove Karin through the banks of snow to see if she could get into her half-basement office. As we rounded the corner at the bottom of the stairs to put the key into her office door, there was an eerie coldness to the door, which appeared almost blue and reminded both of us of the *Dr. Zhivago* movie. As we opened the door, we discovered the window she had left ajar, a window near the ceiling of her basement office, had blown wide open. A mountain of snow stretched from the top of the window to halfway across the room, even covering the thermostat. The church custodian helped us shovel the massive accumulation of snow into nine large garbage sacks. Some of Karin's education materials and a few of my theological works still bear watermarked evidence of the storm. Two-and-a-half feet of snow were dumped on the city, but an efficient snow removal system soon had everything and everyone back to normal and we were enjoying Minne*snow*ta.

At Christmas even native-born Minnesotans ask, "Will we have a White Christmas?"

Annetta and Randy were in Minnesota for business, to see the sights, to celebrate Thanksgiving 1992 and to see SNOW! Sights they saw, but NO SNOW! They had to be content seeing only the Mall of America and driving to Claremont to see my church.

When St. Paul's annual winter carnival began we took part. The Ice Palace early in 1992, our second year in Minnesota, offered us two months of fun. Karin and Jack spent New Years Day and as much as possible of January and February watching the construction of the 165 foot tall Ice Palace on Harriet Island in the Mississippi River in St. Paul. Each ice block weighed at least 550 lbs., making the four-wing, 220 ft.-wide Palace weigh over 15 million lbs., as much as 20 Boeing 747's! The large 550-pound blocks of clear ice were trucked in and placed upon a solid foundation on the bank of the Mississippi River. A forty-foot spire rose above the Palace. When the unique structure was complete, we were present for the light and sound show, which took place within the crystalline building.

Opening night Karin stood in 5-degree weather at the foot of the palace. Tears beneath her sunglasses shielding her eyes from the glare of the ice slid down her cheeks and froze as the castle's multi-colored lights blinked in rhythm to music which ended with the *1812 Overture*! Karin wanted to buy the Palace, but we could not find the down payment. (Two down jackets were all the down we could manage!)

We enjoyed the unique ice sculptures, which were featured in the park across from the St. Paul Hotel and could be viewed throughout the celebration of winter's grip upon the land. On one of Karin's days off, when the carnival was over, we sat on a street above the Mississippi River where the massive accumulation of the huge blocks of ice that had been the frozen castle was clearly visible and watched as the Palace was unceremoniously dumped into the Mississippi waterway which flowed to New Orleans. The wrecking crew was supposed to take care of it in just a few hours. However, it had been so cold and the castle, lighted from the interior, was so well engineered that it had melted and frozen in place and it took them the good part of a week to destroy the fairy land. It was as though a magnificent fantasy had come and gone within a period of a few weeks.

Weather in Minnesota is as unpredictable as Texas weather. Halloween of 1991 was the Mega Blizzard, 33 inches of snow. January of 1992 I enjoyed every thing at the St. Paul Winter Carnival. Twice I made the trip in an ice sled down the two-block long ice slide built on the state capitol's steps. I was never able to coax Karin to join me in that exercise. She wisely stood at the bottom of the slope to help me off the sled and took pictures. I posed behind a cutout of the costume of Vulcanus, the mythical god of fire, who each winter tries to bring on summer by melting the Ice Palace of Boreas, King of Winter. A friend in Claremont saw me in that posed picture and said he could not believe I posed in a costume of Vulcanus. As much as we enjoyed the St. Paul Winter Carnival, Vulcanus had bad timing during the 1992 Palace year: the snow and ice did not melt until after Easter, there was a killing frost June 28, summer consisted of 5 days when temperature was above 80 degrees, leaves began turning in late August and it snowed 8 inches November 1, snow which Vulcanus melted completely in a week and then clouded over the sun for three weeks!

A truly unforgettable and Great Adventure happened in the Northland, when Minneapolis friends invited us to visit their vacation home on an island in the boundary waters of Rainey Lake. We drove north to International Falls, went through Canadian customs, and carefully followed the instructions given us. Suddenly there was nothing ahead of us but water. We were about to turn around, thinking we had taken a wrong turn when a woman emerged from the forest. She had received a call from the island asking us to wait. Soon a sailboat appeared which took us to the island home for a several day stay in the midst of unlimited natural beauty.

By day we saw loons on the massive lake. With my binoculars I was able to watch two adult loons teaching their offspring to dive into the water to catch food swimming in the depths. Once the loon infant had secured an adequate repast, the tiny creature mounted the back of a parent to rest before taking another lesson in diving. Eagles soared above, occasionally descending from their perches in towering trees near the rocky shoreline. On board a motor driven boat we visited the mermaid statue that marked the boundary between two nations that had long been at peace. We swam in a narrow channel that separated the small island owned by our Minneapolis friends from a much larger landmass that was the property of Her Britannic Majesty, Queen Elizabeth II. At night we gloried in the wonder of a star-studded sky overhead while noticing the distant glow of the Northern Lights on the far horizon.

Karin's mother, Ina Kinsey, wanted the family to celebrate together. And so we were there for a grand day in March 1992 when the family gathered in Lubbock, Texas for the wedding of her youngest daughter's son, Marilyn's son, Ina's grandson.

Only 29 days later the same group gathered in Sweetwater, Texas for Ina Kinsey's funeral.

She had not been ill, but told Karin Saturday, April 11, she was "extremely tired". Later that same night, Karin had a sudden urge and, despite the late hour, decided to telephone again to see if she was feeling better.

The conversation was short: "I'm just very tired. I don't have any more to say."

"Go back to sleep. We love you," replied Karin.

The next morning, April 12, Palm Sunday, 1992, the message came during Church School to Dr. David Sawyer who was serving Oak Grove as Interim, that Ina Kinsey had quietly died in her bed during the night. David went downstairs where Karin was helping the nursery attendants prepare for the morning activities. He stood at the door waiting to speak to Karin. She glanced up, saw him and came to the hallway. She spoke before he did.

"My Mother died, didn't she?"

Karin knew. David told her she could go home to prepare for a second trip to Texas. Instead, she went into the sanctuary to pray and attend Palm Sunday worship. The service began with a musical fanfare and the words, "Enter into His Gates with Thanksgiving". It was as if the angels were announcing Ina's arrival in heaven.

Texas wildflowers covered the countryside for the two trips we made. Even airport runways were a colorful patchwork of bluebonnets, Indian paintbrush, primroses. Texas (Lubbock and Sweetwater) had never looked so beautiful. Karin's Mother's yard was a field of her favorite flowers, blue bonnets, waist high. Even more beautiful was time we enjoyed with our family, which after the death of Ina consists only of our two children and Karin's two sisters and their families. After the death of Ina, neither Karin nor I have a home in Texas to which we can return.

General Assembly was held in Milwaukee in 1992 and Karin and I attended opening ceremonies and the election of the moderator. That year it was especially meaningful to see friends from everywhere and to enjoy the unique architecture of the many cultures in Milwaukee within driving distance of our home in Minneapolis.

August 31 that year we celebrated our anniversary in Door County, a string of small communities on a peninsula jutting into Lake Michigan; sea shore to rival North Carolina; countryside to compare to New England; buildings with goats on the roof; shops as much fun as New Orleans and cherry orchards to entice us.

# The Great Adventure   233

St. Paul, Wisconsin
Winter Carnival
Ice Palace
Each block weighs over 550 pounds!

## St. Paul Winter Carnival

*Sliding Down the Steps of the St. Paul Capitol!*

*What Fun!*

*Hi! Do You Recognize Me ???*

*Twenty-Seven*

# At One P.M. The Snow Began To Fall
*December 1993*

When I completed my seventeen-month service in Claremont, I was asked to accept a similar position in St. Paul, Edgecumbe Presbyterian Church. This proved to be a much more difficult assignment than Claremont in spite of the fact the St. Paul church was only a few miles from my apartment home.

One of the church members commented on my last Sunday, "At least you did settle all of us down."

I realized that the elder who made the remark was one who had needed a bit of "settling down" on more than one occasion. My final ministerial act was that of presiding at a congregational meeting, which issued a unanimous call to an able woman minister who has had a very successful pastorate in the years that followed.

I continued my writing, making this my primary activity while Karin focused on her work as a Church Educator at Oak

Grove in Bloomington. My efforts resulted in the publication of my third book, *Photographer Under Fire, The Story of George S. Cook*. This was produced by Bolger Publications of Minneapolis and marketed under the imprint of Historical Resources Press.

Karin assisted me during her vacation in my research in places such as the Library of Congress. On one of our visits to Washington, the Library was undergoing a total renovation. All facilities had been moved across the street to an annex. Karin spent most of the day in the building's sub-basement sitting on a cold cement floor. There she used her Trinity University cataloging experience to locate leads for materials and books, which I could take to the comfortable fourth floor reading room. I could sit in a heavily padded chair and call up printed works or manuscripts she found that would aid me in completing my current project while she sat on the basement cement floor searching through card catalogue trays. This effort produced a fourth book in 1996, again by Eakin Press, *Jean Laffite, Prince of Pirates*.

It had been three-and-a-half years of transition in Oak Grove. From the moment of arrival there was transition in Oak Grove (by actual count, 15 people retired or left for other employment during Karin's time). Finally, the new Head of Staff arrived June 1993, the very month Karin had completed recruiting all the teachers for the fall education program! At the same time the Floods of 1993 were hitting the Mid-West and Karin had an irresistible urge to go help. With the Education Program in good order in Oak Grove and with things in dis-order in flood territory, Karin resigned so she could volunteer to help in the flood area. It was a good transition.

Karin became the Volunteer Coordinator for Volunteer Efforts in the State of Iowa. From the office of Ecumenical Ministries of Iowa she worked with the Presbytery of Des Moines, the Emergency Management for the State of Iowa, the Federal Emergency Management Administration (F.E.M.A. offices, Washington), the American Red Cross, the Salvation Army, the Mennonites, the national offices of C.R.O.P. (familiar because of the CROP walks and the Hearts of Love Care Packages General Assembly promotes), the Mayor's offices of Des Moines and others. Karin found all these to be real people. They won her heart. Working with them was sheer joy. Their patience in the midst of adversity was an inspiration.

As a person who grew up in territory which is usually drought-ridden instead of flood-ridden, a person who requires sunshine, perhaps the hardest fact for Karin to accept was the fact that it rained 29 out of her first 30 days in Des Moines! She became *Flood Weary,* as were many people in Iowa. She lived through the Flash Flood that followed the original flood. That happened after the shelters had been closed for only two days, believing the need for them was no longer real. For the first time in over six weeks merchants had planned to take the weekend off and think of something beside floodwaters!

Karin said, "Talking on the telephone to people all over the world, I was convinced people wanted to hear a live voice coming from national level offices. I needed to fill that spot, even for a short time."

Since my interim work was one third of the way between Minneapolis and Des Moines, I was able to get to Karin's headquarters without great difficulty. On one such trip, she put me to work distributing clean-up kits and mops to sites where the flood had left its mark. On another journey from Claremont to Iowa, I was volunteered for the job of running an electrical rust-removing tool to help a family-owned plumbing supply company get back into business.

By October she was back in Bloomington and we were able to take a vacation, to return to Texas while the Texas State Fair was open, to see our Texas friends and our children at a delightful time of year.

An unexpected treat was a visit in Fort Worth with the person for whom we named our daughter, Mrs. Robert F. Jones, Annetta Jones, Karin's sponsor of the Synod of Texas Youth Council.

Robin treated us to some wonderful times, meeting us with

Kathy, Jared and Jena at the Fair, taking us to see him in a Dallas court room, having breakfast and farewell lunch with us, and bringing Kathy and Jena to a cafeteria meal at the Mall. Annetta & Randy also met us, bringing pictures of remodeling (childproofing) they were doing in anticipation of Ian's arrival on November 24, 1993.

After completing her flood relief service in Iowa, Karin received a call to serve as Church Educator for a congregation in Green Bay, Wisconsin. Once again we packed our possessions and moved the first Monday in July 1994. We rented a comfortable townhouse on the northeast corner of the city of Green Bay.

Once again I joined a new Presbytery, Winnebago. For a time I was Session Moderator and occasional preacher for a country church east of town, one, which originally had been a Huguenot congregation where French was spoken as the primary language. By this time, English was the only language allowed in Wisconsin. Yet I was not sure my sermons of moderation were fully understood. The church had a history of withholding funds from the Presbytery since some of the elders felt the area's governing body was a bit too liberal for their liking. Although I never got the local Session to officially approve full support of Winnebago Presbytery, the church treasurer told me he was making regular financial contributions to the Presbytery without mentioning this fact to his fellow elders.

I was then invited to serve as interim pastor for the Crivitz Presbyterian Church in the heavily forested lands fifty miles north of the city of Green Bay. This was my most delightful temporary position. Although some Sundays involved drives through ice and snow with temperatures that could reach forty degrees below zero, the roads were well maintained and always passable. I enjoyed making monthly communion visits to shut-ins in isolated areas. The church deacons assisted me, sometimes helping me through heavy snowdrifts to farmhouses and cabins well off the main road. I will always remember one of my communion assistants, a robust deacon named Ernie Guth, who would use his heavy boots to trample out a pathway through accumulated

## At One P.M. The Snow Began To Fall 239

snow for me. He took delight in telling his fellow church officers that he had finally found a preacher who would "walk in my footsteps" rather than the other way around.

I used the kit I had inherited from my minister father. This included communion glasses, a small silver tray, an airtight container for bread, and a bottle for the "fruit of the vine". In northern Wisconsin this last item would always be grape juice. Most of the isolated communicants were elderly. They were deeply appreciative of the simple service I conducted, realizing the significance of the fact I made use of my father's kit.

Since the town was in the middle of a resort area, two worship services were necessary during the summer months. Even in the worst of winter weather, people filled the church sanctuary each Sunday. I realized this was not because of great sermons but simply because the worship service was an effective antidote to cabin fever.

One of the parts of our Spouse Trailer arrangement, which was discouraging for both Karin and to me, especially in Minnesota and Wisconsin, was the fact that each of us was involved in separate activities, not working together on the same church projects. On a few times when her schedule in Green Bay allowed, Karin went to Crivitz with me. On one occasion, on a day other than Sunday, she conducted one of her workshops that assisted persons in writing their own life story.

She advertises these workshops as *This Is Who I Am* with a slogan, "If you don't tell us who you are, someone else will."

After the workshop in Crivitz, Wanda Wiedemeier called her and asked her to write her life story. Karin told her that she didn't do that; she merely taught people how to write their own. Wanda said she had already done that, but she needed more help. She had never told her children who she was and she wanted to give them booklets for Christmas. Her story was wonderful. She had grown up, thinking she didn't know who her mother was, but she did! Karin helped her and published her booklets called, *Wanda, Who Is She Anyway?* After that Karin helped her husband, Bob, write his story, equally as interesting: *Bob's Log*. Bob had been raised in a Logging Camp after his mother died when he was a very small child. After the booklets were published, Bob and Wanda invited us for a special Karin appreciation day: Bob let her run the Sawmill all by herself. Bob was proud of his Sawmill that he had equipped with a laser to guide the saw to efficiently cut selected trees from the forest with its six-foot cutting blade. I got to take pictures, but Karin is the only person he has let run his Sawmill. Even Wanda has not had that privilege. Bob, the fourth generation sawmill owner, has been recognized for his Sawmill design for operating the entire mechanism. Once he explained the basics of the program to Karin, she was able to strip and cut an entire tree into a usable stack of lumber.

Karin and I became Packer Backers, even buying, though never wearing, a cheese head. We bought complete Packer outfits. Even though every home game had been sold out in advance for years, we did see the Lambeau Leap at first hand at least three times. This was the dramatic jump most running backs made into the stands when a touchdown was made, a jump only possible in the stadium at Green Bay. A season ticket holder in Karin's congregation allowed us to use the ticket privileges she had inherited.

A neighbor, Antonio Freeman, lived directly across the side street from our townhouse. He had just completed his rookie year as a wide receiver. Karin noticed he did not take the Milwaukee newspaper. When a front-page article included a photograph of Freeman in action on the football field, she clipped it out and took it to him. At first he thought she wanted him to autograph the picture. She told him that was not what she intended. She had clipped it out so he could send it to his mother in Virginia. When Freeman broke his arm while scooping up a pass on an opponent's goal line, Karin took him cookies during his recuperation. While at the hairdresser's, Karin learned her cookie therapy was widely known among ardent Packer Backers. Karin's cookies were possibly a contributing factor to the teams' success that year, for the go-ahead touchdown at the New Orleans's Superbowl was a pass caught by Antonio Freeman.

We made countless trips to Door County. On one occasion we were present for a Fish Boil, a traditional event in the area. The fresh fish caught that day were placed in a large, outdoor cooking pot. Once the pot had been filled with water and other appropriate ingredients, a vigorous fire was built under the vessel. When fish and contents finally boiled over, all present were served. We took the tour of the twelve lighthouses by boat, and learned how the area had gained its name. On the final leg of our voyage, the small ship passed over the deep underwater chasm, which had once sucked native canoes to doom, thus giving the passage the direful name, "The Door to Death".

Summer 1995 we visited in Dallas and Denton and Annetta and Randy proudly introduced us to their second son, Camden Ramsay Hunt born June 3, 1995. Camden's brother, Ian, who was not quite two when Camden was born, celebrated the birth of his brother by breaking out with a full-blown case of chicken pox.

1995 was a year of conventions: Association of Church Educators in Atlanta, Georgia and the American Book Sellers Convention in Chicago, Karin as Publisher, I as author. I spoke to the Optimist Club of Minneapolis on "My Second Career".

Soon after Karin joined the Green Bay church staff, a major renovation and building program began. Karin had not known this was about to happen when she accepted the job. The renovation included adding an elevator in the very center of the building, an elevator which really was needed because the sanctuary was on the second story and the stairs were old and very hard for most anyone to climb. As a result, the builders had to virtually tear out something in nearly every room in the entire facility. Karin's boxes arrived and many of them were never unpacked. Dust from 50-year-old cement permeated everything. Karin's office was moved several times, many treasures getting broken in the process. She ended in the basement where nothing could be locked or kept ready for the next activity.

The most difficult part of the situation was that for two years there was not really a place to keep curriculum and supplies for the education program. Karin had to sort and try to keep safe every education resource the church had ever purchased. In desperation, she finally decided to pack everything and take advantage of the unusual situation. She designed a curriculum based on the fact that Moses and his people were "on the move" for 40 years! As a result, some of the young children decided Moses was their hero, better than Hulk or Superman! While the curriculum was originally designed for the teachers to hold classes in rooms by age level, the builders eventually tore up so much of the building that teachers never knew where they would be from one Sunday to the next. She rose to that challenge by designing an intergenerational educational program that could be held in a large open area. Instead of teachers' guides, she made bulletins that the children could illustrate and/or take home for parents to discuss the story with them. At first, when a few bulletins remained after Church School, she took them upstairs for the children to use during worship. Adults, yes, Senior Citizen Adults, discovered the bulletins which had teaching helps for all ages on the back. Each week she had to produce more and more bulletins. Some of the most elderly ladies confessed to her that they have complete sets of "Moses & The Journey Through The Wilderness".

Green Bay First Presbyterian Church completed their renovation of their building, creating one of the best facilities any church could imagine. They had spent a year "Crossing the Red Sea" and finally had entered the "promised spaces" and from their own ranks developed leadership to carry forward regular programming they dreamed. Karin accepted her final paycheck on September 7, 1995 and moved into the publishing field.

The new pastor for Crivitz arrived September 15, 1996 just in time for us to go to a September Never-To-Be-Forgotten Reception and Double Book Signing sponsored by the Carolianana Society of the University of South Carolina. We had begun the year with a trip to Richmond for reunion of my Seminary Class and a Book Signing for my book at the Valentine Museum in Richmond. We ended the year with The Small Press Book Fair in New York City where we had a booth for our books in the same building where the *New Yorker* operated 25 years earlier.

Though the experiences of Moses had challenged Karin creatively, it had also discouraged her. Both Karin and I began to talk about the advantages and disadvantages of our Spouse Trailer adventures. When Karin began trailing me in 1951, we both felt the support of Presbytery and Synod. We especially looked forward to those meetings, nearly always over night meetings that included worship as well as a time to see friends and encourage each other. While the Presbyterian Church in 1951 did not recognize the wives of ministers as staff, meetings of Presbytery and Synod left both of us feeling affirmed and supported as pastor and wife by the greater church.

After I became the trailer in 1987, I still had the support of a Presbytery. Karin found other educators were feeling the same as she did, generally unsupported unless they had a Senior minister who was especially appreciative. When she had worked for Roy Zuefeldt at Northminster she had experienced the best of both worlds: a feeling of appreciation from two pastors and she was running back and forth between Roy and me, helping each of us use the best of the other's denominational offerings. Even though she had been warned that the education and worship committees of Chapel Hill were in conflict, she and David Hoffelt had become partners both in worship and education. In every church she served, she has negotiated with the committee and officers in charge, requesting that there be no conflict between education and worship schedules. She maintained that part of her call was to attend worship as a role model; adults and especially young people and children needed to see her attend worship. When she had interviewed for the job in Bloomington, she had called the pastor of Oak Grove and asked him point blank, "If I come, are you going to move soon?" He told her he loved where he was and hoped to retire there. Less than a year after she came, he announced his departure. David Sawyer, who is now on the staff of a Seminary, understood the role and possible frustrations of educators. However, he was an Interim to be followed by other Interims.

APCE (Association of Presbyterian Church Educators) was designed to help educators feel supported. An issue to encourage Educators had been before General Assembly for years, repeatedly voted down by the General Assembly: the issue of ordination which would give educators vote and voice in Presbytery, the same privileges and support ordained clergy and newly recognized lay preachers presently receive. Karin originally attended these conventions and I went along on the trip but found other things to do while she was in convention. Research for books I like to write is rich in the places conventions are held. However, when the issue of ordination of educators was first proposed and needed understanding and support, and when extra convention attendees would make conventions more financially feasible, I was urged to join APCE, and did. As a result, Conventions were more spectacular but Karin and I felt like they had become a conference for church leadership, a need, but left no special place or convention where an educator could feel support for the specialized work they do.

One issue that discouraged Karin was the issue of pension. After Karin had worked a few months with Northminster in Dallas, it was obvious that she was doing as much or more than any full time staff person could do. It was then that she was issued a formal call from the Session of Northminster, changing from part-time to full-time status and a change to include full payment of pension benefits. Perhaps I should have followed up on this since none of these payments were ever received as far as either denominational office could tell or Social Security now shows. Soon after this Roy Zuefeldt left Dallas. He moved to Abilene where he became a pastor of a strong congregation that had come together through the union of what were then called *Northern* and *Southern* churches. As best we could determine Karin's pension payments had been lost in the reuniting process.

Both Karin and I were invited to participate in the work of Twin Cities Area Presbytery. At one meeting of Presbytery, Karin spoke before the assembled Elders and Ministers. In view of all

## At One P. M. The Snow Began To Fall

that happened since we left Covenant, I think the issue on which she spoke may be the real issue that discouraged her. She received a standing ovation for her objection to a policy paper that did not allow the family of a retired minister to participate in the life and worship of their former congregation. The Presbytery immediately voted to return the document to committee and only approved the paper when the statements that Karin found offensive had been deleted. The Presbytery recognized both her professional position as a Church Educator and her standing as an ordained Presbyterian elder. On more than one occasion, she was asked to preach and lead worship in churches in the Minneapolis area.

Whatever the reason, after three years in Green Bay we decided it was time to return from our feeling of isolation to civilization. We were determined not to retire and die. Perhaps we should both concentrate on writing books and publishing. Attendance and participation in national book fairs in Chicago and New York and membership in SPAN (Small Press Association of North America) and PMA (Publishers Marketing Association) had given us a sense of belonging and productivity. We seriously considered Minneapolis as a permanent home and made an appointment with a real estate agent to visit a potential residence at three o'clock on an April afternoon the week containing Good Friday. At one P. M., the snow began to fall. Within an hour nearly a foot of snow was on the ground. I called the agent and postponed the appointment indefinitely.

In 1997 we continued south, looked at a score or more apartments in Dallas and San Antonio and finally settled on a comfortable one on Cowboys Parkway in Irving. Our Green Bay friends made me promise I would wear the Green and Gold with a large "G" on my chest on Cowboys Parkway. This I did a few days before the Packer game in the Irving stadium on October 31.

One young lady saw my garb and shouted, "Rah, Rah, Go Packers".

Her companion, a heavy set young man who looked like

he could have played right guard for any pro team, and may have, for several Cowboys lived in our complex, responded, "That looks like a Halloween costume to me."

The move back home to Texas was the most difficult one of all. The moving van company lost all of our possessions for eight days. When the truck finally arrived after an unscheduled detour to the Canadian border, over two thousand dollars worth of damage to our furniture was apparent. The van line paid off at last and we bought new furniture vowing never to move again. Nine months later we broke our vow and moved to Corinth, just south of Denton.

I rejoined Grace Presbytery. I met with the Committee on Ministry and once again went through the necessary procedure for becoming a member of the governing body in which I had served twenty-eight years. I told the committee that I was interested in occasional preaching. I was invited to preach at St. Andrews Church in Denton. I filled the pulpit at the Presbyterian Church in McKinney when the local pastor was on vacation. I accepted all invitations in churches all the way from Stephenville south of Fort Worth to Honey Grove well north of the Metroplex. In the early fall of 1998, I preached at Glendale Presbyterian Church. This had been my mother's church during the years she lived at Presbyterian Village. Her funeral had been held there. I offered to continue to preach at Glendale as long as I was needed. This was a relationship that lasted for six months. At one point I was offered an interim contract. This I turned down. Although making the trip across downtown Dallas was quite easy on Sunday morning, I knew I could no longer fulfill a contract that would include the responsibilities of making necessary hospital visits by driving from Corinth/Denton to the downtown Dallas and Oak Cliff areas and back home again, sometimes daily. My last sermon there was preached on Palm Sunday of 1999. This concluded my preaching ministry, one that began as a student pastor in Anson in 1944 and continued for a total of fifty-five years.

We had enjoyed apartment living. We felt we had a community, particularly in Minnesota! We were enjoying out apartment in Irving when Robin and his wife, Kathy, took us out to see the house they were in the process of building on the north side of Corinth. Kathy was the one who suggested that Karin and I talk to their real estate agent. Both of us thought we really were not interested when Karin later suggested to me that Kathy had given us the greatest compliment ever. She had never before made a suggestion we could live near them, near family again. Karin commented that we should go just to show Kathy we appreciated the compliment. I think that we were more surprised than Robin and Kathy when, in less than two hours of viewing and talking, we purchased a model home, within four blocks of the house they were building.

This was one of our easier moves since we had family help. Robin drove a rented U-haul truck two nights in a row from Cowboys Parkway to the new house in Corinth. Off-duty firemen provided professional assistance making the transfer of heavier items possible without a single scratch.

The model home was landscaped and needed only Karin's touch to make both house and garden truly beautiful. When a drainage problem developed, Karin sought an adequate solution to the problem. She found a landscape designer who was a native Texan with an understanding of water problems in the Texas soil who would supervise a redirection of the water that poured down in torrents on our garden area. After several tons of New Mexico river rock were brought in and skillfully added at appropriate places, the backyard became a site of unique charm. Although we were willing to give up the excitement of vagabond life we had so enjoyed, we knew there could be great adventures ahead back in Texas.

*Welcome To*
*2104 Post Oak Court*
*Corinth, Texas*

*Twenty-Eight*

## The Last Bicycle Ride
*October 1999*

Karin and I found our new home, 2104 Post Oak Court in Corinth, comfortable and enjoyable. Although it was not as large as the Lavita Lane house in Farmers Branch, it was ideally suited to our needs. In addition to the master bedroom, there were three smaller bedrooms, one of which would be designated as Karin's office and another could serve as a place where I could continue my efforts as an author. This had been a model home that the builder had used to display potential upgrades: white tile kitchen floor, top quality appliances, a spacious outdoor deck and extensive landscaping.

Obstacles to the move appeared during the weeks in which we sought to coordinate the necessity of breaking our apartment lease with the closing date for the new home. The builder's project manager called and told me his company was losing twenty-two hundred dollars on the sale because of the many amenities in the new house. He would have to increase the price.

I stayed on the telephone quite a while trying to negotiate but finally turned him over to Karin.

It didn't take long before I heard her, in a resolute and determined tone say, "I know we probably can't get our money back, but how do we go about canceling the contract before we lose more money?" The project manager immediately gave in. He agreed to let the contract price stand.

One more problem arose in the new home buying process. On one trip to the new house to measure floor space for furniture placement, Karin noticed that the air conditioner in the garage used for an office while the house was a model had been removed and that the upgrade dishwasher was pulled forward as though it were being removed. A boxed dishwasher of lesser quality was sitting in the front room. She immediately contacted the sales agent, stating she had been led to believe her agreement affirmed that all appliances the house contained at the time of contract signing were a part of the deal. The cheaper dishwasher suddenly disappeared and the quality appliance remained, though the air conditioner in the garage was already gone.

Three weeks after settling in our new house, a violent thunderstorm swept through the area. The weather forecaster, in a casual tone of voice, had mentioned the possibility of hail. Yet no one was prepared for the heavy pounding that the house received. Just after I had coaxed Karin to quit her yard work and come in from the garden, a deadly barrage of hailstones descended upon our home.

Glass panes in the front and side windows were broken, gutters were dented and window screens hopelessly injured, the deck and fence pocked. The attractive front door was scarred, the carriage light fixtures broken and the roof destroyed. All trees in the area were stripped naked of the beautiful spring foliage, which had made the area so attractive. The circular paved area in front of the four model houses was a beautiful solid green, completely covered with a four-inch layer of leaves that had been striped from the trees. A heavy coating of broken greenery covered the entire neighborhood.

Our moving boxes were not yet completely unpacked and we had met our neighbors only casually, but the next morning, when we could survey in daylight what the storm in the night had done, we found out how fortunate we were to have caring persons living near us. We did not even own a rake or enough garbage bags to start the task before us, so we told our neighbors we would return just as soon as we were able to buy some cleanup tools and supplies. While out, we decided to stop to buy some Texas barbecue to take home from a market we remembered when we last lived near the area.

We left to buy a rake, but when we returned our fellow dwellers on Post Oak Court had completely cleared our yard and were returning to clean their own yards. We celebrated by sharing barbecue with them. The rake still hangs on the garage wall hoping it will never be used for cleanup after a violent hailstorm.

The insurance adjuster gave as liberal an estimate of repair costs as possible, one that he knew would be hard to believe in an insurance office outside of Texas. He took a picture of a large flowerpot that had a hole in the side larger than a Rio Grande valley grapefruit. This he used to prove the validity of the damage claim. Although our homeowners' policy had an extremely high deductible, we were finally able to get all essential items properly repaired including a completely new roof. Karin made some of the repairs herself such as the repainting of the home's front door. An electrician replaced the shattered light fixtures with ones that were carefully selected by Karin. These were even more attractive than those installed by the builder.

I had continued to ride my bicycle while living on Cowboys Parkway. On occasion I rode past Jerry Jones' Cowboy headquarters wearing my Green Bay Packer jacket. Since the apartment complex was on a hill, I usually gained considerable momentum going toward the exit gate. One morning I saw the gate open and accelerated. Suddenly the electronically controlled device closed. I slammed on my brakes and went head over heels to the pavement. My helmet saved me from serious injury, but the accident left me with heavy swelling below my left eye. Karin took me to the best eye doctors available who concluded that only minor damage had been done to my eyesight. Thereupon I promised to never again race an electronic gate.

As far as I was concerned, one of the appealing factors about the new home site was the fact we would no longer be in a gated community with gates unable to respond to a bicycle trying to exit. The multi-speed Cannondale I had bought in Minneapolis rode exceedingly well in the area that the builders had named *The Knoll*. There was enough up and down slope to make a ride delightfully exhilarating.

On the morning of October 28, 1999 I made my last bicycle ride. I had been told years earlier that my heart murmur was an indication that I would eventually need extensive surgery to correct a problem with my aorta valve. I would have warning symptoms such as swelling of the ankles, extreme shortness of breath or sharp chest pains. Since none of these had occurred, I had decided not to worry about the direful forecast both Wisconsin and Dallas doctors had placed upon me.

On this particular morning I did not feel my usual enthusiasm for the ride I was about to take. Once on board the Cannondale, I pedaled up hill to take advantage of a half mile of down slope. Even the downhill run left me with none of the exhilaration I had anticipated. I got off the bike at the point that I normally would have begun another gentle climb. There I saw a sign I had never noticed before: "Call 911 for emergency."

For a moment I wondered if I would have to make such a call. I decided to cut short my usual ride. I returned my bicycle to the garage storage rack little realizing I would never again set forth on another bicycle trip.

I was scheduled to attend a Writer's Conference at North Texas University the following morning. Karin had suggested I take part in the event, which would offer professional suggestions for publishing a manuscript I had been working on for years. I took her advice. I sent in the required materials to be judged. I

# The Last Bicycle Ride

had been trying to write all of my life, yet I had never before dared enter a contest.

Since I had heard nothing from the conference leaders other than information about which garage I should use for parking, I felt sure the two-day event would result in nothing other than criticism of my efforts.

I dressed carefully, a business suit with a white shirt and a conservative tie.

Karin looked at me and said, "Since you are going to a writer's conference, why don't you dress like a writer? Why not wear that white turtleneck I gave you?"

I took her suggestion and headed out the door. I had a feeling of uneasiness, one that I attributed to my uncertainty about the location of the university conference center garage. I had no difficulty in finding my assigned parking slot. I pulled my six-year-old Honda into place, got out and suddenly had the feeling I might never be able to return to that location. I counted the spaces from the entrance ramp in case I had to tell someone where to find my car. Still I had not felt any of the symptoms my doctors had promised, only a heaviness in my chest. I realized I had to get to some place where there were people. The feeling of uneasiness took over my whole being.

I walked the three hundred feet to the Conference Center's door with difficulty. Once inside the building, one of my fellow conference goers tried to make friendly conversation. I fear I must have appeared utterly boorish. I followed the arrows to the registration desk. I gave my name and was handed my packet. I looked for a place to sit down. Finding none, I went back to the registrar's table and said, "I am a heart patient and I need help."

Two stalwart security guards immediately appeared. They helped me remain upright until the paramedics came. The next thing I knew I was in a fast moving ambulance.

I asked, "Where are we going?"

The driver replied, "To the nearest hospital".

"Could you take me to the new hospital?"

"Why?" The driver asked.

I vaguely remember I made a response that may have sounded something like this, "Because the new hospital is very close to where I live."

I knew Karin was at home without transportation. The ambulance seemed to swerve, perhaps make a "U" turn.

The only other conversation I can remember was that of the paramedic hovering over me. He kept saying, "Raise your tongue up so we can put this tablet under it."

A very comfortable feeling had swept over me. Why make any effort to do anything when I felt as though I was in warm cocoon, one that seemed to be carrying me away from all pain and difficulty.

Another thought laid hold upon me. If I gave in to the gentle flow of serenity, would I see Karin's beautiful face this side of death? The paramedic's request to raise my tongue became more and more insistent, but how do you raise up your tongue when you are lying flat on your back?

This was a situation from which I did not want to depart; yet I sensed I must do something to see again the one person who had brought so much joy and outright pleasure into my life. How dreary my existence would have been without her! I had to make some effort.

I tried again and again until the paramedic said, "Good, good".

The next thing I knew I was looking into the face of the beautiful person I had married so many wonderful years ago.

*Twenty-Nine*

## Kissed By An Angel

*November 1999*

Karin and I had received a printed invitation to the grand opening of the Denton Regional Hospital, an event that would take place in mid-October. Since the brand new facility was less than a mile from Post Oak Court, we considered taking the tour that would have included a visit to the new emergency room and intensive care unit though, for some reason we failed to attend.

In the forty days that followed October twenty-ninth we saw more of the new medical facilities than we would have seen on the tour or ever have imagined possible. Our tour of the facilities started on the day I was carried there to begin two sixteen day visits with nine days at home between the two admissions. Karin would travel to the hospital every one of those days I was in Denton Regional Hospital, returning home only for rest at night and occasional errands or meals outside the hospital.

When I awoke from the ambulance ride to find myself in

the brand new emergency room, I saw what I above all else wanted to see: the face of the person who most mattered in my life. The staff had called Karin and told her I was there and she should come as quickly as possible. All they would assure her was that I had not been in an automobile accident. She called Robin's work number and was told that he could not be reached that morning since the judge had just begun a session in the city courtroom.

"Okay", said Karin, "Please tell the judge that his father has just been taken by ambulance to the new Regional hospital".

Suddenly the wheels of justice for Denton ground to a complete halt that Friday, October 29, 1999. Within minutes the Judge was on his way to Post Oak Court where he picked up Karin and took her to the hospital. Nine days later he brought his court to Jack's room. The medical staff required on file a Living Will for all seriously ill patients scheduled for open-heart surgery. I also needed an updated conventional will. The two documents were sworn to with the highest possible level of due process.

Four days after I entered the hospital I had a cardiac catherization that was followed by a heart attack. My doctors came to my bedside to explain the necessity of open-heart surgery. I responded that was what I had been told six years earlier by my Wisconsin doctor. He had insisted such a procedure would be necessary within five years. At least I had succeeded in getting a little more mileage out of my old heart valve than the Wisconsin doctor had expected me to get.

I also admitted I had discussed with my Dallas cardiologist the type of valve replacement I should receive. I could choose between an animal heart and a mechanical device. The first probably would last no more than seven years. The other could be good for decades, but would require special medication as long as I lived. I had already decided to go for the long haul in order to have as many more years with Karin as possible.

Complications from the catherization and the heart attack developed and I remained in bed, flat on my back in intensive care for days, medical personnel constantly watching all sorts of monitors. Finally a date was set for my grand opening. On the night before surgery my nurse, Shane, performed the necessary body shave. All hair below my eyebrows would be removed. During the process, Shane told me that the entire staff was delighted I had reached this point. At the beginning of my week of total bed rest no one believed I would be able to under go the proposed procedure.

"Suddenly all the numbers came together", said Shane. "We are all certain the surgery will be successful".

I had met my surgeon, Dr. Tea E. Acuff, who, according to Shane, was one of the top three heart surgeons in the nation. In addition to that rating he was a fellow Davidsonian. Acuff told me he was a "Tennessee boy who had gone to Davidson College hoping to become a Presbyterian minister but had been sidetracked into medicine." I had gone the opposite route. In any case, I knew I was in good hands.

Sixteen days after I entered the hospital, and five days after my grand opening, I was released from the hospital in Karin's care. Nine days later, when I even could not eat Karin's cooking and did not have the strength to walk around the culdesac with her help, I agreed to return to the hospital where I remained for sixteen additional days. I was later told Karin had saved my life by insisting I go back to the emergency room for evaluation after my brief stay at home.

Once back in the hospital my life hung by a thread. On my second admission the head nurse granted Karin special privileges in the new Intensive Care Unit because "you are family". Karin witnessed three code blue emergency calls that first day of the second admission where doctors and hospital responded for assistance in keeping me alive. She was in the cafeteria when she heard another one and she raced back to the intensive care to ask how many times they had called for help. She learned that this was but one of a number of similar occasions during which my heart had been restarted, so many that they had quit counting. One nurse who had been an attendant during my first hospitalization called in on another matter, and when she heard I was in the hospital again, she came to the hospital on her day off and sat for two hours with Karin. The cardiologist told his office staff he was prepared to give up Thanksgiving family activities since he was almost certain I would die on that day.

Annetta and Randy had planned on taking their two sons out of town for a brief holiday the day I returned to the hospital. They came by the house to tell me they were going, and when they found the house empty, they came to the hospital. I was in the emergency room where they saw both Karin and me. I was waiting for the results of a test the emergency room had ordered. They decided that I would probably be home as soon as the results were known so they went on to Galveston. While touring the battleship *Texas*, permanently anchored in the San Jacinto River near Houston, Annetta had a feeling that all was not well. She left her family and went to a telephone booth near the entryway to the ship's anchorage area. She placed a call to the Denton hospital. Though she called and asked to speak to her mother, Shane, the nurse who cared so much, intercepted the call and told her they should drive carefully but they should not waste any time getting back to her father in the Intensive Care Unit. Shane merely told Karin Annetta had called to check on her father.

Annetta asked the help of the battleship ticket taker in rounding up her family. A bullhorn was used to alert Randy and sons and tell them they would have to return home immediately. The ticket taker then told Annetta that she had nothing to fear. She had been praying for Annetta's father and she was confident that he would live.

The hospital chaplain sat with Karin for several hours, Karin says five or more. Robin and his family were in Mexico, and though the hospital wanted to contact them, Karin insisted that they were coming back Thanksgiving Day and a call would not speed their ability to leave Mexico any more quickly. Roy Sherrod, my seminary roommate and our best man, called to check on my condition and when told that Karin was alone with only hospital friends, even though it was the day before Thanksgiving, came to sit with Karin. He refused to leave until the Bailiff of Robin's court came at 5:30 or 6 P.M., and insisted on sitting with Karin until Annetta arrived, that not happening until 1:30 in the morning.

Annetta was able to be with Karin for Thanksgiving dinner in the hospital's cafeteria. It was a feast worthy of any five star hotel. Indeed, it should have been, for the chef for the new hospital was a five star chef associated with chefs who appeared on television almost daily. Both Karin and Annetta who really were "not hungry" nevertheless found themselves filling their plates with food from the beautiful and abundant Thanksgiving buffet tables.

Suddenly Annetta, with full plate in hand and tears in her eyes, came to Karin and said, "Mother, they won't let me pay. They said it is free today!"

The two of them returned to Intensive Care. My condition remained "critical". Roy Sherrod was back again late Thanksgiving Day in time to wait while the hospital staff prepared me for the first time Annetta and Robin would see me.

I had no consciousness of these events or of anything else in the days that followed my return to the hospital. I did recall one nightmare in which I thought I had fallen into an abyss entangled in attachments to both arms. This seemed so real that I have sometimes wondered if I actually fell from my bed. Karin has reassured me that this could not have happened since I was constantly under the observation of a very able staff.

I can remember only one action that I am sure did occur during the fortnight or more I was in a deep coma. The surgeon and his heart specialist had talked with Karin, explaining that there were no bodily sounds. Karin, having worked in a cardiologist's office, asked about brain activity and insisted, contrary to their opinions, that she was sure that when she slid her hand under my hand, which was attached to tubing, I responded by rubbing her hand with my thumb. They were not convinced, but did give the instructions at the nurse's station to allow Karin permission to visit my room any time she wanted plus the instructions that they were to watch my monitors and record any activity they saw.

The next day, the day before my birthday, she made one of her daily trips to the hospital and found me alone with equipment pushed back, further away from me more than usual. She tucked her hand under mine and spoke to me. She told me that it looked like she could reach me more easily than she had ever been permitted. She asked me if I wanted a kiss. She told me I was to respond by winking my right eye, an eye that was swollen shut, as my whole head was swollen beyond belief. I must have had enough consciousness to make the right response.

"Let me be sure", said Karin. "If you really want a kiss, wink your left eye."

Again I gave enough response to convince her I was hearing. She reached over the railing, stretching to reach me, and kissed me on the forehead.

My head came six inches up in the bed. My feet came up under the sheet. My hands reached out. I tried to spit out the tube that was taped to my mouth. Lights above my head flashed orange, red, green, yellow. Buzzers rang. My movements scared her so much that she stumbled across my lifeline on the floor as she retreated from the room.

"Fix him, I think I killed him," she cried out to the nurses as she ran down the hall to the retreat the head nurse had given her, tears streaming down her face.

Almost immediately nurses came to her side, with the news, "You didn't kill him. You did what you've been doing for years. You gave him the will to live. You brought him out of coma."

Nurses tried to cheer Karin. The same nurse who had come on her day off even told Karin a joke about a parishioner who had asked his priest if it was okay to have sex on Sundays and was told it was okay as long as he didn't do it in the aisle and get in the way. Another nurse stopped by just to give Karin a hug. By 5 p.m. they had moved me to another room in the ICU. The next morning they had the window curtain back so nurses could bring other nurses by and look through the window to see that I was sitting up in my bed. Karin was beside me. We were talking to each other. It was my birthday and though I didn't care to eat any cake, Annetta brought a cake for the nurses to eat in their little dining room behind the nurses' station. Karin had achieved what the medical staff had been unable to do: awaken me from my long stupor.

Although the doctors believed several dialysis procedures that removed toxic fluids from my body had brought about my seemingly miraculous recovery, I am convinced there were other factors in the healing process. I learned later that dozens of persons in several different denominations were praying for me. During my ministry I had often seen the efficacy of effective medical procedures coupled with persistent prayer, a combination that time and time again had produced amazing results.

In my own case I was certain there was one more factor that saved me: the power of the daily presence of a saintly person. Months later when I gave my long time physician, David Sikora, an account of my recovery, the trusted doctor replied, "A bit of tender loving care goes a long way to aid the healing process".

On the afternoon of the day I first entered the hospital I was questioned about items I had abandoned when I took my ambulance ride. I was able to tell Robin he could find the car on the second level of the University garage, five spaces from the up ramp. Robin, amazed that I had the presence of mind to remember where I had parked the car, took care of the Honda's recovery.

When Karin questioned the hospital about my white turtleneck which she found missing, they told her it had been cut off and thrown away. When she asked me, I remembered hearing the paramedics say they needed to open my shirt by cutting it off of me. Karin reassured me she would buy me a new shirt. I think I now have at least a half dozen turtlenecks hanging in my closet.

Though I remember seeing Karin in the emergency room, I was completely in the hands of the Intensive Care after that and Karin, Robin and Annetta could do nothing except to wait and pray.

On the first day I was hospitalized Annetta remembered the writer's conference I had started out to attend. She suggested that Karin go to inform them of what had happened, to thank them for the help they had been and to redeem the materials I had sent there. The conference leadership warmly greeted her and urged her to come back the next day for the closing session, "Come for the luncheon. He has already paid for it. We will let you tell how he is doing. It will be good for them to see you, for they were concerned."

Karin asked to pick up the materials I had entered. They replied that those materials were still in the hands of workshop leaders who would meet before the luncheon in small groups where critics from national publishers would hear authors read a small section of what they had submitted. They were scheduled to meet immediately before the luncheon, and since she was coming to the luncheon anyway, they suggested she substitute for me and read a portion of my manuscript before the critics. The invited her to plan to stay a few moments after the meeting to talk with publishers who would be available at that time.

Karin didn't want to do that, she had not even read any portion of my manuscript, but the convention leaders were so gracious that she agreed to come back for both the luncheon and to read before the critics. She really planned to skip the meeting with publishers after the luncheon.

The next day she went to the workshop and saw my manuscript for the first time when critics handed each author what they had written. She had never done anything like this and the word *critic* scared her. She hastily looked at what I had written. She decided not to start with my first chapter. Rather, she picked what I had written as a third section, the section about a woman named Jane Long who I was presenting as someone who had been slighted in previous presentations of Texas history.

The other authors read first. Critics were harsh. Karin became even more nervous, thinking, "Why does any author ever try? If critics told me what they are saying to these poor people,

I would go home and cry and then quit writing!"

When they asked her to read, she had no choice. She read the section she had chosen and then waited for their comments.

Comments were few. "Why did he choose that title? We think he should chosen something which would cause readers to want to read or buy."

Karin said she didn't know why.

"Why did the manuscript he submitted start with something other than what you read? It was our opinion that the book was more about Jane Long than those he used in the first section. There are many books about the ones in the first section. We didn't even know anything about Jane Long other than that she was the *Mother of Texas*."

"I don't know", responded Karin.

Karin enjoyed the food and the friendliness of those at her table at the luncheon. She made a thank you announcement to the conference when the emcee graciously asked her to inform the conference of my condition. She then sat down and fidgeted during the remaining program, anxious to get back to me, as she sat and heard the presentations and acceptance of award after award, my name not among the prizewinners. When her mind was completely on other things, she was jolted as the grand prize for "the manuscript most likely to be published" was announced: "Jack Ramsay"!

Karin was then presented with the award for the "Best Non-fiction", an engraved ballpoint pen, quickly followed by a second award, the Grand Prize, a cash prize for the "Most Publishable Manuscript"! Only two critical suggestions had been made: concentrate more on Jane Long and change the title in order to attract readership.

Karin decided to stay for the brief meetings after the luncheon where possible publishers were waiting to talk to prospective authors. She was greeted warmly, especially by one of the judges who told Karin, "When he recovers, have him call me". After the conference we received a gracious letter of concern from the sponsors of the conference, along with the check I had sent for the conference.

During the week I had to lie on my back while waiting for the surgery that would make recovery a possibility I had plenty of time to think.

Upon Karin's early morning arrival midway through that first week, I greeted her with the announcement, "I have a title".

Karin who may have been concerned with matters other than my book, which was still only a manuscript, replied, "A title to what?"

"A new title for the book you said the writer's conference wanted", I replied.

"How about this? *Texas Sinners and Revolutionaries: Jane Long and Her Fellow Conspirators*"?

My doctors heard I was mentally working on my book and, realizing the precariousness of my situation, used this as an incentive for increasing my will to live. One mentioned to me I would need to get well to publish my fifth book. Yet publishing one more book was not the essential incentive I needed. Although I later was told I was near death on several occasions, I did not fear death nor did I welcome it.

During the second admission to the hospital, the two weeks or more I was in a coma, I remember only one event: I was kissed by an angel.

I am certain that my final recovery was only possible because of Karin's life-giving kiss.

*Thirty*

## Two Bicycles On a Garage Floor
*December 1999*

After repeated tests and many strength-building escorted walks through the hospital, I was once more dismissed from Denton Regional. Karin received precise instructions on what she needed to do to care for me. By this time my chest incision had begun to heal, but a four-inch wound in my thigh would require continuing attention.

The hospital staff recommended that a visiting nurse arrangement be established. My plastic surgeon that had been called in on the case agreed and then later changed his mind. He decided Karin could do all a home nursing service could possibly do.

Dr. Kadi was not the only one who had become an admirer of Karin. Shortly before my second release from hospitalization, Karin and I were walking on one of my prescribed walks through the building's hall when a nurse passed us and said to her, "That's a beautiful sweater you are wearing."

"Thanks," she replied. "Romeo gave it to me".

The nurse whirled around to look at us a second time.

"Oh, you are the Juliet I have been hearing about, the one who gave your husband that kiss."

Once at home, an effort was made to make use of the available nursing service, but, after several tries in both arms, the first visiting nurse was unable to draw blood so Karin had to drive me to the hospital to have blood drawn and she had to agree to have the nurse come to the home daily anyway. When she was also informed that to qualify for nursing service I must stay at home with constant care, leaving only for trips in the car to the hospital, Karin called Dr. Kadi who immediately told her that he was convinced she could do what he wanted done. She might as well do it all: she would become my nurse. The guest room was turned into a hospital facility. I would spend all of my nights and much of my daylight hours in what before had been called our guest room.

My thigh wound, which had been caused by testing prior to the heart surgery, had to be dressed three times a day. Stacks of dressing and medical supplies filled the dresser. This was a piece of furniture that served as a replacement for the massive medical equipment that had been wheeled into my room at the hospital. In addition Karin had to purchase all the prescribed drugs I would need, carefully sort these out and give me nine scheduled pills each twenty-four hours.

Not only was she a substitute for the highly skilled nursing staff, but also she was replacing equally able dietetic advisors. I could only eat foods, which did not contain an excessive amount of Vitamin K, a substance that could clog my mechanical heart valve.

In addition Karin had to see to it that she not feed me anything that contained considerable amounts of soy, a widely used food additive that could counteract the drugs that were keeping me alive. This requirement made it necessary to read all grocery store labels. The simple act of food shopping became a lengthy and tedious task.

I had lost twenty-six pounds during my hospital stay. Karin had the job of restoring me to normal strength while seeing to it that I did not eat any of the foods that might cause additional difficulties. She met this challenge with considerable skill.

I returned to computer word processing, an activity which two decades earlier had replaced my dependence on my trusty Underwood. While I was still a full time pastor in Carrollton, Jim Macphearson, a retired electrical engineer, offered to bring the church office into the electronic age.

He secured the donation of two Apple 2-E computers. An Epson dot-matrix printer and a ten Meg hard drive were purchased. Each week, Jim came to the church office. There he drilled both the pastor and the secretary on the complex task of word processing on an Apple. Since the particular Apple device placed in the church office had no function keys or a mouse, progress was slow.

At last I had enough confidence with my electronic skills to suggest to Karin that we purchase a home computer. Together we went to both soft and hardware demonstrations. Once we had learned something about the computer world, we purchased an AT&T Six-hundred along with an IBM Quietwriter printer.

Later I bought an IBM XT and a Radio Shack laptop. The portable computer was carried into libraries where I could copy data on a floppy disk that could be inserted into the XT and downloaded into the text of whichever book I was writing at the time. I later upgraded to a Dell computer and a Compaq notebook.

Karin and I attended every computer event we could, once taking part in a Minneapolis seminar led by Bill Gates who was just beginning to be recognized as the chief mogul of the electronic world for that day and time. When the laser printer became standard, I purchased an HP Three and Karin bought her own Dell and an HP Four.

She soon became so skilled at laser printer design that she was featured in a Hewlett Packard publication called *Reflections*, a journal that was sent to a mailing list of several hundred thousand computer specialists.

Kirby, her printer father, would have been proud.

Soon after moving into the home on Post Oak Court, I upgraded to a Compaq Presario with a larger monitor and twenty gigabits of hard drive space. On this I had produced the final copy of the book I had been working on which won two awards at the North Texas Writer's event.

I followed the suggestions of the conference experts. I rewrote the introduction explaining why I had used the word *sinners* in the book's title. I made several stylistic changes in the manuscript before final submission to the publisher.

Two days later I lost most of my eyesight. I was able to adjust the thermostat on a mid-January evening before going to bed. The next morning I could not see the device I had reset a few hours earlier. I had suffered a severe coughing spell during the night that resulted in breaking a blood vessel behind my retina. Coumadin, a blood-thinning drug, was a contributing factor to my loss of sight. The necessary medication allowed a massive hemorrhage in my right eye. My already damaged left eye would have to do it all.

Karin and I did not give up easily. Karin drove me through the worst of the early morning traffic between Corinth and Dallas's Greenville Avenue area for treatment by retina specialists. For a time I was involved with an experimental process that was believed to be a remedy for eyesight loss for a person on the medications I was required to take.

After over a year of treatment, it was decided that my eyesight would never be restored. I was declared legally blind. The only bright side of this event was that the IRS would give us a deduction on our ten-forty. The tax collector's concession approximated the allowance that resulted from having a baby. I figured that was a measure of compensation since giving birth at this stage of life might have been even harder on Karin than putting up with a near blind husband.

Nonetheless there were numerous disadvantages. I could never again drive an automobile. I could not read a newspaper, write checks or even proofread my books. Karin took over these important chores.

Since Karin had performed as a professional bookkeeper in three of her jobs in North Dallas, she soon reorganized my files in an orderly manner. She saw to it that no checks were written for unnecessary causes. She proved that if she had been writing the checks all along, we would be far better off than we would have been if I had continued to write all the checks.

When it came time for proofreading the book I had revised a few hours before I lost my sight, Karin not only out-proofed the professionals, but also secured sixty-one illustrations through the Internet. In addition, she produced a highly sophisticated index.

The Republic of Texas Press published *Texas Sinners and Revolutionaries: Jane Long and her Fellow Conspirators* in the spring of 2001. This press was a subsidiary of Wordware, a company that originally published computer workbooks. A national publisher, Rowman and Littlefield, bought the Texas book portion of their business and the book continues in print. I could go to book events and spread out all five of my works, expound at length on any one and occasionally make a sale or two.

About this time, another fortunate event took place: my Ph. D. thesis on the Darien Scheme, originally published on Microfilm by a British company, made a comeback. Scottish nationalists had revived interest in Darien in order to re-establish a Parliament in Scotland. At least one American University is currently advertising my thesis along with other British works. I could now claim that I was the author of six books that were readily available on the world market. In addition, I could claim articles I had written for historical journals and biographical synopses. The Davidson College librarian offered to be my bibliographer, keeping my books and papers in a special section in the Davidson Library. Karin gathered up copies of the various Darien articles and sent them to North Carolina.

Since I could no longer ride a bicycle, my two bikes continued to hang on a rack in the Post Oak Court garage beside the odometer that gave proof I had once ridden another bicycle over ten thousand miles.

When a new car replaced the seven-year-old Honda, the larger vehicle left no room for the rack that had long held the Trek and the Cannondale. The two bicycles were placed on the garage floor along with other items, which no longer had value. Eventually I gave both my Trek and my beloved Cannondale to my grandsons, Ian and Camden. I hoped they would get as much pleasure from my bicycles as I had during my years of bicycling.

By Easter the deep wound in my thigh began to heal under the supervision of Dr. Kadi, the Denton plastic surgeon recommended by the hospital staff. On each visit, the doctor carefully inspected my thigh and finally told me Karin's four months of three times a day treatments had been completely successful.

Once my thigh had gained an endorsement from the plastic surgeon, I was able to join a cardiac physical therapy program. I worked out under the careful scrutiny of a skilled staff person at Denton Regional Hospital. After each workout, I was given instructions essential to my recovery. I learned to manage stress and diet. I gained help in planning future exercise activities.

Kyle, the leader of the program repeatedly gave us the following advice, "Be sure to walk your dog every day even if you do not have a dog."

# Thirty-One

# A Bundle of Joy

## May 2000

Karin and I took Kyle's advice seriously. Karin had decided if she could take care of me, she could also take care of a pet since I had said I wanted one. On National Pet Adoption Day, May 6, 2000, she suggested we visit a nearby pet store and look over the possibilities. I thought a cat might be the best house pet for me. I tried to pet one that was up for adoption. The animal turned toward me and snarled and hissed. I was about ready to give up when we found ourselves in a back room of the store where animals were being displayed by a group who called themselves *The Stars*, an acronym for *Saving The Animal Rescue Society*.

Suddenly Karin found a small auburn-haired dog in her arms. One of the rescue group members suggested that we take the dog for a walk around the store. We did and our new friend put on a real show for us. She did not just walk; she strutted.

A few minutes later we were paying the fee and signing

the papers that would make her a member of our family. She was a Longhaired Chihuahua that had been rescued from the Fort Worth Pound and had been given the name "Lena". Karin found the name "Chalena", a Hispanic name that meant "A Bundle of Joy". We decided the name fit, for she had already proved that she could bring laughter and love into our house. When we noticed that "Lena" was the last part of "Chalena", we renamed her. We decided her full name would be Chalena Chihuahua Ramsay.

The new member of the Ramsay household immediately took charge. Karin and I had begun regular walks in the neighborhood, an activity that was designed to build up my strength. Chalena insisted on leading us on our treks. Sometimes, when we forget, she reminds us that is time for our walk. Communication is not a problem for Chalena; she is able to make her wishes absolutely clear. I have been slower in learning to understand Dog Language than Karin, but Chalena has insisted that I can and will learn. Sometimes, realizing I am legally blind, she comes in front of me and stomps on my foot with the full weight of her ten pounds. Other times, she comes behind me, takes her foot and catches my house shoe, sometimes causing it to come off my foot. If necessary, she has a special bark just to capture my attention. None of these things does she ever do to Karin, for whom she merely stands still in front until she is sure Karin sees her, then she lowers her head and front legs to the floor, her version of a full court curtsy and a way of saying, "Please".

One afternoon, three weeks after Chalena's adoption, heavy storm clouds developed. We thought this made the usual walk impossible so I was sitting in my large lounging chair in a relaxing position with my feet on a footrest that extended well beyond the seat. Karin went out to get the mail before the rain came.

Some time later, I realized I had not seen Chalena in a while, so I asked Karin, "Where is the dog?"

"Why do you ask?" responded Karin.

"Well, you took her out with you when you got the mail

# A Bundle of Joy 273

and I haven't seen her since. Did you bring her back in with you?"

Karin panicked. Though she was sure she had brought her back in, she went to the back room to get her outside shoes. I panicked even more, so while she took the extra time to go to the back room, I jumped up, closing the foot support of my chair so I could get out of the chair, and rushed outside. It had been time for our usual walk but because of the storm clouds we had not gone. I assumed that Chalena might have taken the trail and gone by herself. I took off down the trail.

When Karin came through the house and out the front door she could find neither Chalena nor me! Nurse Karin called both for Chalena and me, and hearing or seeing neither of us double panicked. Fearing for both of us, she ran to the telephone and called Robin. Kathy answered.

"I can't find Jack. I think he may have gone for a walk and something happened!"

That is all it took. Kathy, Robin and Jena all started searching the neighborhood. Karin alarmed the neighbors who joined the search. Immediately, Kathy found me and brought me back to the house. Karin was crying. I promised that I would stay on the porch while everyone else searched, some by foot, others by car. Karin was on foot.

Just then the storm struck. Thunder boomed. The search continued, those searching on foot, calling Chalena's name, describing a little dog that looks like a little red fox to everyone they saw. The heavens literally poured rain as I stood in the shelter of the porch and all those searching were drenched, everything they were wearing soaked to the skin. Robin, in a car, found Karin and insisted she ride with him. Neighbors who knew how upset I was continued searching on foot, water no longer a factor: they were as wet as they could get.

Karin was afraid that Chalena had crossed into the expressway area adjacent to the residences, so Robin drove over to the expressway and stopped at the Lincoln dealer through whose car lot she would have entered the expressway area. Karin got out of the car and went into the dealer's showroom.

"What happened to you?" asked the salesman as he spotted Karin in his spotless showroom, a puddle of water developing at her feet. When Karin told him he promised not only to look for Chalena, but that he would deliver her should they find her. Karin got back in the car with Robin. By this time, over an hour had passed. It was still raining. Robin suggested they go back and check on me.

We stood, comforting each other, and finally decided to abandon the neighborhood search and send the neighbors home to dry clothes. There seemed to be no hope. Karin and I, clasped each other, standing in the rain on the front lawn. We added our tears to the wetness of our rain soaked clothing, believing there was no possibility of finding the dog we had come to love.

Robin opened the door for us. Karin heard a soft yap. She listened again. She heard a yap, yap! She recognized what the dog talk meant. She raced to my chair, Robin behind her. Karin spied a small patch of red fur pushed against the back of the footrest of the chair.

"Look, Robin! I think Chalena is under Jack's chair!"

Together they carefully lifted the heavy chair in the air and the small dog, once free from the underside of the chair, began to jump. On the third try she made it all the way to Karin's arms. There she cuddled up close to Karin.

This time the tears were tears of joy. Somehow, Chalena knew Karin and Robin had rescued her. While she was certain she had a home with Karin and me, it was weeks before she was as friendly with me as before. It was even longer before she would approach my lounge chair.

This was not our first pet. I had a dog during my teen years, Bolivar, named not for the South American hero of independence, but for the fact he appeared to be a ball of fur when I first got him. Each time I went off to college or graduate school, "Bollie" warmly greeted me on my return.

Soon after Karin and I married, we were given a white and tan cocker pup which we named "Tessie from Odessie" since she had been born in Odessa. Tessie died soon after she came to live with us. We were then given a kitten born in the alley behind the same Odessa home. We chose the most energetic member of the brood. We named her Lilliput, Lilly for her mother and "put" since she was a "putty cat". She reigned supreme in the small Crane home for a while until Mr. D. came to live with us.

Karin gave our dog his name, "Mr. D., 'D' for 'Dog", for all you could say about him was the fact he was a dog, yet one due proper respect. One ear stood up, one ear flopped down. His nose, no longer black, was worn off and looked like a worn, formerly pink, pencil eraser. Both elbows were calloused; heaven knows how he managed that. His tail was curly, bent to the side, making him look like a yellow helicopter that might take off in a sideways flight. Obviously a decrepit creature, Mr. D. selected the Ramsay's front porch one winter night as a refuge from a cold norther. He gave evidence he was in trouble, barely able to make it up the two small steps. We had been out that night and when we returned to our little shotgun house in Crane we found him on the porch where he had collapsed, his back two legs seemingly paralyzed.

Ranchers had been putting out arsenic to rid the area of rodents. Karin gave the forlorn animal egg whites and placed him in a large cardboard box so he could die peacefully and easily be carried out the next morning. When dawn came he was very much alive. He jumped out of the box and made it plain he was glad to have a home. When Lilliput had kittens she elected Mr. D. her baby-sitter. Once he was curled up for a good night's sleep, she brought her offspring one by one and dumped them on top of him. With each additional kitten he rolled his dark brown eyes and sighed but did not move. He was forever grateful and always loyal. We left him outside. He was already an outside dog. He would ride in our car when we went to buy groceries and watch a movie. On those trips, we left him in the car with all the windows rolled down. He always had to be begged to get out of the car, so he would stay, waiting for us to return. We would never try that with any other dog, and I am not sure how he convinced us it would work with him. When we would go out of town we would find him hiding under the hanging clothes, hoping to go with us. We would make him get out even though he went, tail dragging to sit on the porch while we left. Mr. Shaffer, the Crane grocer, said he made my rounds twice a day, hunting me. He would go first to the Post Office, then to the Church, then to the Grocery Store and then back home. Everyone knew him and knew he had adopted us. They would tell him, "Sorry, Mr. D, they are out of town." When we would roll back into town after being gone, he would be sitting on the side of the highway outside of Crane. We would stop the car; he would hop in and ride the rest of the way home with us. When the aging dog died, we adopted a registered Cocker Spaniel, Laird Lotapup, and later owned a French Poodle, Mimi LaPoodle.

We also had cats. Annetta, when in the second grade, came to us, complaining because we had promised her that, because Lilliput was already old when she was born, she "could have a kitten when Lilliput died." She continued, "Liliput is not going to die!" Her argument worked: we let her adopt Chim Chim Cheerie, a Blue Persian who reminded us of the color of a chimney sweep. Karin's favorite cat was Cheerie's kitten, to which we gave a name to fit him perfectly. There were two reasons: (1) he was full of mischief and (2) she could preach a whole sermon just by calling the kitten's name: "Sin Sin"! We also had Sin Sin's son, "Tem", short for "Temptation". Oh yes, Liliput finally did die. We think feathers killed her. She died quietly in her sleep soon after she climbed up the chimney from inside the house, caught a bird and ate it. She was twenty-one, yes, 21!

When we left Texas for our ten years in the east and the north, we decided to give up all pets. After living in a townhouse and three apartments where neither cats nor dogs were welcome, we were ready to accept a dog into our lives once more.

Since the small animal was an important part of my therapy, we were delighted to have our beautiful new Long-Haired Chihuahua. In many ways Chalena represented the best of our past pets: she had the friendliness of Bollie, the faithfulness of Mr. D., the charm of Mimi and the loving quality of all our previous animals, cats included. Without a doubt, Chalena was a bundle of joy.

My health continued to improve. Once I graduated from the twelve-week physical therapy program, I was able to keep up with Chalena and Karin on our neighborhood walks. Our route led us through a playground area where small children ran out to stop our progress asking, "What is the doggie's name?" and then for permission to pet the spirited small dog. Children along the trail love it when we say, "Her name is Chalena Chihuahua." Even the youngest children try to say it after Karin picks her up and Chalena gladly accepts all petting. Eventually almost every child in the area learned her name and called out "Chalena, Chalena" as we walked the trail.

When I was asked to speak at the dedication of the Juan Seguin statue in South Texas, Chalena went along. She proved herself an excellent traveler, willingly accepting the travel crate strapped to the new car's back seat as her home away from home. Her only desire was to of go in the car with us wherever we went. Obviously this was because her single reason for living was simply to love and be loved.

On the book signing tours that followed the publication of my fifth book, Chalena went with us. When overnight accommodations are necessary, we make a point of staying in motels that readily accept small pets. On more than one occasion when a motel manager hesitates, I take Chalena to the registration desk. Almost always her dogged charm wins out. Few can resist her pathetic brown eyes.

*Thirty-Two*

# When Nightmares Became Pleasant Dreams
## *2004 and beyond*

When I was finally released from the hospital, I was told I would often have severe nightmares. I found this prediction accurate. Although my physical health continued to improve and my daylight hours with Karin were delightful, I dreaded the night in the loneliness of the front bedroom.

I tossed and turned when I slept. I knew I was not ready to return to the large antique bed that Karin and I had long shared. I realized the unfairness of imposing my fretful night hours on her. I desperately hoped I could overcome on my own my dread of the time of darkness.

The hospital staff had provided me with a mild medication that aided relaxation. This added to my hours of sleep, but the nightmares continued. Generally my unpleasant dreams involved the feeling of loneliness, separation from human contact, the dreary feeling of being unable to participate in normal activity.

One morning I awakened convinced I had experienced an angelic visitation. It was more than a dream for it was very different from any I had ever known. It was an event that vibrated with reality. After breakfast, I told Karin what had happened. In the dark hours a beautiful being entered my room, lying beside me for a time. Then she placed a tender kiss upon my forehead.

"That was no angel", Karin said.

"You were so restless. I went to your room and watched you for a moment. I decided to lie down beside you. You seemed to settle down, almost in a peaceful sleep. I gave you a kiss and went back to my bed."

Karin placed that tender kiss upon my forehead, one that was identical to the kiss that had awakened me from my lengthy stupor! There have been no more nightmares. From the time Karin kissed me, all of my dreams have been pleasant.

My seventy-eighth birthday marked the one-year anniversary of the date my doctor had believed I would die. The actual date of my chronological birthday and my more important new birthday already coincided. I asked Karin to buy a cake and place only one candle upon it, forget the seventy-eight. We invited the neighbors to my birthday party. I declared that I was starting all over again. One year later I had two candles to blow out. I would add candles until a medium sized cake was filled to capacity. This would be one means of guaranteeing more birthday cakes and, more importantly, more time to spend with Karin who kissed away all unpleasant dreams.

Any author dreams of book tours. Since Karin's kiss, I have enjoyed tours I never dreamed possible when I sent my manuscript to be judged. Since my hospitalization and the loss of most of my eyesight my dream of touring has continued!

One of my book tours took me to the Austin area where I spoke to over a hundred fourth graders in Round Rock, Texas. My young audience sat in rapt attention. Those forth graders gave me the courage to accept other invitations to tell the story of Texas to school audiences across the state.

After Round Rock, Karin and I went to Houston for a book

signing in a large urban store. The next day we crossed the causeway to Galveston Island where I spoke to the Laffite Society. Three weeks later we went to San Antonio for a signing at a bookstore that specialized in Texas history. On the same trip we went back to Galveston where I was a featured author at the famed Art Walk. Invitations to speak at Fort Bend Museum in Richmond, Texas two years earlier had been the result of my first full-length book, a biography of Mirabeau Lamar, which had established me as an authority on the life of the second President of the Texas Republic. After the publication of *Texas Sinners and Revolutionaries*, I was asked to return as featured speaker again at the museum that displayed the artifacts I had earlier researched for my book relating to Jane Long. There were other trips: several speaking engagements and book signings in the immediate area and a five hundred-mile round trip to Abilene. On the West Texas trek, I was one of the speakers for a book festival sponsored by the Abilene Library.

Just as my dream of touring with my books continues, so does my dream of invitations to speak about the books I write, the history I research.

Though I can no longer type an outline for a talk and deliver a speech from my notes, I have learned a new technique for public speaking. Karin bought a portable tape recorder and a box full of tapes. We research together and I tell her the facts I need. She makes notes and later records basic facts including exact dates on tape. I replay whatever tapes I need in order to get essential information I need to keep in mind for any one talk.

I have prepared several different talks from data tapes. When an invitation comes, I simply listen to the recording that best suits the upcoming event. I then tailor my talk to an audience all the way from an assemblage of fourth graders to a group of mature adults. When I need to review an article or printed matter I need for research, Karin scans the material I want into her computer, transfers the scanned text to a disk and my computer then enlarges it and reads it to me.

In the months that followed my near death experiences, I

spoke to a dozen or more different audiences. I autographed and sold copies of all five of my books. Although my first book had been published in 1985 and had been out of print for several years, Eakin Press decided to go to a second printing. They also made available all my books, including those that the Austin presses had produced in 1990 and 1996. I am now able to accept speaking engagements at which I display all of my books on a single table, all currently available in bookstores and on the Internet: any author's dream.

Although tests proved I had lost all sight in my right eye, my doctors believed I would be able to retain some vision in my left eye. I was told by one of my doctors that the eye has amazing healing ability. My initial eye accident at the electronic gate could have been a blessing in disguise, one that shut off flow of additional blood to the eye before I was on a blood thinning medication.

One of my eye specialists recommended, and we bought, a specialized computer program called *A-I Squared*. With this program I enlarge the text on my computer monitor to a usable size, eight times what a screen usually shows. I can then edit what I write by listening while my computer reads back to me what I have written. When the computerized voice cannot pronounce a word I have written, I know I have misspelled something. I back up the cursor and usually I find the squiggly red mark showing where I need to make a correction. Once I have completed a document, I sit back and listen while the computer reads aloud to let me hear and review several pages of material at a time.

In addition, I have discovered with *A-I Squared* and a program called *Bible Works* I can read the Bible in any version, including Hebrew. Though I always prepared for any sermon based on a Hebrew text by studying the scripture in Hebrew, I have used the excuse of my blindness not to read my scriptures in Hebrew any more. Instead, I have done something I have never done before and never urged anyone else to do. I am reading the *Bible* from cover to cover. At this time I have read from *Genesis* to *The Gospel of John*. I must say that I have enjoyed the luxury of reading my *Bible* for myself and I have learned a lot I did not know or realize.

I can continue to write, another dream that began when I was in college and continues today. At first I attempted brief letters and short articles. Eventually I became able to put my thoughts and reminiscences into readable form. This true love story, which has become the book you are reading, could not have been written without this unique program.

On one of our trips along the expressway to the hospital for blood work, Karin pointed out an early spring Redbud tree in full bloom, one of the most colorful signs that spring has arrived in Texas.

"I see a whole row of Redbud trees", I told Karin, expecting her to rejoice that with my one eye I had been able to see the beauty she saw.

Instead, I heard, "What row of Redbuds?"

When I pointed to the row of trees along the expressway, she said, "The Redbud tree I pointed out to you was the only tree with any color. All the other trees are bare, twisted, dull grey branches, waiting for spring."

My one remaining eye had developed a unique ability: I now see only what is genuinely attractive. I see neither scars nor blemishes. I am blind to all that is lacking in beauty or charm. When Karin looked into a mirror and thought she saw a wrinkle or two, I looked into her face and told her with sincere honesty that I saw nothing other than her smooth, delicate beauty, the same beauty I had relished on the night of our wedding. For me, her exquisite beauty will last for all eternity.

I had once been tempted to allow my anguish to sweep me into the serenity of a warm cocoon state. When I realized Karin was the angelic personage who had ended my post hospitalization nightmares, I felt a continuing sense of peace. Lying beside her, I can reach out in the night and touch her vibrant being. She was truly the beautiful angel that had come into my life over five decades earlier, one who had brought to me untold joy and strength. I am determined to add an additional candle to my birthday cake each November. Yet I realize such actions will eventually lead to futility.

In April 2004, the doctor who had expected me to die on Thanksgiving Day 1999 insisted that I undergo tests that might discover some medical problem still unknown to me. Ten days later his assistant called back and left a message on my answering machine: blood was reaching all portions of my heart as it should and the bypass and mechanical valve was showing no signs of clotting. I suppose that this is about as clear an indication as any that I will be able to live in good health for at least a time.

Since Karin has always been in perfect health and I have not, given our difference in ages, I have always assumed she would outlive me. This was true with both sets of our parents: Ina and Kirby as well as Lilian and John. I think I have taken comfort in this fact, simply because I cannot imagine life without this magnificent being. I now realize that this is something over which no human has control.

In my last sermon at Covenant, I made reference to an event that had taken place fifteen years earlier. I had attempted to play the part of King Arthur in a musical presentation written by the youths of the Church. I took a line from the script, the "Brief Shining Moment". I suggested that my ministry had been but a moment in the history of the congregation, yet I hoped it would be remembered as one that reflected the glory of God in a unique fashion, a "Brief Shining Moment".

There have been many shining moments in my life and Karin's. From the time we first walked hand in hand beside the waters of the Mississippi on our honeymoon, there were moments of wonder. Others occurred in Crane and Crestholme as well as at Covenant, and still more in Chapel Hill, Bloomington, Des Moines and Green Bay.

Although I know not that which lies ahead, there is one fact that I hold with confidence, I could never have won Karin without some form of Divine Assistance.

I am confident my heart is beating because I was kissed by an angel.

# INDEX

**Abilene** (TX), 37, 42, 83, 244
**Acuff**, Dr. Tea A., 257
**Adams**, P.B., 213
**Adler**, Connie, 198
**Alexandria** (LA); 1st Presby. Ch., 3-4; Kinder., 6; Central Elem. Sch., 6; manse, 5-6; Sun. dinners, 6; Sun. Sch., 5; Bible Teacher, 8; rivers, 8; my father, pastor 23
**Allison**, Carolyn, 124, 133; The Allisons, 131
**Anson** (TX), 37, 44, 246
**APCE** (Assoc. of Presby. Ch. Educators), 244
**Aunt** Bessie (Elizabeth Lavinia Cook), ii; 3, 6-9, 23, 38, 49; bed, 24-25
**Aunt** Bessie (Gordon), 41-42, 44
**Austin** (TX), 29, 36, 43, 197
**Austin** College, 31
**Automobile**, See "Car"
**Avenger** Field (TX), 20-22, 52
**Babcock**, Jim, 172-173, 176
**Baillie**, Dr. John, 43
**Baine**, Billy (William Allen), v, 5, 36-38; 170; Margaret Truman, v, 5, 36-37
**Banker**, Linus, 35
**Barth**, Dr. Karl, 66
**Bartlett**, sisters, Frances & Helen, 44
**Barton**, Jim, 195-196
**Bates**, Seth, 17; Bates, Silas, 17
**Between** years break, the, 62
**Beverly**, Jim, 103-104, 216
**Birdsong**, C.D., 83
**Birdsong**, Carol Jean, 97
**Birkner**, Jimmy, 124; PICTURE, 128
**Black**, maid, 6; Yth., 9; slaves, 26;

Covenant's policy, 139-140; bus driver, 177-178
**Blind,** legally, ix; 268, 272, 280; computer programs, 282
**Bloomington** (MN), 226-227, 237
**Bodie**, Mr. Sam, 109; Bodie, Mrs. (Evelyn), 126
**Boren**, Ted & Janet, 197-198
**Bower**, Nancy, 97
**Brady**, Mathew, ix, 4, 24
**British** Royal Air Force (RAF) cadets, (Avenger Field) 20-21, 52
**Broadhurst**, Col. Dick, 183
**Brownwood** (TX), i; 11, 17
**Bunteen**, Jeanne, 160, 184
**Burleigh**, Dr., 67
**Burns**, Connie, 135
**Burton**, Burt, 173
**Car**, Hudson-Terraplane, my, 44-45; Ford 6, my, 78-79, 83; our Ford 6, 98, 107; Studebaker, our, 107, 115, 125; station wagon, our, 143; Honda, our, 206-207, 224; Nisson, our, 216, 224; PICTURE, Honda & Nissan, 209; Prelude, our 253, 261; never drive again, 268
**Car**, my father's, Model T Ford, 2; Essex, 3-4, 25; Chevrolet, 25, 27-28; Dodge, 28-29; Ford V-8, 76
**Carpenter**, Marj, i
**Carrollton** (TX), 133, 135, 212
**Catechism**, Westminster, 9
**Cavillini**, Manlio, 179
**Cavness**, Miss, 30, 35
**Chapel** Hill (NC), 213, 215, 225-226; Univ. Lib., 215; PICTURES, 209
**Chapman**, Monroe, 27

# 288 INDEX

**Chapman**, Ruth, 114
**Church** (Jack), Claremont Presby. (MN), 226-227, 230, 237
**Church** (Jack), Covenant, Carrollton-Farmers Branch (TX), 131-212; 249
**Church** (Jack), Crane (TX) 1st Presby., 76-100
**Church** (Jack), Crestholme Presby., San Antonio (TX), 98-133
**Church** (Jack), Crivitz (WI), 1st Presby., 238-240; 242
**Church** (Jack), Glendale Presby., Dallas (TX), 180, 246
**Church** (Jack), Meth., 45
**Church** (Jack), of Scotland., 43, 60-61, 70-71; Richmond Craigmillar, Scot., 54-56, 160; Yth. group, 62, 201; choir, 62; PICTURES, 50, 202
**Church** (Jack), Roscoe (TX) 1st Presby., 41-48
**Church** (Jack), Yanceyville (NC), 215; 224-225; PICTURE, 221
**Church** (Karin), Chapel Hill (NC), Univ. Presby. Ch., 204, 206-207, 212, 214-219, 223-224; Confirmation, 214-215; Kerygma, 218; *pig pickin'*, 225; basketball, 225; Hurricane project, 216-218; PICTURES, 222
**Church** (Karin), Green Bay (WI) 1st Presby., 238-239, 241-242, 245
**Church** (Karin), Northminster Presby., Dallas (TX), 184-191, 194, 203, 244 Picture, clowns 191
**Church** (Karin), Oak Grove Presby., Bloomington (MN), 223-224, 226, 228, 231, 235-236
**Church**, Presbyterian: U.S. (Southern), 194; Presby. in the U.S.A., United, 184; reunion, 127, 194, 204, 244; threat to leave, 158
**Churches**, circuit rider plan in Texas: Meth., Presby., Disciples of Christ, 17-18
**Churches**, other: Baptist, 90, 216; Crystal Cathedral (CA), 189; Disciples of Christ (TX), 90; 1st Presby., Fort Worth (TX), 123; Greek Orthodox (WI), 175-176, 216; Holy Family Catholic, Ft. Worth (TX), 144; Mennonite (KS), 175, 188-189; Meth. (Idaho), Sergeant Bluff, 175; Meth. (TX), 18, 44, 90, 98, 104; Northwest Bible, 158; Pentecostal, 116; Sullivan's Island Sunrise Presby. Ch., 216-218; PICTURES, 222
**Churches**, Texas Conference of, 196-197
**Cisco** (TX), 35, 43, 126
**Claremont** (MN), 226-227, 229
**Clausell**, Lena, 42-43; Clausell, Mrs., 42
**Clowns**, 186, 187, picture, 191
**Colgrove**, Bob, 115
**College**, Austin, Sherman (TX), 31, 34, 43
**College**, Davidson, (NC), 34, 36, 43, 257, 269; Diploma, 37; roommate, 123-124
**College**, New (Scotland), 60-61, 68, 71; faculty, 43; Principal, 53; theological branch of U. of Edinburgh, 55; Ph. D. Committee, 71; Lib., 201
**Committee**, Pulpit Search, 97, 131
**Cook**, Elizabeth Lavinia (see Aunt Bessie)
**Cook**, George L.; grandfather, my 4
**Cook**, George S., great grandfather, my, 4, 24
**Cooper**, Winston, 135
**Corinth** (TX), 246-247, 249, 268
**Cousin** Maude's son, Laredo; 34
**Covenant**, Carrollton-Farmers Branch, (131-213); pastor, 203, 205, 211-212, 245, 267; membership, 137, 149, 184; Andrew Club, 141; weddings, 152-153, 193-194; Session, 199, 207; elder, 212, 245; officer's retreat, 150; Every Memb. Canvas, 137; Building Program, 145, 149, 199; budgetary problem, 152; Stewardship, 153-154; Palestinian Supper, 154; Faith Budget, 154-155; Women of the Ch., 155; West Dallas project, 155; migrants, 135-136, 145-146, 163; Denton State Sch., 136, 155; New Years Party, 137; Weekday Kinder., Mother's Day Out, 159-160;

# INDEX 289

Yth. Meetings, 137, 141, 150; Yth. Trips, musicals, *Covenant's Godspell*, 167-173, 175-178, 185, 187, 191, 194; Holy Land trip 157-158; Dispensationalism, 158-159; Scottish dance 160; Tornado relief, 188-189; Scottish heritage, 212; Trip to Scot., 212; Mariners, 160; Sr. Adults, 161; Sr. Citizen residence, 199; burglaries, 200

**Cowden**, Gib, 77-78

**Cox**, John R., 12

**Cozby**, Vivian & Jim, 136; 147; Jimmy Cozby, 175-176; 216

**Crane** (TX), i; 204; 1st Presby., (76-100); construction boss, 78, 94, 96, 98; Courthouse, 97- 98, PICTURES, 98

**Crestholme** Presby., San Antonio (TX), (97-133) anniversary, 107; new members, 119; Yth. fellowship, 103-105, 120, 124, PICTURE, 128; relocation, 108-116, 119, 120; fire, 113; *Crestholme Crier*, 114; attendance, 119, 125, 132; Wed. Night suppers, 119-120, 125; Eventide, 124; Andrew Club, 125; Every Memb. Canvas, 120, 125; weddings, 120, 122; Women of the Ch., 124; hosted Presbytery WOC, 132; hosted Presbytery, 125; Christmas, 132; hosted Presbytery Yth. Rally, 132; reunion, 198; PICTURES, 117, 118, 128, 129

**Crofoot**, Wendell, 110, 112

**Cunningham**, John, 185

**Currie**, Dr. Ed, 123, 124

**Currie**, Dr. Thomas, 36

**Currie**, Jr., Dr. Tom, 43

**Dallas**, (TX) Explo 1972, Campus Crusade, 165, 172, 176; office buildings, 187; West, 196; North, 197; 204; church, 203; visited, 241, 245; Presby. Village, 246

**Darien** Scheme (Thesis, see also), colonial plan, 53-54, 56, 59, 67-72, 201, 269; South America, 53; Parliament, 53, 70, 72; Bank of Scot., 59, 70

**Davidson** (NC), (see College, Davidson)

**Davis**, Mrs. Reuben, (Lola) 95

**Demler**, Richard Wayne, 97

**Denton** (TX), 194-195, 241, 246

**Depression**, The Great, ii, 12, 25

**Disney**, Walt, 21-22

**Door** County (WI), 241

**Dowdle**, Louise, 183

**Draper**, Lillian, 111

**Durk**, Bob, 183; Mickie Durk, 183

**Duval**, Troy, 159

**Dwight** (see Fortier)

**Edinburgh**, Scot., (city), 53, 55, 57-58, 61, 70; Scottish church, paying position, 54; Nat. Lib., **55**; Gen. Assembly Hall, 55; McEwan Hall, 55, 75

**Educator**, Church, 43, 185, 214, 238, 243, 245; Min. of Ch. Ed., 79, 190, 198, 203

Edwards, Marge, 159

**Farmers** Branch (TX), 133, 204, 212, 249; Lib., 95

**Fayetville** (WV), 37

**Fifinella**, 21-22

**Fireman**, Vol., 76-77; Firemen's Aux., 92

*Fools, Thee Holy*, 186-187, 190, picture, 191

**Ford**, Jewel & Clayton, Melba & Sonny, 125-126

**Fortier**, Dwight, 170, 172; 177, 178

**Foster**, Dr., 123

**Gardner**, Bill, 198

**Garner**, Harold & Inabelle, Anne Garner, Nancy Garner, 97

**Garrison**, Jeff, 142

**Geigenmiller**, Mrs., 132; granddaughters, 133

**Gibson**, Ruth Ann, 124; PICTURE, 128

**Godspell** Tours, Covenant's, 167-173; 216; pictures, 173

**Goering**, John & Orletta, 175

**Goering**, Valerie, 173

**Good** Shepherd Community Center, W. Dallas (TX), 196, 205

**Goodenough**, Walter, 124

**Gordon**, Mr. & Mrs. William (see "Uncle

Bill" or "Aunt Bessie")
Grassley, Mrs., 123-124
Green Bay Packers, 240, 245, 251
Green, Evelyn, 126; Green, Papa, 126
Harris, Beverly, 124; PICTURE, 128
Hart, Houston, 12-13
Haunted House Party, 103, 120, 150
Hawkins, Bob, 83
Haws, LeRoy, 124
Hay, Marion Macgill, 56
Hendricks, Liz, 175
Hermann, Joan, 124; PICTURE, 128
Herriot, Larry, 151
Hill, Dr. P. B., 107
Hinkle, Jennifer, 173
Hoffelt, David, 214-215, 243
Hohner, Sue, 124
Holiday, Christmas, my parents, 3; 5
Holiday celebrations, Kinsey, 20
Holidays, Christmas, my 35, 57; Advent, 68; after marriage: 94, 132, 135-136, 155; Holy Land, 157-158, 181; Charleston, white, 216-218
Hospital, Norfolk (VA), Mt. Sinai, 2; San Antonio Robert B. Green, 111; San Antonio Baptist, 111; San Antonio Nix, 123; Dallas Masonic Children's Hospital, 136; Farmers Branch, Brookhaven, RHD, 178; Denton Regional, 255, 265; Kyle (rehab), 270-271
Hotel, Bluebonnet, 81; Fairmont, 84; Gunter, 108; Roosevelt, (Room 553) 84; Wardie, 54; 58; Wooten, 83; St. Paul, 229
Hubbard, Larry, 82
Huie, Wade, 54; 60, 63-65
Hunt, Camden Ramsay, 241, 270
Hunt, Ian Ramsay, 238, 241, 270
Hunt, Judge Trish, 218
Hunt, Randy, 193-194
Hunt, Richard, 194
Hutchison, Alexander, 56, 201; Nanette, 201; PICTURE, 202
Hyde, Hal, 108, 111

Idol, Rev. Kathy, 197
Innes, Bill, 95, 212
Insh, Dr. George Pratt, 67, 70-71
Iowa (state), floods, Des Moines, 236
Irving (TX), 245, 247
Jensen, Mel, 136
Jones, Dr. Robert F, 123; Jones, Mrs. Robert F. (Annetta) 123; 237
Jordan, Barbara, 167, 198
Kadi, Dr., 265-266, 270
Kelly, Sandra, 135; Kelly, C.D. & Mary, 162-163
Keywood, Arthur, Jr., 135-136, 159
Keywood, Arthur, Sr., 159, 161, 183-185
King, Sandra, 135
Kinsey, Ina Wood, 11-22, 79, 183; death & funeral, 231-232
Kinsey, Karin, birth, 11; 14-22, 46-49, 51, 57, 60, 62; 72, 75-76, 78-88; 1st & 2nd birthdays, Zephyr, 12; Sweetwater 14-22; printing shop, 14; choir audition, 19; *Pony Express Editor*, Kirby & daughters, 15; pen-pal, 21; valedictorian, 20; editor, *Howl O' The Hills*, 16; Editor, Society, *Sweetwater Reporter*, 15; editor, *Tex-Syn News*, 16; Presbytery Yth. Council, Mid-Texas, 19; Synod of TX Yth. Council, 19; KXOX 16; proposal, 79-80; Trinity Univ., 82; PICTURES, KK, 48, 58, 80; KR, 86, 87, 88; 98, 118, 128, 129, 191, 192, 202, 207, 208, 220, 233
Kinsey, Kirby & Ina, 11-15; Ft. Parker heritage, 16-17; grandparents 138; British Cadets, 52, 53
Kinsey, Kirby Luther, ii; 11, 46-47, 79-84; 225, 268; *Printer*, 12-15; Fifinella, 21; Football tickets, 13-14; East 12th St., 22, 49, 75, 81; Presbyterian, 18; Watson-Focht, 12, 15; death, 178; brother, 178
Kinsey, Marilyn, 15-16, 183; 231-232
Kinsey, Nelda, 15-16; 83; 183; 232
Kriehn, George, 186
KXOX, 82
Laney, Hubert; Laney, Holli, 169-170, 191

## INDEX 291

**Language**, Spanish, 28; Latin, 43, 53; German, 60; test, 60
**Larrabee**, Dr. Clyde, 175; Clyde Larrabee, 177, 216
**Lawther**, Lynn, 131-132, 139-140
**Legally** blind (see Blind)
**Leroy**, 7-8, 23
**Leslie**, Miss, 71, 75
**Lib.** of Congress, 215, 236, Lib., UNC, 215
**Loch** Ness monster, 61, 202
**Lynn**, Dr. Matthew, 99, 196
**Macphearson**, Doris, 198; Macphearson, Jim, 212; 267
**Maddox**, Ginny, 135
**Magee**, James, 124
**Mann**, Ed, 27
**Manse**: Alexandria, 5-6, 25, 28; Taft, 29; Roscoe, 41; Holyrood Palace, 61; Crane, 89-90, 97; PICTURE, 98; Crestholme, 101, 124; PICTURES, 128, 129; Child/children of the manse, **126**; Covenant, 137, 141, 155, 178
**Maunder**, Pearl, 21, 53, 200; Geoffrey, 21, 53
**Maxfield**, Dr. Jack, Sugie Maxfield, 156, 197
**McCabe**, Ted, 135
**McCain**, Charles, 49, 58, 63
**McCall**, Dr., 35
**McCrary**, Jim, 83; 198
**McDougall**, Mr. 109; Lee Allen McDougal, 124; PICTURE, 128
**McGaughy**, Mr. 109
**McGeath**, Leila, i
**McLaurin**, Dr. Eugene W., 180
**McLeod**, George, 63
**McMichael**, Jack, 79
**Mercer**, Tommy, 124; PICTURE, 128
**Midland** (TX), 80, 99, 165
**Migrants**, (see Covenant, migrants)
**Miles**, Dan J., 97
**Mills**, George & Mozelle, 160
**Minnesota**, 215, 247; Minneapolis, 223, 230, 236-237, 245; speaking Minneso-

tan, 224; St. Paul Winter Carnival, 230; PICTURES, 233, 234
**Mo Ranch** (TX), 75, 78-79, 150 (see also Westminster Conference)
**Moncada**, Georgia, 179
**Montreat** (NC), 19, 142
**Mooty**, Bob, 124; Melody, 173
**Moran**, Dan, 78
**Nelson**, C. Ellis, i
**New** College, Univ. of Edinburgh, 55; Old College Quad, 55
**New** Orleans (LA), 84-85, 161, 167, 179, 207, 230, 232, 240
**New** York City (NY), 4, 12, 35, 49, 138, 243
**Nolan** County (TX), 41, 45
**Norfolk** (VA), 3
**North** Carolina, 35, 37
**Nuevo** Laredo, Mexico, 165-166
**O'Neill**, Peggy, 198
**Odessa** (TX), 80; 92
**Ofton**, René, 114
**Oil** fields, 76-78, 90, 93-94, 97
**Overton**, Mr. J. G., 19-20
**Pan** Amer. Sch., Kingsville, TX, 166
**Paris**, France, Pigalle, Follies, 63-64
**Parker**, Cynthia Ann, wife of Peta Nocona, 16, 30; Commanche captive, 17; son, Quanah, 30; Soldier's Mound, Spur, 30;
**Parker**, Fort, massacre, 16; Texas Rangers, Rachel Plummer, 17
**Pentecost**, Dr. Percy, 151
**Phillips**, Ellen & Harry, Jean Phillips, 95
**Pitchford**, Jeanie & Sylvia, 173
**Pledger**, Clayton, 135
**Pogell**, Wendell, 27
**Police**, Carrollton & Dallas (TX), 139
*Pony Express*, editors, Kirby, Karin, Nelda & Bus. Mgr., Marilyn, 15
**Pope**, blessing, 65-66
**Port** Isabel (TX), 74
**Poteet**, Robert (Bob), 104, 132, 145-147, 152, 216
**Presby**. Village, 138, 180

# 292 INDEX

**Presby.**, Gen. Assembly, 99, 102, 108; ruling from, 110; new church development, 111; constitution, 113, 198; meeting, 115; met in Dallas, 137; rejection of Dispensationalism, 158; commissioner, 194, 1992 Assembly, 232; educator issue, 244

**Presby.**, Kirby Kinsey: Ch. Treas. 18; Deacon, 18; Elder, 18; Men of the Ch., 18; 22

**Presby.**, ministers, 83; 100; 257; Candidate for ordination, 103-104; Southern, 64, 194

**Presbytery**, Candidates Committee, 35

**Presbytery**, Executive 39, 185, 203, 211-212, 226

**Presbytery**: Covenant (TX), 170; Grace Union, (TX) 194, 196, 211-212, 246; John Knox (TX), moderator, 128; Mid-Texas, 42-43, my home Presbytery, 43, my Examination Committee (for ordination), 43; Orange (NC), 215, 221; Twin Cities (MN), 226, 244; Western Texas, 102; meeting in Kingsville, 112, 115; met at Crestholme, 125; moderator, 128; Winnebago (WI), 238; my father's presbytery, Norfolk (VA), Home Missions Supt., 1-2

**Price**, Ruth & LeRoy, Rickie, 115

**Prozanski**, Dorothy, 121

**Prozanski**, Mrs., 106

**Publisher**, Univ. of Edinburgh, Thin, James, 75

**Publishers**, my, Microfilm Limited of London, 72; Eakin Press, 200, 206, 216; Republic of TX, Rowman & Littlefield, 269; American Univ., 269

**Queen** Elizabeth, R.M.S., 49, 51, 68; PICTURES, 49

**Ragsdale**, Bert, 100-101; Margaret, 121, 127; Ann, 121; Johnny, 124

**Ramsay** apartment (VA), in Pre-Civil War home, 25

**Ramsay** home (TX), Laredo, 27, 74-75, 78, 95; Grandfather's estate, 34; The Heights, Laredo, 28; (VA), Larchmont, 1-2

**Ramsay**, Annetta Jean, 123, 143-144, 157-158, 161, 178, 211, joined Covenant, 143; Godspell, 168, 180, 187; married, 192-194; A & Randy, 229, 238, 241, 258-259, 261-262, 276; PICTURES, 129; 173, 192, 207, 220

**Ramsay**, Elizabeth, 3-4, 6, 92-93, 138, 180; death, 181, 183, 184; PICTURE, 4

**Ramsay**, Foster M., grandfather, my; death, 27; estate, my summer job 34

**Ramsay**, Jack, birth, my, 1-2; birthday, 5, 260, 280; $1^{st}$ grade, 6; friends, 7; $4^{th}$ grade, 7; Jr. Hi Sch., 28; Hi Sch., 28; sports ed Taft Hi newspaper, 29; Spur Hi Sch., 30, 33, 34; speech contest, 31; grad, 33; Memb. of the Ch., 9, 23; ministry, decision, 34; ministry, candidate for, **35**; Davidson diploma, 37; preach, 37-38; Scarboro (WV), 37; Summerlee (WV), 37; Kenbridge (VA), 39; Victoria (VA), 39; Seminary degree, 38; missionary, decision, 38; ordination, 44, 198; Latin, 43; adult Yth. Advisor, 47; swimming party; 47-48; audience, Pope Pius XII, 65- 66; grad U. of Edinburgh, 75; firefighter, 76-77; 136; Lions Club, 76; hepatitis, 155; hosp, 155-156; bicycle, 156, 252, 269-270; Rotary Paul Harris Fellow, 197; Thesis or Dissertation (see Darien Scheme); other writing, 235, 252, 262; doctors, 252; hosp, 255-257; hosp chaplain, 258; nightmares, 259, 279; turtleneck sweater, 253, 261; writing conference, 263, 268; visiting nurses, 265; computer, 267; Chalena, 276; therapy, 276; resumed speaking, 277, 280-281; PICTURES, 4, 49, 58, 86, 87, 88, 192, 208, 233, 234, 285

**Ramsay**, Jack, my pastoral duties: sermons, 205, 212; preach, 44, 56, 76, 180; Baptisms, 205; Infant, 47, 56, 97; Adult, 97; Baptism, $2^{nd}$, 134; weddings,

# INDEX 293

56, 97, 120-122; 152-153; 193-194; 205; funerals, 132, 180, 183, 205; pastoral visits, 102, 110, 133, 144, 205; receive members, 205; communicants' class, 104; communion, 105, 111; lead Bible study, 105, 226; Sun. morn, 135; committees, 134-135; 196; V. Bible Sch., 123; admin. skills, 150-151; speaker, 194; Presbytery & Gen. Assembly, 115, 194; moderator, Western Texas Presbytery, 127, moderator, John Knox Presbytery, 128; Building prog./fund raiser, 145; Teach & Direct MoRanch Women's conference, 150; work schedule, 185; ecumenism, 197; retirement, 203-205, 211, 220; left Texas, 276; Bryn Mawr Presby. Ch. (MN), 226; Interim min.: Claremont (MN), 226, 235; St. Paul (MN), Edgecumbe Presby., 235; Crivitz (WI) Presby. Ch., 238; preach, occasional, 246; ministry concluded, 246; PICTURES, viii, 98, 128-129, 207, 208, 220

**Ramsay**, John Cummins; my father, ii; 1-4, 6, 23, 27, 29, 34, 36, 38, 76, 83, 138; spouse, Lilian 1-3; Parent, my 1-4, 26; pastor, Alexandria, 23-24; Union student, 25; pastor, Taft, 29-30; Spur, 30; death, 138; inherited from, 239

**Ramsay**, Kathy, Jena & Jared, 195, 238, 247, 273

**Ramsay**, Lilian Cook, Mother, my, ii; 1-4, 6, 23, 35, 76, 78-80, 138, 142; Parent, my 1-3; bed, 24-25; teaching, career 25; Presby. Village, 138; death, 180, 183, 246; PICTURE, 4

**Ramsay**, Robin Andrew, 125-126, 132, 134, 140, 142-144, 157-158, 161, 200, 211, 237-238, 247, 258, 273; adopted Corny, 136; joined Covenant, 155; Godspell, 168, 180, 184, 187; Deacon, 140; Attorney-at-law 195, 256; court bailiff, 259; my father's car, 261; Chalena, 272-274; PICTURES, 129;

173, 192, 207

**Ramsey**, Susan, 176
**Ranch** families, 44; Rancher, 37, 45, 77; Ranches, 45, 76, 90, 170
**Rand**, Joe, 132, 154
**Richmond** (VA), 1-4, 25, 27, 36-37, 43, 115, 198, 214-215; Valentine Museum Bk. Signing, 242
**Rimmer**, Gene, 124; PICTURE, 128
**Rivers**: Brazos (watershed), 45; Colorado (watershed), 45; Mississippi, 8; Red, 8; Bridge, Alexandria Red River, 25; Rio Grande, 27, 74; Shining, 8-9
**Rock**, Edwin (Ed) 100, 101
**Rodriquez**, Elizabeth, 135-136
**Rogers**, Dr. Isabel, 214
**Roommates**, my 36-37, 54, 60, 81
**Roscoe** (TX), 41-42; ordination, 44; my record book, 205
**Ruffin**, Jac, 63-65
**Ruffin**, Vesta, 185-186, 197
**Runkel**, Betty, 169-171
**Sadler**, Harley, 16
**Saint** Paul (MN), winter carnival, 229, 230; PICTURES, 233-234
**Sampson**, Leone & Bill, 135; Billy Sampson, 135
**San** Antonio (TX), 76, 78, 85, 100, 106, 116, 204-245
**Sawyer**, Dr. David, i; 231
**Schecter**, Robert, 135
**Schilling**, Fred, 179
**School**, Crane High, 91; Crane system, 92
**School**, Gen. Assembly's Training, 42
**School**, Laredo Martin High, 28
**Schuemaker**, Arthur, 27
**Scotland**, 43, 66, 75, 103, 200; Glasgow, U. Lib., 68; Iona, Isle of, 62; Regent Terrace, 61; weather, North Sea, 56, 58; Gulf Stream, 55
**Seguin**, Juan, statue speaker, 277
**Seminary**, Austin, " a Texas", 37, 104; Columbia Theological, Atlanta, GA, 54; Dallas, 159; Fuller, 194; San Francisco Presby., 172; Union, NY, 138

# 294 INDEX

**Seminary**, Union, Richmond, my father, 25; apartment, 25; President, 26-27
**Seminary**, Union, Richmond, my years, 36, 41, 43; Middle Yr, 37; roommate, 37, 170; 258, Final yr, 38; Degree, 38; Classmate, 49; reunion, 198; 242; Confirm. Class, 214
**Seminary**, Virginia, 37-38
**Shaffer**, Mrs., 97
**Sharp**, Dwight, 83
**Sheridan**, Laura, 15, 82
**Sherrod**, Roy, 37, 81, 83, 198, 258-259
**Shields**, Alexander, 71
**Sikora**, David, 261
**Sinclair**, Miss, 7, 9, 26
**Smith**, Newman & Pauline, 151; Pauline, 198
**Smith**, Sarah, 183
**Smith**, Sue, 198
**Snipe** hunt, 46-47
**Speigel**, Sandra, 135
**Spillers**, Jack, 81
**Spouse** Trailer, 204, 216, 239, 243
**Spur** (TX), i; 30, 31, 36; High Sch., 30; Spur, Soldier's Mound, 30
**Stalder**, Jack, 173
**Stanford**, Pat, 27
**Stappenbeck**, Lois, 124
**STARS**, Saving The Animal Rescue Society, 271
**Steinbommer**, Henry, architect, 114
**Stewpot**, 196
**Strange**, Beulah, 187, 194
**Strickland**, J.B. & Thelma, 91
**Stuart**, Dr. James, 43
**Sweetwater** (TX), i; 11-22, 39, 44-49, 75, 79, 95; Airport (see Avenger Field); Broadway, 12; Cotton Oil Mill, 14; 1st Presby. Ch., 46, 198; Football Bowl, 13; Municipal Auditorium, 16; Printing Shop, 12-14; Chapel, Westminster, 44, 46, lake 47-48
**Synod** of Texas, 16, 78-79, 243; Synod's Yth. Council, 47, 123; met in Midland, 138

**Taft** (TX), 29, 36, 170
**Tait**, Katherine, 152, 159, 184, 197
**Teachers**, my: Aunt Bessie, 6-7; Cavness, Miss, 30, 35; Sinclair, Miss, 7, 9, 26; Baillie, Dr. John, 43; Burleigh, Dr., 67; Stuart, Dr. James, 43; Thomas, John Newton, 38; Watt, Dr. Hugh, **53**-54; 60, 67, 69
**Texas** (state), Centennial, 28; my return to 27, 39, 47; Bluebonnets, 104, 232; border, 213; funeral, 232; move back to, 246; pets, 276
**Thesis**, Darien Scheme (Dissertation), 34, 67-72, 201; 269; Church, Tron on High Street, 60, 71; Church & State, study of, 71; Covenanters, 71; Duke of Hamilton, 69; Equivalent, 59, 70; Examiner, External, 60, 67, 71; Examiner, Internal, 67, 69; House of Lords, 53; Panama, Isthmus of, 53, 70; Parliament, Scottish, 53, 59, 71; shipbuilding, 68; (see also, Darien Scheme)
**Thomas**, John Newton, 38
**Thornburg**, Alex, 216, picture, 191
**Todd**, Bennett & Beverly, 124; PICTURE, 128
**Tucker**, Vicki, 167-168
**Typewriter**, 34, 60, 68, 267
**Uncle** Bill (Gordon), 41; J. of Peace, 42; elder, 42
**Univ.** of Edinburgh, Scot. (Jack), 38, 43, 48; Ph.D.Candidate, 53, 75; Principal of the College, 54; European Univ., 56; graduation, 71, 75; diploma fee, 75; registrar's office, 70; Lib., 201
**Univ.** of Texas, my father 25, 34; my major, 36; Typing Contest, 29
**Univ.**, Glasgow's Teachers', 67
**Univ.**, Oxford, 57
**Univ.**, St. Andrews, 56
**Univ.**, Texas Tech in Lubbock, 31
**Univ.**, Trinity (San Antonio, TX, Karin), 48-49, 76, 104, 163, 236
**Varga**, Mrs., 102
**Valentine** Museum, 242

# INDEX 295

**Virginia**, (state), 1, 27, 39, 215
**Walker**, Mary, 169, 171
**War**, Civil, 25, 26; WWI, 2; WWII, 52, 82; Pearl Harbor, 35, 36; ROTC, 36; Draft Board, 36; Navy Chaplains, 38; Sea Bee Base, 38; Avenger Field, 20; "War, The", 36, 38, Pen-pal, 52; tour Ger. to Holl., 66
**WASP** (Avenger Field), 20; Fifinella, 21-22
**Waterstreet**, Lewis, 83
**Watson**, Wayne & Patti Lee, 124, PICTURE, 128
**Watt**, Dr. Hugh, 53-54; 60, 67, 69
**Weather**: 230; Tornadoes, 188-189; Hurricane, 216; PICTURES, 222
**West** Texas, 30; 37, 41, 45, 75, 79, 165
**West** Virginia, 37
**Westminster** Conference, Kerrville (TX), 33, 47, Mystery Ramble, 33, cross ceremony, 34; Mo Ranch, 75
**Wiedemeier**, Wanda, 239; Wiedemeier, Bob, 239, 240
**Williams**, Clifford, 39, 44, 46-47, 79, 83; John Rowland, 47; Mary Agnes, 47
**Williamsburg** (VA), 27; Sea Bee Base, 38
**Wilson** sisters, Dawn, Sandra & Janis, 132-133
**Wilson**, Craig & Yth. Specialties Conventions, 189
**Wohkittle**, Marty, 197
**Wolfe**, Peter, 179
**Wood**, Al, 135
**World** Council of Churches meeting, Amsterdam, 66
**Wright**, The Very Rev. Ronald Selby 61, 65, 69, 70, 201
**Zephyr** (TX), 12, 17-18; 21
**Zoella** Lykes, S.S., 71, 73, 74
**Zorn**, Warren, 197
**Zuefeldt,** Dr. Roy, 184, 190, 243, 244

**Other Books by Jack Ramsay**
IN LIBRARIES, BOOKSTORES, ON THE INTERNET AND BY MAIL FROM

HISTORICAL RESOURCES PRESS
2104 POST OAK COURT
CORINTH/DENTON, TX 76210-1900

TELEPHONE 940. 321.1066
FAX 940. 497.1313
www.booksonhistory.com

### *Thunder Beyond the Brazos*, the story of Mirabeau Lamar

Before election as second President of the Republic, he led the charge on Santa Anna's Army at the Battle of San Jacinto. His friends were devoted; his enemies declared him a better poet than politician.
Winner of the T.H. Fehrenbach award for
"Best Biographical/Family History Publication 1985".
Reprinted in Soft Cover 2001   $24.95

### *Photographer... Under Fire* THE STORY OF GEORGE S. COOK (1819 – 1902)

(My great grandfather, historian, honored as famous photographer, parted ways with his associate, Mathew Brady; and
recorded the human side and terror of the Civil War in the South.)
"A fascinating trip through American photography with one of its earliest and perhaps most well-known 'forgotten practitioners'." James M. Caiella, Richmond Times-Dispatch.
Hardback, $34.95

### *The Story of Cynthia Ann Parker, Sunshine on the Prairie*

"Heavily-researched history of the wilderness life of Cynthia Ann Parker." Judith Rigler, San Antonio Express. "Story well told…" Larry Swindell, Fort Worth Star-Telegram.
Soft Cover $22.95

### *Jean Laffite, Prince of Pirates*

"Over the years, … a number of historians have stated flatly that an accurate biography of Jean Laffite would be impossible. …
Jack Ramsay seems to have accomplished the impossible."
C.F. Eckhardt, Book Bag Editor, The Tombstone Epitaph.
Hardback, $34.95

### *Texas Sinners And Revolutionaries*: Jane Long And Her Fellow Conspirators

Jane Long, Sam Houston & Mirabeau Lamar, three founders of the Texas Republic, who each could be considered "sinner" and "saint"; this is the story of their intertwining lives through revolution and victory at the Battle of San Jacinto. (Texas history, 1819 – 1880)
Soft Cover. $18.95